Inter-tech(s)

Inter-tech(s)

COLONIALISM AND THE QUESTION OF TECHNOLOGY IN FRANCOPHONE LITERATURE

Roxanna Nydia Curto

UNIVERSITY OF VIRGINIA PRESS *Charlottesville and London*

the modern language initiative

THIS BOOK IS MADE POSSIBLE BY A COLLABORATIVE GRANT FROM THE ANDREW W. MELLON FOUNDATION.

University of Virginia Press

Printed in the United States of America on acid-free paper

First published 2016

9 8 7 6 5 4 3 2 1

Library of Congress Cataloging-in-Publication Data

Names: Curto, Roxanna Nydia, 1979– author.
Title: Inter-tech(s) : colonialism and the question of technology in francophone literature / Roxanna Nydia Curto.
Description: Charlottesville : University of Virginia Press, 2016. | Includes bibliographical references and index.
Identifiers: LCCN 2016002823 | ISBN 9780813939223 (cloth : alk. paper) | ISBN 9780813939230 (pbk. : alk. paper) | ISBN 9780813939247 (ebook)
Subjects: LCSH: French literature—French-speaking countries—History and criticism. | Technology in literature. | Colonies in literature. | Postcolonialism in literature.
Classification: LCC PQ3897.C87 2016 | DDC 840.9/356—dc23
LC record available at https://lccn.loc.gov/2016002823

Cover art: Amanda Burnham

For the three loves of my life: Paul, Sienna, and Sebastian

CONTENTS

ACKNOWLEDGMENTS

This book is the culmination of many years of research conducted in multiple locations: New Haven, Connecticut; Paris, France; Bloomington-Normal, Illinois; and Iowa City, Iowa. During the course of its fruition, I experienced the joy of finding employment at the same institution as my husband and of having two wonderful children. Although these life events no doubt slowed the progress of this work, they have brought me tremendous happiness and made completion of the project all the more satisfying.

At Yale, I had the great fortune of having Christopher L. Miller as my dissertation advisor, whose guidance at the early stages was truly indispensible. I am also grateful for the teaching and mentoring that I received from other faculty in the Department of French, including Ned Duval, Jean-Jacques Poucel, Julia Prest, and the Director of Graduate Studies at the time, Maurie Samuels. I also learned a great deal from my discussions with fellow students, especially Marc Michael, Alexandra Gueydan, Rebecca Ruquist, Jeffrey Boyd, Ryan Poynter, and Alexandra Parfitt.

During my three years at Illinois State University, I had a truly wonderful cohort of colleagues who played a fundamental role in the development of my career. I greatly appreciate the guidance and friendship of my colleagues in French, Mary Trouille and Jim Reid; and in Spanish, Bruce Burningham, Julie Lynd, and Jim Pancrazio. And of course, I will never forget the dinner conversations with Elke Segelcke at the Garlic Press and evenings spent writing at the Coffee Hound.

I am also grateful for the mentoring I have received from many colleagues in the Division of World Languages, Literatures and Cultures at the University of Iowa, including Russ Ganim, Roland Racevskis, Mercedes Niño-Murcia, Cinzia Blum, Geoffrey Hope, Wendelin Guentner, Deborah Contrada, Denise Filios, and Adriana Méndez, as well as the support of my fellow junior faculty member in French, Émilie Destruel Johnson, and the former Dean of the College of Liberal Arts and Sciences, Linda Maxson.

I would also like to acknowledge the enriching discussions with colleagues following presentations of parts of chapters in various venues throughout the years, including the University of Oxford in September 2010 and June 2011; Fort-de-France, Martinique, on the occasion of the Césaire Centennial in June 2013; London at the Society for Francophone Postcolonial Studies Annual Meeting in November 2013; Long Beach and Atlanta for the 20th- and 21st-Century French and Francophone Studies International Colloquium in March 2012 and March 2013; at the MLA Convention in Philadelphia in December 2009, Los Angeles in January 2011, and Boston in January 2013; and the University of South Carolina for the French Literature Conference in March 2009.

The research for this book was funded through fellowships and grants from a number of institutions. At Yale, a John Enders Fellowship and a Kenneth Cornell Research Grant allowed me to spend a summer conducting research in Senegal, and a Yale Dissertation Fellowship and a scholarship from the École Normale Supérieure funded a year of writing in Paris. I also benefited from a Jacob K. Javits Fellowship in the Humanities for four years. At Illinois State, a New Faculty Initiative Grant allowed me to spend a summer researching the project, and at Iowa, an Old Gold Fellowship funded another summer of writing and revising.

I was fortunate enough to have received help from research assistants at various stages of this project. I am recognizant of Natalie Benson for her valuable work revising and editing; of Stephanie Kupfer for her translations; and of Jason Hong for verifying references in the final stages.

Amanda Burnham, a most talented artist and dear friend, painted the beautiful image that appears on the cover.

At the University of Virginia Press, Cathie Brettschneider and Eric Brandt were most helpful in bringing this project to completion. I am also very grateful to the two anonymous readers for the Press, whose careful comments improved the manuscript immensely.

I acknowledge permission to reprint portions of chapters that have appeared previously. A section of chapter 1 appeared as "The Science of Illusion-Making in Aimé Césaire's *La tragédie du roi Christophe* and *Une tempête*" in *Research in African Literatures* 42.1 (2011): 154–71. Part of chapter 3 appeared as "Senghor and Heidegger: Negritude's Appropriation of German Phenomenology" in *French Literature Series* 37 (2010): 27–41. Part of chapter 4 appeared as "Tech Transfer, Modernization and Independence in Bhêly-Quénum and Loba" in the *Journal of the African Literature Association* 5.1 (2010): 144–60. And part of chapter 5 appeared as "Technology Transfer, the Railway and Independence in Ousmane Sembène's *Les bouts de bois de Dieu*" in *Trains, Literature and Culture: Reading/Writing the Rails*, ed. Steven Spalding and Benjamin Fraser, 53–75 (Lanham, MD: Lexington, 2011).

I would like to thank my family for their love and support. My parents instilled in me a passion for learning despite our different academic backgrounds and have been such wonderful grandparents to my children. My older sister, Carina, has led by example and given much helpful advice. My younger sister, Vilsa, has provided warm friendship and wisdom beyond her years. And, of course, I am grateful to my husband, Paul Dilley, for his help reading and editing the manuscript, and the endless love and support that he has shown me during our fifteen years together.

Inter-tech(s)

Introduction

Although questions of modernity are often at the forefront of debates in francophone studies, current scholarship has largely neglected the representation of technology, including its fundamental role in community formation, development, and globalization for African and Caribbean authors. Yet an examination of how postcolonial francophone literature represents technology transfer from the metropolis to the former colonies is crucial for understanding how these authors approach questions of modernity, extricate themselves from the vestiges of colonial rule, and propose a means of integrating their cultures into a global community. Technology, both the product of a culture and a means of transforming it, brings individuals into close proximity to one another, produces objects that circulate between the metropolis and the colonies, and creates images that represent the peoples and territories of distant countries.

In this book, I propose a new understanding of the relationship between the inhabitants of the metropole and the colonies, by showing how a number of major twentieth-century authors depict technology as a mediator, both productive and destructive, between them. As the "inter" prefix of the title suggests, this book examines how various "techs" (technological innovations) act as intermediaries between colonizers and colonized, urban and rural cultures, French and African or Caribbean communities, and individuals networked together into a global society. My analysis focuses on how francophone literary texts, primarily from West Africa and the Caribbean, represent the complex relationship between colonialism and technology.

Although technology is broadly defined as the application of scientific knowledge to practical use, I use the term primarily in reference to the innovations developed from the second Industrial Revolution (1870–1914) to the present (including the current information age) and commonly referred to as "modern technologies":[1] systems of transportation (railways, motorboats); mechanical modes of representation (photography, film); technologies of industry (dams, machines) and transmission (radio, television, and the Internet). I examine the relationship between the representation of these innovations, and "colonialism," understood as the various forms of domination that the metropole exerted upon the colonies, from the time of initial exploration and subsequent colonization to the ongoing relations of power and dependence in the age of globalization. This definition of colonialism comprises three different elements, each of crucial importance to assessing the impact of technology on the relationship between France and its colonies. The first element is colonialism as a discourse: the myth and ideology of the "civilizing mission" that corresponds to a series of images of itself that France presented to the world;[2] and the presumed technological superiority of the West that formed an integral part of these images. The second element denotes the practices described as colonization, in the sense of the political and economic domination by one country of others. Technology, as the means by which the French empire conquered its colonies, constitutes a fundamental part of this process.

The third element of my definition comprises the legacy of these forces, and their effects on the former colonies. Colonialism, as presented in the title of this book, refers to both the political and administrative authority that France exerted upon its colonies; as well as the forms of social, economic, cultural, and political domination existing in the postindependence period beginning in the 1960s, when almost all of France's former colonies gained independence. These forms of domination, which are generally denoted by "postcolonialism," "neocolonialism," and "imperialism" (terms that evoke simultaneously the process of moving past the violent era of colonization and its persistent legacy in the former colonies), constitute the vestiges of colonialism and are thus included in my definition.

My analysis of literary texts focuses not only on the literary representation of technology in colonization but also on the way in which the diffusion of scientific and technical knowledge is either politicized as a mode of colonialism or depoliticized as an endeavor altogether separate from it. In my readings of these authors, I explore both how they represent modern technologies as mediators between cultures of the metropole and the colonies; and how the relationship between technology (as a theoretical concept) and colonialism is portrayed in literature. Ultimately, I seek to trace a literary trend emerging in the wake of decolonization, when a series of key francophone African and Caribbean authors began to portray modern technologies as a liberating, democratizing force, capable of erasing the hierarchies of the old colonial order and promoting economic development, through the mass circulation of goods and peoples.

During the colonial period, modern Western technologies were generally associated with colonialism and exploitation for francophone authors, who were reacting against the ideology of the "civilizing mission." But following political independence in the 1960s and continuing into the present era of globalization, francophone literature (including Negritude) saw the emergence of much more favorable attitudes toward Western technologies. For the authors I study, Western technologies are capable of being dissociated from the culture that produced them; writers begin to equate their acquisition with liberation from an Old Order. Ultimately, the representation of technologies by francophone authors represents an opportunity to explore their own conflicting sentiments about the use of the French language to express themselves; and the problematic place of the francophone literary work, which is generally written by an African or Caribbean author, published in Europe or North America using Western technologies, and inaccessible to the vast majority of the population in the former colonies.

Chapters 1 and 2 consider the representation of technology transfer from Europe to the colonies in the work of the two most influential writers of the Negritude movement, Aimé Césaire and Léopold Sédar Senghor. In my readings of Césaire and Senghor, I build on the extensive corpus of literary criticism dealing with Negritude,[3] but by focusing on the understudied issue of technology in their work, I argue that Negritude—too often considered outmoded and obsolete—is still highly relevant today, especially to current debates about modernization, ecology, and globalization.[4]

In chapter 1, "Science, Modernization, and the 'Theater of Development' in Aimé Césaire," I show how Césaire's shift from poetry to theater as the genre of choice for expressing his politics of Negritude was accompanied by a move toward an extremely favorable view of technology, as reflected in his plays, essays, interviews, and political speeches from the 1960s until his death in 2008. In particular, I situate his work within the tradition of protest and consciousness-raising of the "theater of development" movement, by examining speeches and interviews, identifying influences from Bertolt Brecht and the Colombian playwright Enrique Buenaventura, and showing the central role of development through the acquisition of technology in his classic plays *The Tragedy of King Christophe* (1963) and *A Tempest* (1969).

My discussion of Senghor in chapter 2, "Technics and Poetics in Léopold Sédar Senghor," begins by demonstrating how his close readings of Martin Heidegger, especially "The Question Concerning Technology," shaped his notion of the ideal role of technology within culture and provided him with a means of separating modern innovations from discursive reason, which he adamantly opposed. Subsequently, I show the important role of technology in Senghor's politics (which constituted an all-out drive toward modernization, without regard to the ecological consequences hinted at by Heidegger) and the utopian vision of a "Universal Civilization." Finally, I examine how his frequent comparisons of French language and literature with technological innovations reflected his conception of each as an ideal means of fostering cultural contact in his imagined Universal Civilization of the future.

Chapter 3, "Radios and Revolution in Frantz Fanon," examines the questions of modernization and technology, especially the radio, in Frantz Fanon's writings on Algeria. Fanon's frequent emphasis on the role of the *fellah* (the indigent agricultural peasant class) in the Revolution, his critique of capitalist exploitation of proletariat workers in urban areas, and his adamant rejection of the colonizer's culture have all led many scholars to assume that these ideas imply a complete rejection of technology and modernization, which, in turn, forms part of a broader critique of modernity. In reality, in his essays from *Toward the African Revolution* and *A Dying Colonialism* (many originally written for newspapers), as well as in his classic work on decolonization, *The Wretched of the Earth* (1961), Fanon advocates, even glorifies, modernization and technological development in colonized societies. He forcefully argues that any rejection of modern technology, science, and medicine results from the negative associations evoked by their initial introduction within the context of colonization, and that these marks of modernity are wholeheartedly embraced once this context has been removed.

Chapters 4 and 5 consider the arrival of modern Western technological innovations—the railway, motorized boats, radios, and a dam—to African communities in the works of francophone African novelists of the independence/postindependence era. My study adds to scholarly criticism on francophone African literature, which has almost entirely ignored the centrality of technology.[5] This work breaks new ground by examining the representation of technology in several key novels and films of the postindependence era, when the enthusiasm surrounding independence led to an extremely optimistic view of the potential of technology transfer from the metropolis.

Chapter 4, "Machines and Media in Ousmane Sembène," explores the literature and film of the Senegalese author and filmmaker. The first part focuses on the representation of the railroad in his novelistic masterpiece *God's Bits of Wood* (1960), which recounts the strike of railway workers on the Dakar–Niger line from 1948 to 1949. This novel boldly stages the appropriation of the colonizer's means of production, as embodied by the railway, and represents the opposing discourses in the debate about this process through several groups of characters: the white patrons; Muslim leaders; the elders; and youthful workers. Although the novel takes place in 1948, the time of writing and publication—during the era of African independences—illustrates the key role of technologies in nation building for Sembène. The second part examines the portrayal of technologies in two films, *Xala* (The curse) (1973) and *Moolaadé* (Protection) (2004), in order to argue that Sembène advocates valorizing the instrumental function and utility of innovations without fetishizing them (as markers of wealth and social status) and that he believes in the power of media such as radio and television to enact social change.

Chapter 5, "Dams and Motorboats in Olympe Bhêly-Quénum and Aké Loba," identifies and analyzes a set of West African novels and plays from the early 1960s that have been unfairly neglected, probably due to their thematic focus: not primarily on cultural identity formation but rather on issues of modernization, ecology, and economic development. The works exemplifying this ideology are *Le chant du lac* (The song of the lake) by Olympe Bhêly-Quénum, from Benin; and *Les fils de Kouretcha* (The sons of Kouretcha) by Aké Loba, from Côte d'Ivoire. These texts notably reverse the previous associations between race and technology by equating colonialism with backwardness and lack of development, and independence with technological progress. The traditional opposition between colonizer and colonized is supplanted by a conflict staged between two groups, both black African: the educated, youthful students and the national authorities, who seek to induce development through the use of motorized boats and the construction of dams and highways; and the older generation, who oppose bringing in technologies that may disrupt the spirits of nature, and whose defense of animism constitutes an ecological discourse avant la lettre. The glorified victories of the progressive youth at the end of the novels reflect their ideologies about the need for technology transfer for development in the years following independence.

Chapters 6 and 7 focus on the contemporary French Caribbean, exploring the proliferation of new technologies in the twenty-first century, as the question of colonialism and its ongoing influence assumes an integral part of the dialogue and debate about ecology and globalization. In contrast to the unrestrained enthusiasm of their West African counterparts, Édouard Glissant and Patrick Chamoiseau are cautiously optimistic about the revolutionary power of new technologies.[6]

In chapter 6, "Globalization and the Internet in Édouard Glissant," I argue that the shift between the two stages of Glissant's thinking, from the local to the global, corresponds to the emergence of a coherent theory in his works about the role of modern technologies and ecologies in Caribbean globalizations. Each of the major concepts about globalization that Glissant develops in *Poetics of Relation,* and his subsequent writings from the 1990s to the present, including the "Relation," "rhizome-identity," and "*tout-monde*" (everything-world), relate to his views about modern technologies, including television, film, and the Internet, and ecology as both mysticism and politics. In particular, I consider his discussion of ecology in *Poetics of Relation* (1990); the role of the Internet in his totalizing figures of the *tout-monde* and the "*chaos-monde*" in *Traité du tout-monde* (Treaty of the everything-world) (1997); and the place of technology transfer in his opposing conceptions of "globalization" (an imperialist imposition of ideas) and "globality" (a liberating exchange of ideas between equals), which he develops in *La Cohée du Lamentin* (The Lamentin hill) (2005).

Chapter 7, "Urban Space and Cyberspace in Patrick Chamoiseau," examines the portrayal of modernization and technology in Chamoiseau's writings from the 1980s to the present. In his early novels *Chronicle of the Seven Sorrows, Solibo Magnificent,* and *Texaco,* Chamoiseau critiques the technology transfer resulting from departmentalization and champions the Creole culture of orality as the means of combating the forces of standardization. Later on, in *Écrire en pays dominé* (Writing in a dominated land) and *Biblique des derniers gestes* (Bible of the last gestures), he develops the figure of the "Warrior of the Imaginary" in order to assert that communications technologies not only constitute the means of imposing ideas through furtive and silent domination but also provide the instruments for liberation, due to their role in the preservation of orality.

In the epilogue, I reflect upon the field of francophone literature in the age of the Internet, especially how cyberspace opens up domains for the emergence of new forms of literary and artistic expression.

HISTORICAL CONTEXT

The trajectory I trace in my readings of francophone authors is closely linked to the history of technology transfer from Europe to the colonies during the process of colonization.

According to Paul Bairoch, a leading economic historian of the second half of the twentieth century, key differences in the kinds of technologies produced in the first and second Industrial Revolutions caused them to be disseminated in very different ways. During the first Industrial Revolution, which took place from the mid-eighteenth to late nineteenth centuries, emerging technologies remained at a basic level, such that pre-industrial craftsmen could understand their functionality, as well as make reproductions and modifications. Consequently, these techniques spread relatively quickly throughout Europe and sometimes the colonies, by means of migrants who mastered the use of instruments and shared them with others.

This changed, however, during the second Industrial Revolution (sometimes described as a second phase of the Industrial Revolution), which took place roughly between 1870 and 1914, when extensive training in science and engineering became necessary for mastering technology. Ironically, although new inventions such as the steamboat and railway facilitated transportation, the process of exporting the techniques and practices became much more difficult. The French educational system in the colonies focused on teaching the French language and history and did not provide the knowledge of science and technology necessary to import and use technological innovations. Modern technology was also very expensive compared to previous technical instruments and required a great deal more capital to acquire. These factors together contributed to making the acquisition of modern technologies largely dependent on the actions of the colonizer during this period.

In his landmark study *The Tentacles of Progress: Technology Trans-*

fer in the Age of Imperialism, 1850–1940, Daniel Headrick makes a key distinction between the "geographic relocation" of technology and its "cultural diffusion," which proves useful for explaining the differences between modern technologies and previous technical instruments. According to Headrick, the transfer of technology is not one process but two. First, there is the relocation, from one area to another of the technical instruments. Second, it entails "the diffusion from one society to another of the knowledge, skills" (9). The "geographic relocation" of technology, according to Headrick, entails the transportation of machines across borders and continents, without any dissemination in the new place of the knowledge and skills that were used to make them; while "cultural diffusion" involves a spread of the knowledge and skills needed to produce technologies—not just the physical machines.

Headrick distinguishes between four basic categories of technology transfer: "the geographic relocation of technology by Western experts; its relocation by non-Western importers; its cultural diffusion by Western experts; and its diffusion by non-Western importers" (10). Modern technology permitted the geographic relocation of Western experts to occur relatively easily; nevertheless, the high price of machines made the relocation of non-Western importers difficult, and the need for specific scientific and technical knowledge made diffusion by both Western and non-Western agents almost impossible during the colonial era and very difficult thereafter.

The history of technology transfer from the metropolis to the colonies can be divided into three periods, the last two being the focus of this study. The first, beginning in the mid-nineteenth century and extending roughly to the 1930s, is characterized by "the penetration of Asia and Africa by Europeans and the conquest of colonial empires" (5). During this time, crucial innovations allowed Europe to explore and invade other continents; technology transfer involved the geographic relocation of innovations without any mode of cultural diffusion. Headrick argues that both the motives for imperialist expansion and the means by which it occurred fundamentally changed in the late nineteenth century. According to him, "what distinguishes the new imperialism from its many predecessors is that it was so swift, thorough, and cheap" (5) as a result of a few inventions (iron-hulled steamships, machine guns, railways, and telegraphs), which not only allowed European nations to conquer lands on other continents but provided them with the means of controlling those lands from afar.[7]

The second period Headrick identifies is characterized as the "massive transfer of technology from the West to Africa and Asia" (6), with the goal of creating an economy of extraction that would send goods back to Europe. As in the first period, technology transfer in the second consisted primarily of geographic relocation, without any real cultural diffusion. The machines were made in Europe and exported abroad. The agents were Western, and the goal of the transfer was to promote the development of European economies. The negative view of technology held by the African elders in many francophone literary texts such as Ousmane Sembène's *God's Bits of Wood* and related works should be interpreted in the context of this second period.

The third period begins in the postindependence era of the 1960s and is characterized by the desire on the part of the formerly colonized peoples for a cultural diffusion of technology, not just its geographic relocation. The leaders of the newly independent nations sought to use technologies to create an economy that was productive for the needs of the nation, not for the extraction of resources, exploitation of labor, and exportation of goods to Europe. A need arose to appropriate the technologies that Europeans had brought, while at the same time dissociating them from the colonizers who provided them. The desire for cultural diffusion also involved African students going abroad to study in Paris to receive technical and scientific training; there was a demand for knowledge, in addition to machines. Most of the authors examined in my study focus on this postcolonial moment, immediately following independence, or, in the case of Césaire and Glissant, the era of departmentalization, when the French overseas colonies of Guadeloupe, Martinique, and French Guyana became departments of France.

The question of whether colonization helped the spread of technology or impeded it underlies much of francophone literature, in both famous and overlooked works. In Césaire's *Discourse on Colonialism,* for instance, he argues that contrary to the discourse of the "civilizing mission," colonization actually thwarted the progress and development already occurring in the colonies, hindering the kind of positive cultural contact that leads to fruitful technological transfer. Two novels I examine in the third chapter, *Le chant du lac* (The song of the lake) by Olympe Bhêly-Quénum (from Benin) and *Les fils de Kouretcha* (The sons of Kouretcha) by Aké Loba (from Côte d'Ivoire), notably reverse the previous associations between race and technology by equating colonialism with backwardness and lack of development, and independence with technological progress. Another salient example of this debate can be found in Ousmane Sembène's classic novel *God's Bits of*

Wood (1960), which recounts the strike of workers along the Dakar–Niger railway line. While the elders in the story associate the railway with the colonizers, including the slavery and exploitation that was used in its construction, the younger generation views the railway much more positively, as a means of stimulating progress and economic development. Similarly, Fanon, a contemporary of Sembène, argues for the merits of viewing all aspects of modernity (including technologies such as the radio) as universal instruments that colonized peoples have the right to acquire. Glissant, a member of the next generation of writers, considers the Internet to be a communications technology belonging to a globalized community, but he expresses some reservations about it, due to its potential use as a hegemonic instrument.

Although modern Western technologies were generally associated with colonialism and exploitation by francophone authors during the colonial era, following political independence in the 1960s and continuing into the present era of globalization, much more favorable attitudes emerged vis-à-vis Western technologies, which are often presented as part of a universal patrimony that all peoples should have the opportunity to acquire. Moreover, the choice of whether to associate a technology with a particular culture or to consider it part of a universal patrimony is often highly strategic and reflects each author's political ideology.

WHAT IS "TECHNOLOGY"?

An important question to be addressed is how to define the term "technology." A broad definition of technology, which can be found in most dictionaries, describes it as the application of scientific knowledge to practical use. For the purposes of this study, I define the term primarily in reference to the innovations developed from the second Industrial Revolution to the present: railways, motorboats, dams, radios, televisions, and the Internet. Although I choose to define technology primarily as Western technologies developed during this period, it is easy enough to envision a broader definition that would comprise all applications of scientific knowledge to practical use, including the ones developed in ancient Egypt that writers such as Senghor view as part of their cultural heritage, or the innovations that Césaire says were developing in the Caribbean in precolonial times.

In fact, the term "technology," even in English, has undergone many transformations throughout the centuries, since its origins in the ancient Greek word *techne.* As Andrew Murphie and John Potts write in *Culture and Technology,* "'technology' was used sparingly in the seventeenth and eighteenth centuries, referring to a study of the arts; its meaning at this stage remained closed related to its Greek roots. . . . But by the 1860s its meaning began to shift to its modern usage; the word had come to mean the system of mechanical and industrial arts" (3). Thus the modern use of the word "technology" corresponds, not coincidentally, with the advent of the Industrial Revolution. From the late nineteenth century onward, "'technology' has come to describe the overall system of machines and processes (while 'technique' refers to a specific method or skill)" (3).

The use of multiple words and articles in French that refer to the meanings we attribute to "technology" in English provides a further complication. First, "la technique" (that is, the word with a definite article) signifies technology in general, in the sense of the overall practice of using technologies. The word "technique" is also used to refer more precisely to technological innovations, that is, particular objects; for instance, *une technique* is a technology such as the radio. In French, however, the term *technologie* (much like other words carrying the "-ologie" suffix) has traditionally been used to denote only the science and study of technology, not physical objects or inventions. More recently, primarily due to the influence of other languages, many speakers of French have begun to use the word *technologie* to refer to innovations, but this is often considered an *anglicisme* (nonidiomatic use of the word, influenced by its English cognate) and is not the norm in literary texts. Some major francophone authors, notably Senghor, play with the double meaning in French of the word *technique,* which can signify at once a technique (in the sense of "technique" in English, such as a skill) or a technology. The occasional ambiguity in discerning between a *technique* and a *technologie* points to the difficulty in separating the scientific knowledge of how to construct an instrument from its concrete physical manifestation as a machine.

For the authors of my study, the appropriation of modern technologies also implies the assumption of a worldview to be adopted or rejected. An important question with which they must grapple is the notion that modern technologies not only are a set of instruments to be used in a practical sense but often present a particular way of seeing the world. Technological innovation has existed since ancient times, but it was not until the beginning of the twentieth century that the machine began to take on a life of its own and to acquire a meaning that transcended its practical utility. Modern technology differs fundamentally from previously existing technologies, according to philosophers of technology such as Martin Heidegger and Jacques Ellul, in that it transforms a society's mode of experiencing reality and has the potential to control those who created it by producing unintended effects outside of the control of its inventors.

For many philosophers, as well as many francophone authors, modern technologies represent a worldview that is assumed by those who use them; when Europeans transferred innovations from the metropolis to the colonies, they transported not only machinery but also a worldview to be adopted or rejected. The creation of this worldview through the proliferation of modern technologies transformed the modes of interaction between cultures in colonial, postcolonial, and global contexts, as well as the representation of these cultures in literature.

In the foundational text of the philosophy of technology, "The Question Concerning Technology," Martin Heidegger's distinction between "technology" and "modern technology" reflects how fundamentally different modern technologies are from the machines that preceded them. Heidegger describes "technology" as a technical instrument that uses natural resources without consuming them; in other words, a tool that is "sustainable" in current ecological terminology. He gives the example of the windmill, which works with the wind without completely depleting the resource. Moreover, according to Heidegger, such instruments are not mystified: their functioning is easily understandable by the person who uses them, and they do not produce unwanted, unforeseen side effects. "Modern technology," on the other hand, consists of the set of technological innovations that consume natural resources in an irreversible way. For Heidegger, their employment leads to the creation of a worldview according to which the world is perceived only in terms of its potential "use value," and everything is viewed as a resource, a "standing reserve"; Heidegger call this perspective "Enframing," and for him it represents the gravest danger posed by the spread of modern technologies.

In *The Technological Society* (1954), written in the same year as Heidegger's essay, Jacques Ellul outlines seven characteristics of modern technology that make it fundamentally different from the tools and techniques that preceded it: rationality; artificiality; automatism of technical choice; self-augmentation (technical developments automatically engender more innovations); monism (techniques form an interconnected whole); universalism (ubiquity, both geographically and in terms of everyday life); and autonomy (technology is no longer controlled by political, economic and religious forces). More generally for Ellul, modern technology is characterized by the way in which it makes efficiency an absolute necessity; this entails the creation of an artificial system that enforces mechanical organization and subordinates the natural world. Ellul is thus a technological determinist who believes that the advent of modern technology changes our worldview in a way that previous inventions did not, by causing us to view reality in terms of efficiency. For him, if scientists and engineers adopted a sense of morality that dictated their actions and subjected them to a higher ideal than efficiency, they would then become bad inventors.

Heidegger's distinction between "technology" and "modern technology," and Ellul's analysis of a technological society reflect the central question of the philosophy of technology: Is technology a force of its own, capable of ultimately controlling humanity, or rather a set of instruments fully under human control? This question is particularly urgent because those who use modern technological innovations frequently have a complete lack of understanding about how they function. Thus, they can have unforeseen side effects, beyond the control of the humans who invented them, such as greenhouse emissions. Whereas "technology" before the modern era was always completely controlled by human inventors, modern technologies are capable of undermining this control, through unforeseen side effects with potentially catastrophic consequences.

Although most technologies are cultural elements developed in a specific time and place by a particular group, they are often presented as inventions with a universal value for all of humanity. In the case of technologies transferred from Europe to the colonies, the following questions arise: Can technologies be dissociated from their particular cultural origins? Is technology transfer a form of neocolonialism or cultural imperialism? Or do technologies pertain to a universal patrimony, as objects that all peoples should have the opportunity to acquire?

MARX ON TECHNOLOGY

Marx provides the subtext for the discussion of technological issues for most francophone authors. Many of these writers were avid readers of Marx's work,[8] and their approach to the question of technology is largely determined by their interpretation of his writings more than those of any other thinker. Drawing from Marx's own theories about the relationship between race, class, and ownership of the means of production, francophone African and Caribbean authors often insist on the distinction between the capitalist use of technologies to exploit a black proletariat, which is nefarious, and the acquisition of technological instruments and scientific knowledge by formerly colonized nations, which is viewed extremely positively.

Marx predicted in 1853 that the technologies initially transferred to the colonies for the purpose of establishing an economy of extraction, which benefited the colonial powers, would eventually help the inhabitants of the colonies to develop their own independent economies. In "The Future Results of British Rule in India," he argues that the colonization of India by the British will ultimately lead to growth in all its industries: "You cannot maintain a net of railways over immense country without introducing all those industrial processes necessary to meet the immediate and current wants of railway locomotion, and out of which there must grow the application of machinery to those branches of industry not immediately connected with the railways" (5). Focusing on the railways, Marx believed that overall development would be a natural concomitant to the construction of the railway line. As Headrick has observed, Marx's prediction was never realized; technology transfer in the colonial period simply led to the "transformation of traditional economies into modern underdeveloped ones" (5). Empirically, an economy of extraction was never transformed into one of production. Nevertheless, some of the authors examined in my study—most notably Sembène in *God's Bits of Wood*—maintain hope that the instruments of the colonizer (in this case, the railway line) might one day furnish the roots of a new nation.

The theories that Marx develops with regard to colonialism correspond closely to his widely debated views about capitalism. On the one hand, Marx writes passionately about the evils of capitalist exploitation and appears to vehemently oppose the existence of a capitalist system at any point in time. On the other hand, Marx appears to view capitalism as an evil but necessary stage in development that all economies and societies must undergo in order to achieve an egalitarian ideal. Similarly, in his writings on India, Marx seems to consider colonialism a necessary stage in the development of the economies of the colonies, which he characterizes as possessing an "Asiatic" mode of production.[9] Unlike the European modes of production (such as capitalism or "primitive communism"), the Asiatic mode is not a stage in a process and does not describe the relations between classes. For Marx, colonization would seem to be a necessary evil, the only way to transform a stagnant, timeless mode of production.[10]

In contrast to colonialism, which was explored rather superficially in some of his journalistic writings, the issue of technology was central to Marx's work. The debate rages on as to whether Marx was a technological determinist, meaning that he believed technology was capable of becoming a force of its own within history.[11] Although Marx has often been misinterpreted as an opponent of technology in general,[12] in his writings on the subject he points to the evils of technology only as they relate to capitalism, a context that causes machines to produce an alienation of workers from their labor, since they become instruments for the ruthless exploitation of the proletariat. Although this would seem to suggest a negative view of technological development in general, Marx envisions a stage subsequent to this capitalist mode of production in which the proletariat experiences an awakening to "consciousness" that is accompanied by an appropriation of the means of production, including technologies. Many francophone authors view their own works as a fundamental means of provoking this awakening of consciousness that will ultimately pave the way for modernization.

Césaire, Senghor, Fanon, and Sembène all have strikingly similar interpretations of Marx's thinking:[13] they all, to various extents, associate the colonized with a global proletariat, and the colonizer with capitalism. Nevertheless, their writings consistently suggest that, in the appropriation of technology, the colonized, like the proletariat, are obtaining the means of production and therefore instigating the next historical stage that Marx describes, the one in which a stagnant economy ("Asiatic" mode) becomes a productive one. They propose to completely dissociate technology from the colonizers and believe that technology itself should not be considered evil or be confused with the capitalist use of it as a means of exploitation.

NEW METHODOLOGY FOR POSTCOLONIAL STUDIES

The focus on the representation of technology in francophone literary texts from Africa and the Caribbean provides a new methodology for the study of postcolonial literatures more generally by suggesting an alternate approach to the standard models of postcolonial theory, which often describe the politics of identity, including race, as founded on alterity and resistance. These models present an understanding of the interaction between figures of the colonizers and the colonized in literary texts that is based on a binary, hierarchical division between a European colonizer and an African or Caribbean colonized. The basic premise is generally that the colonizer produces an authoritative discourse that is then subverted by the colonized from within. This structure produces the image of a scene of interpellation in the Althusserian sense: the colonizer interpellates his colonized subject; the colonized subject recognizes himself as the object of the interpellation and, in responding, undermines this interpellation in an act of subversion.[14]

The two primary examples from postcolonial theory that have helped to establish this framework are the works of Homi K. Bhabha and Gayatri Spivak. Bhabha's notion of hybridity, a central tenet of classic postcolonial theory, evokes the image of a colonizer who calls upon his subject. According to Bhabha, the colonized subject, in responding, mimics the authoritative discourse of the colonizer, thus calling attention to its inconsistencies and undermining it.[15] Bhabha's analysis provides a framework that has frequently been used for analyzing the works of writers from the former colonies: each act of writing is portrayed as a mode of subverting authoritative discourse through crafty, satirical imitation.

Spivak's "Can the Subaltern Speak?" has provided a similar framework for reading colonial and postcolonial literature. In this essay, Spivak describes the collective awakening of the consciousness of the colonized (like that of a social class such as Marx's proletariat) as an event that necessarily follows from the process of becoming aware of their status relative to their colonizers. The "subaltern" she describes becomes "subaltern" by positioning herself against an authoritative figure. The structure is one of an opposition between a colonizer who oppresses and a colonized who resists, ultimately creating a collectivity.

Thus, traditional models of reading taken from postcolonial theory frequently propose an approach to the study of texts that considers them in terms of domination, subversion, and alterity. While these models are certainly very useful in the reading of colonial and postcolonial literature, their prevalence suggests a need to develop new transnational, transcolonial, and transpostcolonial models that consider cultural elements independently of a binary opposition between colonizer and colonized.

The focus on technology allows us to break out of this traditional framework by highlighting the representation of a cultural element, technology, which acts as a mode of interaction *between* cultures in colonial and postcolonial texts and therefore resists inclusion in a hierarchical structure. This proves particularly fruitful because the use of modern Western technologies is generally not portrayed as a subversive act; for these authors, the primary goal of appropriating technology is not to overturn colonial hierarchies but to instigate progress and economic development in their nations. Technologies are represented as freely circulating commodities that belong to the universal patrimony of humanity and that all peoples should acquire. This approach could ultimately be extended to numerous other cultural elements, including soccer, food, clothing, etc., similarly allowing readers to break out of traditional hierarchical approaches.

Rather than focusing on hierarchies, the study of technology allows us to examine colonizer/colonized interactions in terms of the "imagined communities" and "contact zones" created by the spread of new inventions. Benedict Anderson's notion of nations as "imagined communities," which has frequently been applied to the concept of "Francophonie,"[16] is also highly relevant to the kinds of communities created through the proliferation of new technologies. Every technology that is exported and mass-produced corresponds to new forms of interactions between peoples and cultures that lead to the establishment of a new imagined community. For instance, some of the most significant inventions in terms of transforming East–West relations, the steamboat and the railway line, also created communities of interaction. The most salient examples of how this phenomenon is represented in francophone literature are Sembène on the railway line, Fanon on the radio, and Glissant on the Internet and diasporas. For instance, Glissant writes that the Internet and technologies of communication provide a potential means of establishing transnational identities in the Caribbean. The authors analyzed in my study view technology not only as an instrument or object of representation but as an active element capable of forging new forms of collectivity that exist outside the structure of the nation-state and are often global in nature.

Technological innovations also work to create "contact zones," a term coined by Mary Louise Pratt in *Imperial Eyes: Travel Writing and Transculturation* and defined by her as the "space of imperial encounters, the space in which peoples geographically and historically separated come into contact with each other and establish ongoing relations" (6). This term, borrowed from linguistics, denotes the modes of interaction between cultures and is more or less synonymous for Pratt with an abstract notion of a "colonial frontier." Another potential model for these new modes of interaction is Félix Guattari's notion of "points of transfer and exchange,"[17] to use the terminology he coined in his essay on machines. In this study, I examine how the dissemination of new technologies creates "imagined communities," "contact zones," and "points of transfer and exchange" within the imaginary spaces of literary texts, thus establishing transnational modes of interaction between cultures. These new communities often lead to the creation of new, globalized forms of cultural and linguistic identity.

POSTCOLONIAL CONTEXTS

This study proposes to illuminate some of the broader debates in francophone postcolonial studies, especially as they relate to the omnipresent opposition between tradition and modernity: revivalism versus antirevivalism in African philosophy; feminism and women's rights issues; questions of linguistic choice, writing and orality; the relationship between aesthetics and politics; and the burgeoning fields of ecological literary studies and digital humanities.

First, an examination of the representation of technology in francophone literature provides a means of approaching one of the central questions of African philosophy: the conflict between revivalists and antirevivalists. Revivalists emphasize preservation of the past and tradition, construing calls for modernization and development as forms of neocolonialism; they believe that true modernization can occur only through the revitalization of African cultural traditions. Antirevivalists, on the other hand, advocate for modernity and opening up to the rest of the world; they argue that modernization requires a close connection to the West and the rejection of many African traditions.

The debate between these two groups focuses on whether indigenous traditions enhance or impede scientific, technological, and social progress. The most notable antirevivalists, Marcien Towa from Cameroon and Paulin Hountondji from Benin, posit a strong connection between Western thought and scientific and technological development in Africa. Towa believes that the resuscitation of past cultural values proposed by the revivalists would be contrary to the present goals and concerns of the African people. Similarly, Hountondji believes that "Africans must make a 'clean break' with the premodern past in order to address the most urgent demands of the present" (*African Philosophy* 48).

Kwame Gyekye, in contrast, considers the opposition between tradition and modernity to be a false dichotomy, since so many traditional elements are inherited, cherished, and maintained by modernity (xi).

Much like the francophone authors in my study, Gyekye is a fierce proponent of the forces of progress, including the cultivation of science and technology (xii); emphasizes the importance of appropriating technologies, not simply "transferring" or "transplanting" them (xii); and believes technology to be a universal cultural value that should be shared by all (225). Echoing Césaire's distinction between particular and universal elements,[18] Gyekye writes: "A particular cultural creation will thus have two faces: a particular face—when the appreciation of the cultural creation is confined to its local origin—and a potentially universal face—when that appreciation transcends the borders of the environment that created it" (226). In the following chapters, I argue that although Césaire, Senghor, and Fanon have all at times been classified as revivalists, they in fact adopt a viewpoint similar to Gyekye's, rejecting the simple dichotomy between revivalists and antirevivalists, tradition and modernity.

Second, this study contributes to analyses of the place of feminism and women's rights in postcolonial literature. Although my chapters focus on male authors, their works often represent female characters as extremely progressive in their views toward science, technology, and social issues. This is true in the case of the female protagonists of Sembène's *God's Bits of Wood* and *Moolaadé,* as well as in Loba's and Bhêly-Quénum's novels, in which the women and youth form alliances to advocate for technological development and gender equality. In many instances, women are portrayed as pro-modern and against tradition because they are oppressed in the status quo and therefore more open to change.

This portrayal of women as pro-modern in francophone literature provides a means of exploring the place of the feminine in discourses of modernity. In her classic study *Sciences from Below: Feminisms, Postcolonialities, and Modernities,* Sandra Harding argues that in Western modernity, the feminine and primitive are associated with the traditional, and scientific rationality and technical expertise are presented as "one-way time machines that supposedly enable elite Westerners and men around the globe to escape the bonds of tradition" (1). In other words, Harding highlights a contradiction at the heart of discourses on modernity: they propose to deliver social progress to women and non-Western men and yet measure achievement in terms of their very distance from what is considered feminine and primitive (3). In this book, I consider how francophone writers negotiate this contradiction, by illustrating the ways in which African and Caribbean women and men can become decidedly modern through the appropriation of technologies and concomitant social progress.

Third, this book explores the questions of language selection, writing, and orality that are so central to studies of postcolonial literature. In the works of African and Caribbean authors, technology often serves as a metaphor for the francophone literary work in general, which is usually written in French by an author from a former colony and printed in France using European machinery. Thus the representation of technologies in francophone literature creates a figurative discourse for discussing the problematic place of the postcolonial literary work.

In fact, the great majority of the authors analyzed in my study, including Césaire, Senghor, Sembène, and Glissant, make frequent comparisons between literary forms (theater, poetry, and the novel) and technological innovations, such that the representation of technology constitutes a means of exploring the role of the French language and writing in the context of postcolonial societies. There are countless examples of this phenomenon: Senghor compared his poetry and the French language to technical instruments imported from Europe; Césaire viewed theater as a technology brought from the West to the Caribbean; Sembène compares the novel to a machine in *God's Bits of Wood;* and Édouard Glissant believes that the Internet will provide new forms of poetic inspiration.

Since these authors view technology as pertaining to a universal patrimony that all peoples should have the opportunity to acquire, their comparisons between technology and the French language or literature suggest that they believe that French, too, and writing more generally, constitute universal instruments detached from their particular cultural origins. This provides them with a means of both exploring and coming to terms with their own conflicting sentiments regarding the use of written French as a means of expression. The discussion of technology often serves as a defense of francophone literature itself and a means of justifying and explaining the linguistic choices of the authors, who have chosen to express themselves in French rather than in their native Creole or African languages.

Fourth, this book analyzes the complex relationship between aesthetics and politics in the francophone world by exploring the social function of literary texts. These works are not only artistic objects but also instruments for awakening the consciousness of readers and spectators in a manner that will ultimately prepare them for modernization. Francophone authors realize that it is not enough simply to introduce new technologies into their cultures, since a change in mentality must take place first in order to prepare the public to accept and adopt these innovations. This change in mentality involves undoing the illusionary discourse of the "civilizing mission," which asserts that Europeans are inherently superior to other peoples technologically and scientifically and that they have a "duty" to share their advanced knowledge through colonization.

There are numerous examples of this consciousness-raising: Césaire's theatrical trilogy on decolonization in the 1960s, whose performances are intended to illustrate to the audience, and the public more generally, the value of science and technology; Sembène's *God's Bits of Wood,* which seeks to persuade its readers of the need to embrace modern technologies in the era of independence; Fanon's journalistic writings, which emphasize the revolutionary potential of the colonizer's technologies, especially the radio; and Glissant's manifestos with Chamoiseau, which seek to educate the public about the global "*mise en relation*" (putting into relation) of cultures that results from the proliferation of new technologies, including the Internet.

The works by these authors are directed primarily at the inhabitants of their own countries, not their former colonizers. This marks a significant difference from many other francophone literary texts, which often focus on issues of colonization and strive to write against figures of authority, so that their implied audience appears to be as much in the metropole as it is in the former colonies. In contrast, Senghor, Césaire, Fanon, Sembène, Loba, and Glissant all explicitly state that they are addressing their own people and that they seek to instigate change within their own societies. For these writers, the production and reception of literature is coextensive with the work of the technician. In addition to supporting the transfer of technologies and the advent of modernity on a somewhat theoretical level, they have the highly practical objective of transforming the mentalities of postcolonial societies in a way that will ultimately lead to progress.

Fifth, this book proposes to examine the relationship between technology and ecology, which has emerged as a central issue in contemporary francophone literature, especially for authors from the Caribbean. One of the fundamental questions that these authors face is whether it is possible to develop economically and modernize in an ecologically responsible manner that preserves the landscape. Several earlier authors in my study (Césaire, Senghor, Fanon, Sembène) focus on the role that modern technologies will play in nation building after independence, often with disregard for the environmental consequences of modernization. For instance, when Fanon writes about modernization, there is no concern for the environment; the focus is rather on which social class will control the process and the division of power in the new order. In some francophone African texts, such as the postindependence novels by Aké Loba and Olympe Bhêly-Quénum, the traditional animist beliefs held by the villagers provide an ecological discourse avant la lettre, by ascertaining the importance of protecting the spirits that inhabit the untouched landscape; however, these are presented as backward beliefs that interfere with progress. In the case of the Caribbean, the character of Ariel in Césaire's *A Tempest*—who often speaks in defense of Nature—could likewise be considered an ecologist, although Césaire's work does not generally approach environmental issues. Glissant and Chamoiseau, on the other hand, do address questions of ecology and emphasize the need to perform technology transfer responsibly: Caribbean nations should have control over appropriations, and environmental consequences must be considered.

Finally, this study proposes to shed light on the growing field of digital humanities. Broadly speaking, the term "digital humanities" refers to the act of interpreting literature, culture, and history through new technologies, or, conversely, asking "traditional kinds of humanities-oriented questions about computing technologies."[19] The authors in my study could be considered early theorists of digital humanities for their positive evaluation of technology's potential for deepening humanistic inquiry. They frequently link technology and literature, even comparing the two in terms of their social functions; indeed, the francophone tradition clearly demonstrates how certain areas of digital humanities are firmly rooted in media studies. Césaire's use of mixed media in theater proposes a means of using the digital to communicate his message. For Senghor, the notion of the poet as a technician prefigures the way that the digital can become a source of poetic inspiration in the information age. Fanon's theories on communications systems in revolution highlight the way that technological innovation can shape political action. The radios in Sembène's *Moolaadé* represent the arrival of new media to the village and rural Africa more generally, from radios to television to film to the Internet and beyond. And Glissant and Chamoiseau present theories about how digital media transform human interactions, including the influence of Web browsing on the creation and reception of literary texts.

CHAPTER ONE

Science, Modernization, and the "Theater of Development" in Aimé Césaire

Scholars of Aimé Césaire have often argued that he understands writing as a means of recuperating the primordial unity between the mind and the senses that was lost at the moment of colonization, when the arrival of capitalism, modernization, and new technologies led to an alienation of consciousness, both from the body and from the world that surrounds it. Some of the most notable examples of such readings (which I will discuss in this chapter) include James Arnold's study of Césaire's poetry in *Modernism and Negritude* and Abiola Irele's introduction to his edition of the *Notebook of a Return to My Native Land* (21). Although these interpretations accurately describe Césaire's early poetry, they suggest that a stark dichotomy between a primitive, natural state and a modern, industrialized one is characteristic of Césaire's entire œuvre and thus fail to consider the changes in his attitude toward technology and modernization evident in his literary and political writings. By closely examining the understudied question of technology in Césaire's works, I seek to challenge the understanding of Negritude as characterized by an antimodern, antitechnological ideology.[1]

Césaire's early poetry—composed in the period between 1939 and 1956—frequently idealizes an agricultural way of life while condemning the mechanized existence of the West; yet the *Discourse on Colonialism* (an anticolonialist pamphlet first published in 1950) and his turn to theater in the early 1960s mark a shift toward an extremely favorable opinion of technology and modernization, which he always emphasized in his political speeches. Moreover, even when Césaire's writings do establish an opposition between a modernized West and an underdeveloped Africa, this division is rarely categorical. A close reader of Marx, he often makes a distinction between the Western capitalist use of a technological instrument to exploit the black proletariat, and the technology itself, which he views favorably, as evidenced by the way he consistently equates both the development of technologies in the colonies and their importation from Europe with "civilization" and "progress." Comparing the work of the artist to that of a technician, Césaire argues that the colonized, by becoming writers and engineers, are capable of overturning the fundamental hierarchy between creator and consumer that defines the oppressive colonial relationship. In his speeches as a politician, especially as a representative in the National Assembly in Paris, Césaire spoke adamantly in favor of modernization and industrialization in Martinique, and he believed that they held the key to rapid economic growth.

In this chapter, I will address the following questions: How is the relationship between race and technology portrayed in Césaire's writings? What is the significance of his move from poetry to theater in the early 1960s, in terms of his shifting attitudes toward modern Western technologies? How do his political speeches illuminate his literary works? Does Césaire, as both a writer and a politician, favor a return to the primal, natural state often idealized in his poetry, or rather a drive toward industrialization in forging a postcolonial culture for Martinique?

NOTEBOOK OF A RETURN TO MY NATIVE LAND

More than any other work by Césaire, the 1939 *Notebook of a Return to My Native Land* establishes an opposition between modernization and industrialization, which the narrator associates with the West, and a primordial unity between nature and the body, which he considers to be characteristic of black cultures. This opposition resembles the one found in Léopold Sédar Senghor's writings, probably as a result of their close friendship as fellow students at the École Normale Supérieure during the period (from 1936 to 1939) when Césaire began to write the first drafts of the *Notebook*.

When discussing the relationship between technology and race in the *Notebook*, critics have generally focused on the passage of the poem in which the narrator describes his race as, "Those who have invented neither gunpowder nor the compass / those who have never known how to subdue either steam or electricity/those who have explored neither the seas nor the sky" (111). The debate centers on whether this stanza constitutes either a celebration of the nontechnicity of the black races or an apology for it. In "Black Orpheus," Jean-Paul Sartre calls this declaration "a claim of non-technicalness" (51). For Lilyan Kesteloot, Césaire is implicitly recognizing the inferiority of his own race: "the humble, sorrowful, objective recognition of a genuine inferiority, counted among all the rest of his race's burdens, and, as such shouldered by Césaire" (*Comprendre le "Cahier"* 38). Abiola Irele asserts that the passage is both an acknowledgment of an inherent inferiority and a celebration of nontechnicity: "To situate Césaire's negritude in this way is also to account for what appears to be the apologetic stance implied by the celebration of the absence of technological achievement by the black race" (lv). Both Irele and Victor Houtondji take this notion further to suggest that it proves the existence, in Césaire's writings, of an essentialism akin to Senghor's; that is, the notion of a biologically inherited racial endowment (Irele 67). According to this idea, they believe that Césaire is positing that black peoples are inherently nontechnological. Similarly, Barbara Diese concludes that in the *Notebook*, "Césaire believes, as did Senghor, that Cartesian reason is not effective with Blacks" (44).

The major shortcoming of such interpretations is that they fail to consider the specific context of the innovations discussed by Césaire in this stanza, as well as the relationship between capitalism, exploitation, and technology that he presents throughout the *Notebook*. All of the inventions in this passage were used by Europeans in colonization and the slave trade and are thus inextricably linked to the exploitation of black peoples as workers. In the *Notebook*, the inhabitants of the city have been "proletarized" (to use Césaire's term from the *Discourse on Colonialism*) by the capitalist machines. The masses are asleep because they lack political consciousness: "This crowd which doesn't know how to be a crowd"; "this sorry crowd under the sun, taking part in nothing which expresses, asserts, frees itself in the broad daylight of its own land" (75). For the narrator, each inhabitant resembles the black man he sees on the tramway, whose very face has been transformed by this new form of technological, alienating labor: "It was a restless worker, was Poverty, working on some hideous cartridge. It was quite obvious how the industrious malevolent thumb had modelled lumps into the forehead" (107). Consequently, it is impossible to determine whether these elements—portrayed negatively in the poem—are inherently evil for the narrator or merely put to destructive use.

The close connection with technicity in the West and with nature in the colonies does not necessarily point to an essentialism akin to Senghor's, since the narrator of the *Notebook* never presents a relationship to technology that is independent of this history of suffering. In the famous passage on the lack of technological development of the black race, the narrator appears to be describing particular historical circumstances, which might have parallels to other oppressed peoples in Europe and elsewhere, rather than an intrinsic mode of being.

CIVILIZATION AND INDUSTRIALIZATION IN THE *DISCOURSE ON COLONIALISM*

Written eleven years after the *Notebook,* the *Discourse on Colonialism* is much less ambiguous about the value of technology, emphasizing its liberating potential if successfully appropriated, and more restrained in its exaltation of agrarian society. This shift is marked by a distinction between "colonization" and "civilization" that is introduced in the *Discourse:* although Césaire unambiguously criticizes the former, he nevertheless equates the latter with the modernization, industrialization, technological development, and "Europeanization" he would like to see in the colonies. Césaire is careful here to dissociate colonization and its violence from other forms of cultural contact, such as the transfer of scientific knowledge and technology, which he sees as beneficial and productive.

At the beginning of the *Discourse,* Césaire describes cultural contact in general as a positive phenomenon: "I admit that it is a good thing to place different civilizations in contact with each other; that it is an excellent thing to blend different worlds" (11). In a striking reversal of an Orientalist trope, he argues that Europe's advantage was due to its central position at the crossroads of various cultures: "The great good fortune of Europe is to have been a crossroads, and that because it was the locus of all ideas, the receptacle of all philosophies, the meeting place of all sentiments, it was the best center for the redistribution of energy" (11). Indeed, later on in the *Discourse,* Césaire suggests that scientific knowledge in Africa (broadly conceived to include the Near East) was stolen by Europe and used to create technologies that were then employed for the exploitation of the black proletariat in the colonies. Refuting Caillois's thesis that the West invented science, he writes: "To wit, the invention of arithmetic and geometry by the Egyptians. To wit, the discovery of astronomy by the Assyrians. To wit, the birth of chemistry among the Arabs. To wit, the appearance of rationalism in Islam at a time when Western thought had a furiously pre-logical cast to it" (52). Although Europe has benefited greatly from contact with other cultures, Césaire argues that European colonization disrupted the development of technologies in Africa and elsewhere: "No one knows at what stage of material development these same countries would have been if Europe had not intervened" (24). Despite this claim, he does not argue that African peoples had developed *modern* technologies or that they are in the process of independently producing the kind of technology he feels the colonies greatly need.

Given these circumstances, Césaire advocates a new type of interaction between the former colonies and Europe, distinct from imperialism, that will result in development. In contrast to the destructive violence of colonization, Césaire uses the term "Europeanization" to describe the positive form of cultural interaction with Europe that will lead to development: "The technical outfitting of Africa and Asia, their administrative reorganization, in a word, their 'Europeanization' was (as is proved by the example of Japan) in no way tied to the European *occupation*" (24). Although Césaire does not offer a precise definition of "Europeanization," he uses it as a rough synonym for modernization. At one point in the essay, he makes the paradoxical claim that colonialism made the colonies less "Europeanized" than they would have been without it: "The Europeanization of the non-European continents could have been accomplished otherwise than under the heel of Europe; since this movement of Europeanization *was in progress;* since it was even slowed down; since in any case it was distorted by the European takeover" (24). Thus, Césaire never truly dissociates technological development from Europe.

Given the importance of cultural interaction, rather than breaking with Europe altogether, Césaire suggests that a "non-occupational" mode of contact between colony and metropole provides the only means by which the former can acquire the "material development" that he views so positively. He cites the colonies' demand for construction and Europe's refusal to intervene: "The proof is that at present it is the indigenous peoples of Africa and Asia who are demanding schools, and colonialist Europe which refuses them; that it is the African who is asking for ports and roads, and colonialist Europe which is niggardly on this score; that it is the colonized man who wants to move forward, and the colonizer who holds things back" (25). For Césaire, the building of schools, bridges, and highways in the colonies requires the assistance and consent of the colonizer; he implies that the colonized must demand that their former European colonizers help them acquire what they do not have, because they cannot create it themselves.

In order to justify his eagerness to maintain close ties to the same European powers that were so destructive in the process of colonization, Césaire warns of the dangers in viewing the United States as a possible liberator from European domination ("I know that some of you, disgusted with Europe, with all that hideous mess which you did not witness by choice, are turning—oh! in no great numbers—toward America and getting used to looking upon that country as a possible liberator") and calls American imperialism, "the only domination from which one never recovers" (60). While in the *Notebook,* the European slave trader and entrepreneur is considered to be the greatest enemy of the African peoples, in the *Discourse,* American capitalism poses the most imminent threat to the indigenous cultures of Martinique.

In sum, in the *Discourse,* Césaire places himself in a position from which to advocate the acquisition of European innovations, which he believes to be the best means of improving the standard of living in the Antilles, all the while condemning the colonial violence that has been so destructive. On the one hand, he debunks the imperial ideology that the "obvious material progress" in the colony serves to justify domination, asserting that technological progress was made not because of colonization but in spite of it. On the other hand, he continues to associate technological development with maintaining close ties to Europe.

THE "THEATER OF DEVELOPMENT"

From 1963 to 1969, Césaire devoted himself almost exclusively to the production of plays, which he staged in collaboration with Jean-Marie Serreau, a well-known French theater director. In a series of speeches, interviews, and essays written throughout the 1960s and 1970s, Césaire explained the objectives of his move from the more personal, individual form of poetry to the collective medium of theater. His turn from poetry to theater in the late 1960s was a self-proclaimed attempt to further his political project of Negritude, an effort "to make the visionary poetics of negritude more widely accessible" (Livingston 182), especially given the low rate of literacy in Martinique at the time, which made it difficult for him to use any form of printed material as an effective medium for transmitting his message. In some of these speeches, he explicitly situates his productions within the context of the "theater of development" movement, while employing a heavily technological vocabulary to describe playwriting and production as an important kind of media brought from the West, which must be appropriated by the colonies in order to provoke material development and the creation of a modern, industrialized nation in the wake of decolonization. In a discussion with Jean-Marie Serreau and students that took place in Jouy-en-Josas on November 6, 1967, Césaire proposes to create a "theater of development" that will play a key role in transforming Martinique into a modernized nation (Laville 240). In his speech, Césaire declares that he produces theater for underdeveloped countries because he himself comes from one (240). For Césaire, the acquisition of theater as a mode of expression can mean the difference between development and underdevelopment.

The term "theater of development" was coined in Africa at the beginning of the 1960s to refer to plays performed by NGOs as a means of raising awareness about economic, educational, and health issues. During the spread of the "theater of development" movement, the same nonprofit organizations that distributed televisions, radios, and other technologies to African communities put on plays to educate the public about them. By staging spectacles that could be performed anywhere and involved the participation of the audience, the "theater of development" sought to pave the way for economic progress by transferring to the "people" the means of producing theater, much like NGOs distributed communications technologies to the masses. The use of the term "theater of development" was soon extended to apply to the spectacles created and staged by African and Caribbean playwrights for autochthonous audiences, with the goal of promoting an awareness of current events and contemporary issues.

By referring to his own productions with Serreau as a "theater of development" and emphasizing the importance of their role in decolonization, Césaire seeks to link his own work to this movement, which was simultaneously taking place in Africa. In a speech from 1967, Césaire appropriates one of the foundational concepts of "theater of development," the notion of "conscientization" (*conscientização*) invented by Paulo Freire, a figure of enormous stature in popular movements both in his homeland of Brazil and abroad.[2] In his Marxist analysis of the conditions necessary for modernization in Latin America, Freire asserts in *Pedagogy of the Oppressed* that development is not a given but rather something that evolves through the collective action and reflection of all members of society. For Freire, this action can occur only through "conscientization," or a raising of awareness, which he views as the opposite of the "consumerism" of students who go to school. Freire believes that many activities, artistic or political, that lead to collective action and reflection, can provoke conscientization and thus provide the means of breaking free from this oppressive consumerism. It was precisely by means of his theater that Césaire sought to provoke the conscientization that Freire describes.

Césaire's critique of the creator/consumer hierarchy as characteristic of the colonial power dynamic in "L'homme de culture et ses responsabilités" (The man of culture and his responsibilities) echoes Freire's description of students and audience members as "consumers" of a product that is placed before them by capitalist entrepreneurs. In "L'homme de culture," the "creator" is initially associated with the colonizer, and the "consumer" with the colonized. Césaire writes that colonialism negates the creation of the colonized and establishes a creator/consumer hierarchy that is implicit in the master/servant relationship: "The colonial regime is negation of the act: negation of creation. In colonial society there is not only a master-servant hierarchy. There is also an implicit creator-consumer hierarchy" (117–18).[3] In this power dynamic, the colonizer is the creator of all cultural values, and the colonized is the consumer: "In a proper colonization, the creator of cultural values is the colonizer. And the consumer is the colonized" (118). By forcing the role of consumer onto the colonized, while precluding him from becoming a creator, the colonizer imposes his domination.

Nevertheless, the association between the colonizer, colonized, and the roles of creator and consumer, respectively, are not fixed for Césaire and are certainly not overdetermined by race. In his view, any act of creation undertaken by the colonized is revolutionary since it undermines the foundation of this hierarchy: "All creation, because it is creation, is participation in a liberating struggle. Yet cultural creation, precisely because it is creation, disrupts things. It turns things upside down. Beginning with the colonial hierarchy, for it turns the colonized consumer into the creator" ("L'homme de culture" 118). Césaire writes that all intellectuals or "men of culture" must extract a national sentiment from the people, just as a farmer harvests grain from the earth and stores it in silos: "Yes, when all is said and done, it is up to the artists, the writers, the men of culture, to establish these great reserves of faith, these great silos of strength from which peoples, at critical moments, draw the courage to stand on their own two feet and change the course of the future" ("L'homme de culture" 118). For Césaire, both the artists and intellectuals in the colonies play a crucial role in the process of decolonization and development in the colonies by overturning the hierarchy he describes.

Césaire's essay suggests that the role of creator can be assumed by the colonized by initiating any act of creation, including the development of new technologies, yet when he mentions instances in which members of the colonized culture have overturned the oppressive hierarchy he describes, he only provides examples of intellectuals who have done so by writing, such as René Maran and Jean-Joseph Rabearivelo. Consequently, it is difficult to determine the extent to which Césaire believes that the colonized are capable of producing scientific and technological creations. Nevertheless, by shifting the emphasis in "L'homme de culture" from the dichotomy between technology and nature to the creator/consumer hierarchy, Césaire opens the way for the discourse he will produce on theater, in which the director and the poet will be compared to technicians, as persons who assume the role of creator.

In a 1963 interview, Césaire illustrates the extent to which he views his theater as a potential means of transforming the colonized by raising their awareness of contemporary issues. He declares that the social function of theater consists of combating the current political situation in a country by provoking in the people a "conscientization" (*prise de conscience*) leading to progress: "Consequently, my theater, from the point of view of development, must play a social role. The theater will fulfill its social function, not only by allowing people to see, but also by helping them to understand and to come to consciousness" (Laville 240). According to Césaire, the "problem of underdevelopment" will be overcome once the people emerge from their current state of unawareness: "When I consider the problem of underdevelopment, it seems to me that the welfare of underdeveloped countries will not be assured until their people have moved beyond their current state of lack of awareness" (Laville 240). This is precisely the "inertia" that Césaire famously evoked at the beginning of the *Notebook;* theater provides for him a means of overcoming the problematic "lack of consciousness."

Césaire presents theater as a kind of communications technology capable of producing this "coming to consciousness" by transmitting information about current events to the inhabitants of African nations. Freire writes that in order for "conscientization" to occur, it is necessary to transfer to the "people" the ability to use various modes of communications, including not only books and mass media technologies but also theater. In the absence of mass media, theater is, for Césaire, a key mode of communicating information in Africa. In a 1969 speech, he proclaims, “Africa is entering into the age of theatricality,” and adds, “It is necessary to speak clearly, speak concisely, in order to convey the message [*faire passer le message*]” (qtd. in Owusu-Sarpong 19).

Unlike the language of Césaire’s poetry, which is full of double meaning and ambiguities that show the possible coexistence of “A and non-A,” as Césaire wrote in “Poetry and Knowledge,” the language of his theater is meant to be a technical instrument for the transmission of information. The “message” that is to be transmitted concerns the current problems of the colonies and is forward-looking, promoting progress: “Politics is the modern form of destiny; today, history is lived politics. The theater must evoke the invention of the future” (Laville 239–40). By provoking a collective “coming to consciousness” of the current political situation, Césaire’s theater is meant to transform the passive “consumer” of the spectacle into a “creator” capable of inducing change.

CÉSAIRE, BRECHT, AND JEAN-MARIE SERREAU

Césaire’s ideas regarding the relationship between technology and theater, and their potential role in “consciousness-raising,” were also tremendously influenced by the work of Bertolt Brecht, a German playwright and director whose ideas in turn influenced the “theater of development” movement. In the 1967 discussion in Jouy-en-Josas, Césaire cites Brecht’s thinking as a major influence: “This lines up with Brecht’s ideas. My plays have a critical function, they must make the public judge” (Laville 240). In a 1978 interview, he admits to having read Brecht’s theories about “distanciation” and declares his admiration for a great number of Brecht’s plays, including *Mother Courage and Her Children, The Exception and the Rule,* and *The Caucasian Chalk Circle* (Dunn and Césaire 3).

In his essays, Brecht wrote about the need to create a new theater capable of provoking the spectators’ judgment, while using the latest technological innovations to capture their interest. His “epic theater” is meant to arouse the spectators’ capacity for action by presenting ideas and inviting the audience to make judgments about them. Explicitly linking his work to Brecht, Césaire himself once described his theater as “Epic”: “My theatre is not an individual or individualist theatre, it is an epic theatre for it always presents the fate of a whole community” (qtd. in Bradby 146). David Bradby observes that Césaire’s “plays present all the characteristics that we have identified for Epic theatre: they tell their story by means of contradictions, present their characters in fragmentary form and rely on strong didactic and gestural qualities. Above all, they are plays which aim to arouse the critical reactions of their audiences" (146).

Brecht envisions the creation of a "theater of the scientific age," which, instead of competing against the newer means of communication, tries to apply them and learn from them. He emphasizes the central role of technology in the theater of his day. For him, plays must incorporate these into their scenography to be effective "innovations" or "inventions." He coins the term "apparatus" to describe the instruments of mass communication, including the latest technological developments, such as radio, photography, film, and the telegraph, and describes theater as a communications technology that forms part of this "apparatus" (Brecht 225).

According to Brecht, the theater, like other organs of mass communication, is a means of production, which is controlled by the bourgeoisie but must be brought into the hands of the masses. For Brecht, the traditional conception of theater as a series of hypnotic illusions presents the performance to the spectator as a commodity produced by capitalists and sold to consumers; he thus calls for a battle against illusion making, which he considers to be the instrument of fascist ideology, and views new technologies as an ally in this battle. In the "Manifesto of the Censier Committee," he writes that through the incorporation of radio and technology in his plays, he hopes to democratize and revolutionize theater. Brecht sees the "functional transformation" of theater through technology as a way of liberating the means of production, which are imprisoned in the hands of the bourgeoisie and must be transferred to the "people."

Césaire viewed his collaboration with Jean-Marie Serreau as a way of creating the kind of theater that Brecht describes. Serreau, who had once been involved in the Resistance movement during the German occupation of France, played a central role in the creation of two groups dedicated to the use of theater for political ends: T.E.C. (Travail et Culture [Work and culture]) and C.I.D. (Culture par l'Initiation Dramatique [Culture by dramatic initiation]). He wrote a number of pieces for the journals of these organizations that express a profound belief in the democratic value of a grassroots approach to culture, and he was the first director to introduce many of Brecht's plays to the French stage.

After meeting Serreau in 1960, Césaire wrote his trilogy on decolonization, *The Tragedy of King Christophe, A Season in the Congo,* and *A Tempest,* and became actively involved in the productions of these plays under Serreau's direction. Even before Serreau met Césaire, he already envisioned the creation of a new "consciousness-raising" "theater of development" that would incorporate the latest multimedia technologies to produce a vivid spectacle capable of being transported anywhere. In 1942 Serreau had helped to found the group Travail et Culture, a theatrical company that worked to transform theater into a means of educating the public and creating a popular culture; and in 1969, he established the A.C.T. (L'atelier des techniques de communication [Communications technology workshop]), a group that investigated the problems and benefits associated with the diffusion of new technological innovations. Serreau held the Brechtian perspective according to which theater is considered part of the apparatus of mass communications; he believed that life in the theater had to exist at the center of a communication network of economic circuits (Bradby 128). Serreau talked about the need to create a theater lively enough to compete with television, "these new ceremonies, television's major public broadcasts," and he said that the "new theater" (*le nouveau théâtre*)[4] that he was creating with Césaire would "attempt to establish a synthesis between scientific knowledge and poetic knowledge" (Masson 13; qtd. in Bradby 144).

Césaire's productions with Serreau involved the use of large screens onto which photographic images were projected, recorded music, and short film segments. They constructed a "portable spectacle," a multimedia experience that could be transported to various locales, like a mass media device. Robert Livingston writes about the performance of Césaire's plays in "Decolonizing the Theatre": "Incorporating music, song, dance, choral movement, political satire and audiovisual technology, Serreau crossed Brecht with [Marshall] McLuhan [the communications theorist who coined the phrase "the medium is the message"] to envision a mobile theatre for the global village" (184). Much as Brecht saw theater as analogous to new technologies such as radio in its potential to reach the masses while avoiding the isolation and elitism of the avant-garde, Césaire viewed it as a means of accessing a wider audience and, like Brecht, perceived new technologies to be a means of democratizing theater, as evidenced by his collaborations with Jean-Marie Serreau.

Although Césaire seeks to situate his productions within the "theater of development" movement and tries to appropriate Freire's notions of "conscientization" and "consumerism," he never fully succeeds, because his plays follow traditional theatrical norms, according to which the spectators passively watch a spectacle that is presented to them. Césaire claims, in a 1970 interview, that he turned to theater in an attempt "to bring poetry down to the level of the street" (Fuyet et al. 1110). In fact, fundamental differences exist between his plays and those of other playwrights who more fully integrated Freire's ideology into their practice, most notably the Brazilian Augusto Boal, an influential writer, director, and politician. In another foundational work of the "theater of development" movement, Boal's *Theatre of the Oppressed,* Boal describes his vision of a "dialectical form of theater" that he developed during the 1950s and 1960s, which is meant to transfer the means of producing a play to the spectators by teaching them how to make theater. Boal's main objective was to demonstrate that theater could be practiced by anyone in any place and that any event could be "theatricalized."[5] Boal took to the streets, creating improvisational theater that used ordinary citizens as actors and took place in everyday settings, such as factories, prisons, and markets. Unlike Boal's plays, Césaire's works were performed exclusively in theaters—often in Europe rather than in the former colonies—and therefore failed, for the most part, to reach the audience considered by Césaire to be most in need of "conscientization."

Consequently, Césaire's reference to the "theater of development" movement—which often involved the use of indigenous peoples as actors and producers—as well as his use of Freire's term in his speech, constitutes a means of presenting his plays as more "authentic" and in tune with the masses by linking his theatrical work more strongly to Africa, but he does not necessarily describe the actual function of his plays in the former colonies as a political instrument. Plays such as *The Tragedy of King Christophe* and *A Tempest* attempt to follow the ideology of "theater of development" by presenting characters who represent the "people," with whom the spectators are meant to identify, but the plays fall considerably short of involving them to the extent that the true practitioners of the movement, such as Boal, were capable of doing. Césaire's plays do not incorporate the public directly in the action and are written in a language complex enough so as to cast doubt on their comprehensibility to an illiterate population and on their ability to produce the desired "conscientization." Césaire may have overturned the consumer/creator relationship that he describes, but the passive spectator remains a "consumer" who takes in a spectacle produced by others.

NATION BUILDING THROUGH PERFORMANCE IN *THE TRAGEDY OF KING CHRISTOPHE*

In 1963, Césaire published his first play in collaboration with Jean-Marie Serreau, *The Tragedy of King Christophe,* which they staged together at the Salzburg Festival in Austria the following year. The plot of this play focuses on the construction of an enormous citadel by the Haitian King Henri Christophe, which constitutes an explicit metaphor for the establishment of national consciousness in the newly independent Caribbean and African territories. Throughout the play, nation building is presented as a twofold process involving both the construction of the fortress and a series of performances before the people of the nation and the rest of the world. Many elements of the play can be interpreted in terms of the hierarchy between "creator" and "consumer" that Césaire considers to be so central to the power dynamics of colonialism; in *King Christophe,* both the people of the nation and its leaders undermine this hierarchy—which still exerts an influence over them in the postindependence era—by becoming "creators" of the citadel, performances, and festivals.

The various instances of spectacles in *King Christophe* unlock a game of plays within the play (mise en abyme) in which the performances that take place within the narrative constitute an allegory for the role of theater in nation building in the former colonies. The first scene of *King Christophe* (called the "prologue" in the stage directions) emphasizes the relationship between power and performance by presenting a spectacle, the cockfight, within the performance of the play itself. In this scene, two cocks fight each other while a crowd of people, who are described in the stage directions as "the mob" (*la foule*) cheer them on. One is named Pétion, the other Christophe, and they are meant to represent the two leaders who battle for control of the state. By winning the cockfight, which is a representation of civil war, Christophe's rule gains a legitimacy—albeit one that will be repeatedly called into question—both in the eyes of the nation's people, represented by the crowd that watches the spectacles, and the Western world.

The idea that the Western world is watching the cockfight, or civil war, as a means of determining the nation's legitimate leader, is suggested by the Brechtian figure of the "presenter-commentator." Brecht often had a character in his plays that stood outside the action and commented on it, in order to break any potential illusion created on the stage, by forcing the spectator to assume a distance from it. Césaire's "presenter-commentator" plays a similar role: by analyzing the action and commenting on it, she asks the spectator to reflect upon what has taken place. In each of Césaire's productions of *King Christophe,* the "presenter-commentator," who interprets the action of the prologue and gives a brief history of the nation in her commentary, was dressed in clothes made from the pattern of the American flag, and held many cameras. By presenting the "presenter-commentator" as a journalist from a news organization who reports back to the rest of the world what she witnesses in Haiti, the play implies, from the very beginning, that the events occurring in the colonies are being constantly scrutinized by the West through the media.

Throughout the play, Christophe and the ministers of his cabinet are continually trying to fashion an image of him before the world, since they believe that every one of his actions is being broadcast internationally. Christophe's power is based on a series of performances that are meant to project an image of him as a legitimate ruler before Western cameras and the people of Haiti. As suggested by the "presenter-commentator" in the commentary following the prologue, in order to be considered a king by other nations and the media, Christophe believes that he must conform to the standard image of one, as established by French rulers such as Louis XIV: "Yes, Christophe was king. King like Louis XIII, Louis XIV, Louis XVI and a few others. And like every king, every true king, every white king I mean, he created a court and surrounded himself with a nobility" (9). Immediately before Christophe rides in on a horse to greet the crowds, Vastey declares: "The whole world is watching us, citizens, and the nations think that black men have no dignity. A king, a court, a kingdom, that's what we've got to show them if we want to be respected" (18). By imitating these French conventions, Christophe and his advisors believe that they are projecting an image of his power throughout the world; nevertheless, by following such outdated models, they fail to establish their authority.

In *King Christophe,* Césaire often draws an analogy between the transfer of technologies from the metropolis and the use of theater as an artistic means of expression. In several scenes in the play, the role of moderator (*meneur de jeu*) or play director (*metteur en scène*) is associated with the work of a technician or engineer. Christophe's first act as king is to assemble a court and to receive, from the "International Technical Aid Organization," a "master of ceremonies." This master of ceremonies who arrives in act 1, scene 3, is described in the stage directions as "a White man, sent by TESCO (Technical, Educational, Scientific

Cooperation Organization) in order to provide assistance" (20).[6] His work consists of staging a formal ceremony that will take place in front of foreign cameras in order to give the regime an aura of legitimacy. Upon entering the palace, he takes charge: "Come, come, gentlemen. Forgive me for rushing you, but the King will be here any minute. We really have to begin our rehearsal. I shall call the roll and review the general principles of the ceremony" (20). The master of ceremonies is a director who casts the ministers into various roles and forces them to rehearse their parts. He spends all of his time training the ministers to perform a carefully staged ceremony that he claims will be followed closely by the whole world: "It is a ceremony of the utmost importance, gentlemen. The world has its eyes on us" (20).

The role of the master of ceremonies is reminiscent of that of the professor in Molière's *The Middle-Class Gentleman,* who teaches Monsieur Jourdain how to act in order to switch social classes, a connection that is intentional and that Césaire himself makes in a 1978 interview (Dunn and Césaire 7). Just as the professor in Molière's play would like to teach Monsieur Jourdain how to assume membership in another social class, the master of ceremonies attempts to teach Christophe and his ministers how to join the group of world leaders headed by those in the West. There is no technical component to the work he does; and yet, the fact that he was sent by a technical aid organization suggests an analogy between the director of a play and a technician. The theater is thus associated with a consciousness-raising communications technology that the leaders must master in order to assert their authority. The play suggests that in order to truly become leaders capable of provoking economic and social development, they must adapt to the new modes of representing power that exist in the modern era, by learning to perform in front of the cameras; theater, too, must change in order to become part of a global media culture.

Since the master of ceremonies is very much a comic character, many critics have assumed that his function within the play is entirely satirical. Maximilien Laroche describes "the ridiculous process by which the TESCO representative teaches these exotic gestures" (42), while Robert Eric Livingston calls the scene a "satirical dig on Western aid programs" (65). The analysis of this scene generally hinges on the precise interpretation of Vastey's remarks upon the arrival of the master of ceremonies at the court: "Whom did Europe send us when we applied to the International Technical Aid Organization for assistance? Not an engineer. Not a soldier. Not a professor. A master of ceremonies!" (21). In his commentary on this scene, Albert Owusu-Sarpong writes: "In this process of decolonization, Europe, true to its mission, will send Christophe a white master of ceremonies instead of technical aid for developing countries; it is Vastey who underscores the useless presence of this delegate sent by the Tesco" (131). He continues: "Césaire criticizes technical cooperation and aid to developing countries because this cooperation only burdens a country with protocols they must follow instead of solving real problems. Thus France sends to King Christophe not a professor, nor an engineer, nor an expert, but rather a master of ceremonies" (176). Laroche and Livingston also interpret the phrase quite literally to mean that Césaire is criticizing the West for having sent a theater director to the former colony, as opposed to someone with more useful skills, such as an engineer, soldier, or professor. Livingston concludes that the character of the master of ceremonies represents the kind of useless ties that the former colonies still have with the metropolis and that by means of this character, Césaire satirizes Western assistance in general.

Nevertheless, the conclusion that the primary function of the master of ceremonies is to mock the kind of assistance sent by the metropolis—which presumably sends theater directors instead of more urgently needed engineers and soldiers—ignores the extent to which theater forms an integral part of development for Césaire. We have seen how Césaire adopted the principles of the "theater of development" and sought a means of practicing it in a way that would educate the illiterate masses and provoke their consciousness in preparation for development. The name of the organization that sends the master of ceremonies in *King Christophe,* TESCO, sounds like a combination of UNESCO, and the "TID," or "theater in development," an organization that sent theater troops along with communications technologies to developing countries throughout the 1960s and 1970s as a means of educating the populations on social and medical issues. Moreover, Vastey's comment about how TESCO has sent a master of ceremonies rather than a technician or soldier recalls a line from "L'homme de culture" in which Césaire mocks Westerners who declare that technicians are more urgently needed than artists in the former colonies: "Westerners say: 'It's strange: it is technicians that they need, and it is artists that they produce" (117). Throughout this essay, Césaire attempts to show that the artist's role in raising consciousness is a necessary precursor to the developmental work of the technician; in general, he considers the role of the theater director in development to be just as important—if not more so—as that of the technician, soldier, or professor.

In the productions of *King Christophe,* the role of the master of ceremonies was played by Jean-Marie Serreau himself, a casting choice that unlocks a game of play-within-a-play (mise en abyme). The staging of the play thus established an analogy between the role of the master of ceremonies and that of Serreau: both are theater directors sent from the West as part of a "theater of development" initiative to promote development in the former colonies. While the master of ceremonies works with the ministers on creating a performance that will establish their legitimacy before the people and the world, Serreau came from France to produce a series of Césaire's plays, which were meant to educate the public about current events, as part of a process that Césaire himself viewed as an essential component of nation building. For Césaire, the performance of the play itself is a kind of "technology" brought to the colonies from the metropolis by figures like Serreau, to be utilized in the drive toward modernization.

Christophe sees himself as both a technician whose task it is to construct an enormous fortress representing the nation, and a moderator (*meneur de jeu*) who organizes festival performances and pronounces an epilogue at the end of the play. For Christophe, the work of nation building is at once that of the engineer and the poet; it is a "work" (*œuvre*) as evidenced by his ambiguous use of this term. He declares, with regard to the citadel he is building: "Giving a people the possibility of reaching its full potential, giving it back its proper values, human dignity and desire to work, this work [*œuvre*] must be led by a foreman, a builder, an architect who is both an engineer and a poet" (37). Christophe is continually drawing analogies between the work of constructing the citadel and that of molding the minds of the population to make them subscribe to a national ideology. While speaking to one of his ministers, Vastey, he declares: "There you have it, Vastey. The human material needs recasting" (37). In addition to building the citadel, Christophe tries to instigate a mass plan to educate the people, and at the same time that he builds the fortress, he organizes festivals and spectacles with the intent of allowing them to play a more active role in artistic and political life. In Césairian terms, he could be said to have the goal of transforming the passive population from "consumers" into "creators" through performance, education, and construction; both the performances at festivals and the work involved in building the fort constitute acts of creation that undermine the power of the metropole by overturning the colonial hierarchy.

Christophe valorizes science and technology and sees himself as an engineer, such that his conception of building a nation through construction and performance goes against the idea proposed by the white farmer in the play, Wilberforce, who advocates a more natural, agricultural form of development. As John Conteh-Morgan has astutely pointed out, "Unlike Christophe, who sees development essentially as creation, Wilberforce sees it as growth" (228). Conteh-Morgan perceives a contradiction between Christophe's promotion of industrialization and his status as a representative of Negritude, when one of the basic tenets of Negritude is the valorization of agriculture:

> One thing that is obvious, however, is that by consistently choosing stone and cement as opposed to wood, by likening the political leader of a developing country to an engineer, a constructor, a craftsman as opposed to a farmer (Wilberforce's choice), Césaire's hero would seem to be evincing, unconsciously perhaps, a preference for an industrial as opposed to an agricultural society. Or more precisely, he would seem to be equating development with industrialization. But if indeed such is his choice, (and the evidence from imagery is overwhelming), is it not sharply at variance with the entire ethic of Négritude that he otherwise embodies so well, with its exaltation of the values of agrarian, non-industrial cultures? (228–29)

Conteh-Morgan considers Christophe's advocacy of an industrial state to be a paradox. In what is ultimately an accusation of essentialism, he writes that in the *Cahier,* Césaire posits "scientific rationalism and intuition as distinctive traits of the white and black minds respectively" (229). As evidence of this idea, Conteh-Morgan cites the passage in which the narrator of that work declares, "My negritude is neither a tower nor a cathedral" (115) as well as the stanza beginning, "Those who have invented neither gunpowder nor the compass" (111), discussed earlier in this chapter.

But the different means of representing the relationship between race and technology in the *Notebook* and *King Christophe* do not necessarily point to a contradiction in Césaire's ideology regarding modernization. Rather, they reflect a shift in his attitude regarding white, European colonizers that occurred between the publication of the *Notebook* and his metamorphosis into a playwright. By the time Césaire wrote *King Christophe,* the representation of the relationship between race and technology in his writings had evolved considerably, as evidenced by the *Discourse,* such that the portrayal of a black Haitian leader who promotes an all-out drive toward modernization and industrialization should not be all that surprising. Through the character of Wilberforce, Césaire criticizes the opponents of modernization in the former colonies, such as the French political figures whom Césaire accuses of denying these colonies new technologies and industrialization.[7]

Just as Christophe builds the citadel in order to show the world that he is the leader of a modernized, industrialized nation, Césaire believes that the creation of theater in the former colonies demonstrates their capacity to develop. The parallels between performance and the construction of the citadel throughout *King Christophe* are meant to illustrate the potential role of theater in the nation-building process. Yet the theater that Christophe, like Césaire, envisions for the former colonies is not a grassroots movement that draws on indigenous traditions for its performances but a series of spectacles resulting from a collaboration with a French director from the metropolis who incorporates all of the latest technologies into the performance. Some critics have argued that Césaire's theater calls for revolutionary action that will sever all ties with the metropolis, in order to recuperate the lost, natural state of Negritude. In "The Hero of Negritude in the Theater of Aimé Césaire," for instance, Seth Wolitz describes Césaire's plays as a prime example of socially engaged literature (*littérature engagée*) that expresses the ideal of Negritude and calls for revolutionary action: "All the plays of Césaire are *pièces à thèse* which call for the overthrow of colonial or neocolonial societies and their replacement with the ideals of Negritude exemplified by the martyred hero" (198). Nevertheless, Césaire's theater could not be said to advocate such a complete overthrow of the neocolonial order because it frequently advocates the maintenance of strong ties with the former colonizers as a means of promoting development through cooperative interaction, such as the transfer of technologies from the metropolis and the use of a theatrical mode of production imported from Europe.

SCIENCE, ILLUSION MAKING, AND CAPITALISM IN *A TEMPEST*

Césaire's best-known play, *A Tempest* (1969), a modern adaptation of Shakespeare's *The Tempest,* presents a confrontation between Prospero, the white European explorer, and Caliban, the African slave who also represents a proletariat worker. *A Tempest* presents a Brechtian paradigm for theater in the era of decolonization, according to which the primary struggle between Prospero and Caliban is over ownership of the means of production, which include science, technology, and "illusion making," or theater. Marx writes in *Capital* that those who possess the means of production control the formation of ideas (98); for Brecht, theater represents a prime example of this phenomenon, since he considers the theater to be a technology—a means of production—owned by capitalists who use it to monopolize the role of the producer and force others to become consumers of their commodities. In Césaire's version of the story, Prospero is at once a capitalist entrepreneur, an inventor, and an illusion maker. His ownership of the means of production, which he refuses to share, constitutes the basis of his power on the island by allowing him to govern over those who are economically dependent on him and giving him the ability to trick others through the creation of deceptive spectacles.

The Brechtian paradigm that characterizes *A Tempest* has its origins in a play that greatly influenced its writing and production, Brecht's 1936 *The Exception and the Rule,* which Serreau directed in 1962 immediately before beginning work with Césaire on the production of *A Tempest*. In a 1978 interview, Césaire declares his great love for this Brechtian play, which he describes as "a perfect masterpiece" (Dunn and Césaire 8). In *The Exception and the Rule,* a thirty-minute play written with the intention of performing it in schools and factories as a means of educating the masses, a rich merchant crosses the desert with his porter. When the porter offers the merchant some water, the latter shoots him, believing that he is being attacked. The merchant is accused of murder, but the court then acquits him, stating that he was right to assume that the porter would want to avenge his cruel treatment, a "rule" for which they could imagine no exception. In an interview about his production of *The Exception and the Rule,* Serreau refers to the merchant as the "colonizer" and the porter as the "colonized," thus establishing an analogy between the merchant-porter relationship in Brecht's play, and that of Prospero and Caliban in *A Tempest*. In each of the two relationships, there is one character, the merchant or Prospero, who represents a capitalist with the means of production, ruling over another character, Caliban, who depends on him as a result of the lack of these same means of production. The influence of this play on the representation of the colonizer/colonized relationship in *A Tempest* is reflected in the characterization of Prospero primarily as a capitalist entrepreneur.

Many critics have considered Prospero's power to be a representation of colonial domination in general and have viewed all of the white European characters in the play as serving essentially the same function within the plot. James Arnold, for instance, writes: "Our latter-day Prospero is presented as the agent of European capitalism at its inception. Alonso and Antonio are not essentially different from him in this respect. Quite consistent in their actions, they have merely dispossessed Prospero so that they may better exploit his lands for their own profit" ("Césaire and Shakespeare" 237). Such a reading, though not entirely inaccurate, does not take into account the precise nature of Prospero's power, which differs greatly from the political and administrative authority represented by Antonio (the Duke of Milan) and Alonso (the king of Naples); nor does it consider the elements of the play that highlight its status as a theatrical production and establish a clear distinction between Prospero, as a creator of spectacles, and the other European characters.

In *A Tempest,* Prospero is neither a political leader nor a representative of the colonial administration. Rather, he is a capitalist entrepreneur, an inventor, and a maker of illusions, whose power derives from the scientific and technical knowledge that he acquired in Europe as a Renaissance man, rather than any authority given to him by a government. Prospero holds a tenuous relationship with the European government that supposedly controls the region, represented by Alonso and his advisor, Gonzalo. In act 1, scene 1, it becomes clear that the hierarchies of this government no longer hold in the New World when Gonzalo tries to claim some kind of authority based on his close relationship to the king of Naples. When the master of the ship loses his temper and yells at him during the storm, Gonzalo declares, "I say, my friend, you don't seem to understand to whom you're speaking. (*Making introductions.*) The King's brother, the King's son and myself, the King's counsellor!" (13), to which the master responds, "The King! The King! Well, here's somebody who doesn't give a damn about the King any more than he does about you or me, and he's called the Wind! His majesty the Wind! And just now, he's in command and we're his subjects" (13). In other words, the only form of power that matters on the island is the ability to control nature in order to survive. In act 1, scene 2, we learn the reasons why Prospero originally set sail, in a long speech to his daughter, Miranda: he was exiled from Italy and his life was threatened. After hearing about his plans to take possession of the lands in the New World, two European rulers, Antonio and Alonso, decide to stop him: "They suborned my people, stole my documents and, to rid themselves of me, denounced me to the Inquisition as a magician and sorcerer" (16). They are, of course, unable to do so, since Prospero comes to the island anyway and claims it under his rule. Consequently, the political leader who governs the island officially, Alonso, is the enemy of the actual ruler, Prospero, and the only person on the island with ties to this political leader, Gonzalo, now works for Prospero.

The distinction between a presumed political leadership, represented by Alonso, and Prospero's real ability to govern the island is highlighted in several scenes throughout the play. When the political leaders, Alonso and Antonio, come to the island in act 2, scene 3, their inability to exert any control over its inhabitants—as well as their stupidity in being duped by Prospero's trickery—highlights their powerlessness as government officials. James Arnold remarks that the scene in which the leaders arrive is not realistic: "Even assuming the motivation assigned to Alonso and Antonio, we find our sense of verisimilitude stretched beyond reasonable bounds when we are invited to accept that they themselves, as reigning heads of Renaissance city states, should have made a perilous sea voyage to supervise the progress of colonization" (239). Nevertheless, it is precisely the lack of "verisimilitude" of this scene—that is, the improbability that political rulers in Europe, such as Antonio and Alonso, would have traveled across the Atlantic to visit the land which they governed—that calls attention to the distinction between the tenuous political rule of the island occurring at a distance and Prospero's form of domination, which is closer and has a more significant impact.

In *A Tempest,* although Antonio and Alonso together had enough power in Italy to exile Prospero and put his life in danger, on the island they are just two more sailors among the others. They chat amicably with Gonzalo, who used to be Alonso's servant, and when Gonzalo tries to acknowledge the king's authority by saying, "Ouf! I'll sit down; with your permission, of course," Alonso replies, "Noble old man, even though we're younger than you, we share the same predicament" (30). When Gonzalo declares that it is his hunger speaking, Alonso responds, "I have never claimed to be above the human condition!" (30). The stage directions then read: "Prospero enters, invisible. Strange figures, bearing a laden table, enter as well. They dance and graciously invite the king and his retinue to eat" (30). Alonso becomes frightened and cries: "Heaven help us! Living puppets!" (30). Once they begin eating, the figures return and take away the table. Alonso then declares: "I firmly believe that we have fallen into the hands of powers that are playing cat and mouse with us. It's a cruel way of making us appreciate our helplessness" (31). The table then comes back into the room, and when

Alonso refuses to eat, Prospero, who is hiding, tells Ariel to force them to do so: "They would wrong me by not eating. Let them experience eating out of my hand like chicks. I insist upon this sign of their submission" (32). Although back in Europe Alonso had absolute power over Prospero, on the island the situation is reversed. It is now Prospero who rules, because he has the means of providing the food that will satiate their hunger and is able to create illusions of a supernatural presence, frightening them so much that they leave, allowing Prospero to be the sole ruler of the island. Through his techniques of producing spectacles, Prospero is able to overturn the former relations of power and expel from the island the same rulers who once expelled him from Italy.

In *A Tempest,* Caliban is Prospero's slave because he lacks the means of production that would allow him to subsist on his own; without these means, he is condemned to work for Prospero in order to survive. The relationship between them is very much that of a proletariat worker and a capitalist entrepreneur. In act 1, scene 2, while complaining to Prospero about his servitude, Caliban lists some of his duties: "chop the wood, wash up, fish, plant vegetables" (19). Prospero does threaten violence, with the whip: "If you grumble, you will be thrashed. And if you drag your feet, or go on strike, or sabotage, you'll be thrashed" (21), but his language reveals the extent to which he views him as a worker rather than a slave, since he warns him against going on strike and sabotaging the workplace. Nor does Caliban appear to fear the whip, and Prospero never commits any acts of violence toward either him or Ariel, his mulatto worker, during the play. Prospero appears to have no intention of killing either Ariel or Caliban, since he clearly wants to keep Caliban and Ariel alive as long as possible so that they can serve him. At the end of act 1 he says to Ariel, "I could kill you now . . . [b]ut I need labour. Follow me" (24). Prospero is obsessed with acquiring more labor power in order to increase his wealth and even welcomes the marriage of his daughter, Miranda, to Ferdinand as a way of doing so. He says to his future son-in-law, upon accepting the proposed marriage, "Fortunately, I need more brawn: you'll do as a slave in my hacienda" (24).

Caliban seeks to overturn the master/slave relationship by acquiring the means of production that Prospero possesses and that he needs for his own economic subsistence; without these means, Caliban is forced to work for Prospero. Caliban reproaches Prospero, most of all, for refusing to share this knowledge: "As for your knowledge [*science*], did you ever impart any of that to me? You took care not to. You selfishly keep all your knowledge [*science*] for yourself alone, sealed up in big books like those" (19). The main problem Caliban confronts, as it is represented in the play, is not that of political domination but of an economic dependence resulting from a lack of technological development. Césaire highlights this issue during the scene in which Prospero offers Alonso, Gonzalo, and Sebastian food, only to pull away his hand as they reach for it.

The real form of oppression for Caliban is not direct political rule, which could be said to end with the departure of Alonso and his cry of "Freedom now!" during the play's final scene, but the form of neocolonialism represented by Prospero, who refuses to share his scientific knowledge with Caliban and therefore uses his technological superiority to produce illusions and establish economic dependence. The difficulty in overcoming this form of domination is emphasized in the last scene of Césaire's *Tempest,* in which Prospero does not leave the island, as he does in Shakespeare's version, suggesting that in the era of decolonization the directly political form of colonialism has subsided, but the type of neocolonialism resulting from the inability to access technology remains. The play implies that it is impossible for Caliban to find a way of subsisting on his own without the knowledge that Prospero refuses to give to him. For Césaire, this is the result not of any inherent differences between the races but rather of the state of the island, which has been destroyed by violent colonization. In other words, *A Tempest* illustrates the way in which the colonizers made the island a space that is uninhabitable without the technologies that they brought from Europe, and then established a relationship of dependence with the colonized by denying them access to these same technologies.

Some critics have concluded that Césaire's Caliban is a representative of nature, while his Prospero is one of art. Arnold, for instance, writes of the "sharply defined opposition of Caliban, Nature's ally and grateful son, to Prospero, the antagonist of nature" ("Césaire and Shakespeare" 247). He further observes: "Césaire could doubtless subscribe to Kermode's conclusion that 'Prospero is, therefore, the representative of Art, as Caliban is of Nature. As a mage, he controls nature' (p. xlviii). But as we have seen, Césaire has inverted the value system implicit in that statement" (248). In other words, Arnold suggests that Césaire's play valorizes nature rather than art and invention. Similarly, James Robinson writes that Césaire's play "accentuates the art-nature relationship as a civilization-nature opposition embodied in the Prospero-Caliban conflict" and constitutes a prophetic warning against the dangers of modern technology (439).

Nevertheless, although Caliban may be more in tune to the world of nature than Prospero, he should not necessarily be perceived as the staunch defender of a natural way of living, since he wants, more than anything else, to obtain the scientific and technical knowledge Prospero has brought from the West, in order to develop the island economically. This is evidenced by the way he constantly reproaches Prospero for not sharing his "knowledge" (*science* in the original French): "As for your knowledge, did you ever impart any of that to me?" (19). Moreover, Césaire's Prospero is not, like Shakespeare's, a playwright and magician capable of controlling nature, and thus the representative of art in general; he is an explorer who uses science and technology to produce deceptive illusions. Shakespeare's Prospero is very much in control of both the island and the spectacle itself, and the elements of the narrative that call attention to the work's theatricality are meant to emphasize the extent of his power, which he exerts on many levels. But in Césaire's version, Prospero is completely demystified: he is no longer a magician but a tyrant who practices a crude mode of illusion making with the sole purpose of reinforcing his power through trickery.

The struggle for power in *A Tempest* is as much over the control of spectacles and illusion making as it is over who performs the manual labor necessary to produce the food for survival. Throughout Césaire's play, Prospero's constant struggle to assert himself as a kind of director of a spectacle parallels his effort to exert control over the island and its inhabitants. He sees his work on the island as both a political project and a theatrical one, as evidenced by his ambiguous use of the word "work" (*œuvre*) to refer both to his *civilizing mission* and the spectacles that he creates in order to trick the population into falling under his control. In act 1, scene 2, he cries: "I have a job to do, the methods employed don't concern me!" (18). At the end of the play, in the debate with Caliban, he describes himself as the conductor of an orchestra who must find a way to harmonize the sounds coming from the island: "I am not, in the ordinary sense / the master, as this savage thinks," he explains, "but rather the conductor of a vast score: this isle" (60). In the last scene, referring to his work on the island, he declares: "I will not let my work perish" (61).

Throughout the play, Caliban expresses his desire to overthrow Prospero and overtake the island by creating his own spectacle. In a conversation with Ariel, he describes one such possibility when he says: "From high in the empyrean where you love to soar—you will see this isle, my inheritance, my work, all blown sky high, with, I hope, Prospero and me amongst the debris. I hope you'll enjoy the firework display, it will be signed Caliban" (28). In the final scene, when Caliban has the opportunity to hit Prospero and decides not to do so, Prospero declares, "And now, the comedy's over!" (52). Although Caliban does not consider himself to be an actor in a "comedy," Prospero asserts his power by defining his actions as part of a comedy rather than a tragedy and therefore refusing to take them seriously. Prospero feels threatened by any action performed by Caliban that may undermine his own position as the director of the events occurring on the island, so he declares an end to this "comedy." In *A Tempest,* Caliban is constantly trying to orchestrate events but is ultimately unable to do so because he lacks the means and is thus reduced to fantasizing about revolutionary actions.

As a capitalist entrepreneur who creates spectacles, Prospero represents a bourgeois conception of theater. He represents illusion making in its most evil form, that is, its use as an ideological weapon to force others into submission. Brecht was adamantly against illusion making, which he considered to be the instrument of fascism. He sought to free spectators from the trance that bourgeois theater induced in them through mimetic representation in order to brainwash the population and cause it to conform to a political ideology. Césaire, as an avid admirer of Brecht, no doubt came across the term "culinary art" in his readings of him; Brecht coined the term to refer to a bourgeois conception of theater, which considers a play to be a commodity consumed as nourishment by the spectators, one that leaves them happy and complacent—much like a fine meal at a luxurious restaurant—but fundamentally untouched. The scene of *A Tempest* in which Prospero feeds Alonso and Antonio presents illusion making and nourishment in a way that establishes a comparison between these two activities. Alonso and Antonio consume the spectacle, which they take to be reality, much as they do the meal: they are entirely fooled by it.

In fact, many of the characters in the play—Ariel, Alonso, and Antonio—fall for Prospero's illusion making, taking it for reality. Ariel has bought into the illusions created by Prospero, all the while helping him create them, which is why he is under his control. In act 2, scene 2, Ariel declares, "My master is a sorcerer" (24). In the work of illusion making, Ariel is Prospero's loyal assistant, who is aware of his role as a creator of the ideology rather than a passive consumer of it. In act 2, scene 3, Ariel talks about the marriage between Miranda and Ferdinand as if it were a play put on by him and his master: "So let us turn the page. To end this chapter, it only remains for me to summon you all, on the authority of my master" (35). In act 3, scene 3, Prospero conjures up an "entertainment" (*divertissement*) in his cave with Ariel's help: "Well, Ariel! Where are the gods and goddesses? Let them make haste, your band! I want all of them to play their part in the entertainment I have created for our dear children. Why do I say 'entertainment'? Because from today, I want to instill in them the spectacle of tomorrow's world" (44). Similarly, in the scene in which Alonso and Antonio dine on the island, they are duped into believing that the marionettes represent real spirits and are therefore tricked into leaving. Prospero is a master of using his power of illusion making to reinforce the authority he already possesses as the sole owner of science and technology on the island.

Although many of the characters fall under Prospero's spell, the audience is repeatedly made aware of the false nature of these illusions. In *A Tempest,* Prospero continually tries to assert his power as a kind of director, by claiming that he is controlling all of the spectacles in the play, just as his character does in the play by Shakespeare. In Shakepeare's version, for instance, Prospero creates the storm with his magic, while in Césaire's version, an actor chosen by the moderator (*meneur de jeu*) for his physique produces the sound effects and thus "plays the role" of the tempest: "But there's one part that I must designate: and that's you! It's for the Tempest, you understand. I need a storm that will wreak destruction. . . . So I need a strapping man to be the wind. So, you're game? Agreed! . . . Good, now set to it. . . . Get set! Go! Blow, winds! Rain and lightning in abundance!" (11). In Césaire's version, the function of the Brechtian figure of the moderator is to call attention to the artifice involved in staging the tempest in order to debunk Prospero's claim that he created it.

In the second scene of the play, Prospero takes credit for the spectacle of the tempest by asserting that in order to fulfill the prophecy of conquering the island, which he had foreseen for a long time, he made the storm with the help of Ariel: "I did so, with Ariel's help" (17). He says that, together, they created the tempest: "We unleashed the storm you've just witnessed, so saving my estates overseas and placing those scoundrels in my power at the same time" (17). By describing the tempest as something "you've just witnessed" (*à laquelle tu viens d'assister*) Prospero compares it to a spectacle, thus referring at once to the event in the play and the spectacle performed onstage. In the prologue, however, the spectators were made aware of the fact that the storm was a theatrical illusion produced by an actor, so that when Prospero claims to have created the spectacle, they are able to distance themselves from his illusion making and see it for what it really is, such that they do not fall for his trickery, and his supposedly magical powers are completely demystified.

In *A Tempest,* colonialism is presented as a mode of illusion making that consists of persuading the colonized of his or her own inferiority. Prospero's power as a maker of illusions is emphasized in the last scene of the play, in which Caliban accuses him of being a "great illusionnist":

> Prospero you're a great illusionist:
> you know all about lies.
> And you lied to me so much,
> lied about the world, lied about yourself,
> that you ended up by imposing on me
> an image of myself:
> underdeveloped, in your words,
> incompetent,
> that's how you forced me to see myself,
> and I hate that image! And it is false! (58)

Caliban realizes in the last scene of *A Tempest* that he has fallen victim to Prospero's deception. By highlighting the artificial nature of Prospero's illusions and mode of theater so that the spectator, like Caliban, is no longer duped by them, the play seeks to work against the kind of trickery that forms the basis of his power. The Brechtian distanciation techniques in the work—that is, the elements that call attention to the artificial nature of the spectacle—have the objective of causing the spectators to break free of the harmful illusions, created by the West, that have duped them, by achieving a heightened awareness of them (a "conscientization").

The ultimate illusion that these distanciation techniques are meant to debunk is that of the white man's superiority and inherently scientific and technical nature. Although in *A Tempest* Prospero's ownership of the means of production allows him to rule over the inhabitants of the island, the prologue to the text suggests that this position with regard to science and technology is not racially determined. In this prologue, an anonymous moderator (*meneur de jeu*) offers masks to a number of actors onstage before calling for the storm to begin. A detail of the stage directions that is often overlooked—that the play is written for a *théâtre nègre* (black theater), that is, a company consisting of only black actors—illustrates that Prospero's role as a man of science and technology could be assumed by a black actor. Although Prospero may believe that it is his inherent superiority that has placed him in the position of colonizer, the prologue suggests that this is yet another false illusion, since his position is really the result of the whim of the true director of the play, the moderator. The play thus suggests that the ownership of the means of production by white Europeans is not the result of any inherent differences between the races but of historical circumstances that caused Europeans to develop technologies first.

Césaire's play emphasizes the power of a capitalist entrepreneur who is also an inventor, a scientist, and an illusion maker, while downplaying any form of political authority. This capitalist, moreover, is specifically American: the original production of the play with Serreau was performed in front of the background of an American Western, with the actors dressed as cowboys. *A Tempest* is generally considered the "American" chapter in Césaire's theatrical trilogy on colonialism, and, as Césaire himself suggests in an interview (Dunn and Césaire 7), it can be read as an allegory of U.S. politics at the time. Caliban, who screams "Freedom now!" (the motto of the Black Panthers) and asks Prospero to call him "X," represents Malcom X; Ariel, who advocates a stance of nonviolence, represents Martin Luther King. As the sole owner of the means of production (science and technology), the character of Prospero evokes the evil American capitalist who views black people as nothing more than potential labor power; this capitalist is portrayed as an evil tyrant, and racism as it existed in the United States at the time is equated with slavery.

In fact, *A Tempest* presents a somewhat paradoxical stance: neocolonialism, in the form of economic dependence, is portrayed as nefarious and destructive; while colonialism, in the form of governance from afar, is portrayed as the ongoing presence of innocuous ties to powerless leaders. Overall, the play suggests that the real danger for the colonies does not lie in a lack of political independence but in the failure to produce or assimilate the means of production (science, technology, and theater) on the part of the colonized, as a result of a lack of "self-confidence" (*confiance en soi,* Césaire's term in "Société et littérature dans les Antilles"), which results from the colonizer's illusion making. By calling attention to the artificial nature of Prospero's illusions, the play seeks to provoke a "coming to consciousness" in the "people" (presumably the colonized audience) of their own status as the proletariat, thus paving the way for modernization.

The discourse on technology, science, and illusions in *A Tempest* suggests that if the people of the colonies find a way to break the illusion of their inferiority and develop economically using the scientific and technical knowledge imported from Europe, they will avoid the takeover of American imperialism, with its capitalist ideology. Thus *A Tempest* reflects Césaire's own anti-Americanism: political ties with Europe are presented as largely inconsequential, while economic dependence on the United States is portrayed as a form of slavery. The ideology of the play provided a means of justifying Césaire's own politics (evidenced in his speeches as a deputy in the National Assembly): he spoke in favor of allowing Martinique to become a department of France rather than an independent, completely autonomous nation, in order to avoid falling under American dominance. This perspective, illustrated in *A Tempest,* is consistent with the view expressed by Césaire in his political speeches, to which we will now turn our attention.

CÉSAIRE'S SPEECHES

Just as Césaire came to embrace modernization in his literary works, throughout his political career, both as mayor of Fort-de-France and as a deputy at the French National Assembly from 1945 to 1993, he spoke openly about the need to bring new technologies from Europe to Martinique as quickly as possible. In Césaire's political speeches, from the beginning of his career in office until his death in 2008, he portrays industrialization as a positive force that will induce progress in the Antilles and stresses the need to modernize at all costs. This suggests a remarkable consistency between Césaire's political and literary writings. In fact, one of the reasons scholars have overlooked the positive role of technology in his drama is their disregard of this portion of his work.

In his speeches as the representative from Martinique to the National Assembly, Césaire supported an all-out drive for modernization in Martinique through the acquisition of European technologies. In his very first speech there in 1946, Césaire noted:

> If you want the Antilles and Martinique to get themselves out of the tight spot that the old system, inherited from the colonial pact, got them into, there is only one way to do it: equip them; equip them, so that they are no longer the responsibility of mainland France; equip them, in order to reduce unemployment among our young people, in order to improve the standard of living of laborers, in order to guarantee work and social security to the hardworking masses. We need roads, harbors, airfields, sewer systems, we need hospitals in order to protect our race from degeneration, we need schools in order to satisfy our children's thirst for education. (Moutoussamy 16)

In this speech, as in others, Césaire presents the lack of technological innovations as a central problem that is holding back progress in Martinique and pleads with the National Assembly to provide aid for development.

In his newsletter to his electors before the elections of November 23, 1958, Césaire presents the rapid modernization of Martinique as a key element of his political platform: "Our program? You know it. . . . It can be summed up in a word, the unshakeable determination to put everything into action, to improve the standard of living of the people of Martinique and to ensure the modernization of our country" (Moutoussamy 70). During his campaign for the legislative elections of November 18, 1962, he makes very similar statements (Moutoussamy 70). In another letter to his electors during the Fifth Republic's Third Legislature, Césaire states that the industrial regime that he envisions will create jobs for Martinican workers "by developing the economy of Martinique through a policy of both agricultural reform and the systematic industrialization of the country" (Moutoussamy 96).

Far from glorifying an agrarian society, Césaire attacks French politicians for not believing in the industrialization of Martinique and therefore "condemning" it to remaining a primarily agricultural society: "For if the colonial pact robbed us of industrialization, it left us with—and even more than that, it condemned us to—agriculture, while we are currently subjected, as always, not only to the invasion of European industrial goods, but also to the dumping of Europe's agricultural surplus" (Moutoussamy 106). Césaire speaks so adamantly in favor of modernization, and his speeches focus so much on economic progress, that he appears to be much more passionate about the industrialization of Martinique than about an increase in its political autonomy. His extremely favorable opinion of industrialization, as exhibited in his speeches at the National Assembly, suggests a possible explanation for his efforts to ensure that Martinique would remain a department of France, despite the vehement attacks on colonialism in his literary writings. Césaire feared that the severance of all political ties with France would leave Martinique without the technical resources that it desperately needed in order to industrialize and would therefore condemn it to remain an underdeveloped economy. Ultimately, he believed that colonization had so incapacitated the peoples, land, and cultures of Martinique that full political independence accompanied by economic development was not immediately possible.[8]

In "Société et littérature dans les Antilles" (Society and literature in the Antilles), a speech delivered on April 11, 1972, at Laval University to a pan-francophone audience that included students from Africa and the Caribbean, Césaire articulates a theory about the conditions necessary for a people to modernize, based on the idea that cultures possess both particular elements, such as folkloric traditions, and universal ones, such as modern technologies. He posits the problem of culture in colonial lands as a tension between particular traditions and universal knowledge or practices, "the contradiction between the necessity of an individual culture on the one hand, and, on the other, the necessity to move beyond this individual culture toward the universal" (9), before establishing definitions of culture and civilization that correspond, respectively, to this distinction between the particular and the universal. For Césaire, the term "culture" refers to the specific practices of individuals in their everyday life, which constitute a means of confronting both nature and history: "Thus by culture I mean, not education, but everything that man has done, all that he does and all that he attempts to do each day in order to organize his life, that is to say, to adapt himself to nature on the one hand, and to history on the other" (9). National culture is a collective version of this notion: "It is thus life as it appears in the context of a clearly defined geographical and political entity" (10).

Césaire divides national cultures into elements, saying that the most "vigorous" elements become universal, while the others do not: "Doubtless, all the elements of culture are not universalized, but you could truly say that the most vigorous elements of each particular culture tend to extend beyond their original cultural border and become essential to all men" (10–11). These "vigorous" elements come together to form a civilization, according to Césaire: "That is why it would be risky to set culture in opposition to civilization, civilization, which, from my perspective, can be defined precisely as the total sum of the most vigorous and dynamic elements contained within different individual cultures" (11). Thus, a "civilization" is a kind of macroculture consisting of the most "vigorous" elements of microcultures. Particular cultures and universal civilizations, Césaire adds, must maintain a dialectical relationship of dialogue and exchange with one another: "Let us add that it is our duty to always maintain the connection that unites cultures with civilization, and civilization with culture, like a living dialectical relationship, each sphere fertilizing the other" (11). He argues that constant contact between the particular elements of a culture and "the universal" is necessary to prevent a culture from becoming stagnant: "A civilization unfertilized by individual cultures would wither just as an individual culture cut off from the universal and sealed off from the world would quickly stagnate" (11). So for Césaire, the interaction between individual cultures and universal civilizations is an ongoing process of mutual revitalization.

However, Césaire warns that the cultures of Africa and the Caribbean have not yet produced universalized elements, due not to any intrinsic inferiority but to the violence of colonialism, which destroyed their cultures and caused them to lose their "self-confidence" (*confiance en soi*). Césaire explains that in order to produce or assimilate "universal" elements, such as technologies, a people must possess a particular state of mind, one characterized by a certain "self-confidence." Moreover, a culture under colonial or neocolonial domination is not capable of inventing "universal" elements, since its practices consist of a "subculture" (*sous-culture*) of elements borrowed elsewhere. He writes that in the colonies, the "true" culture of the people has been replaced by that of others: "The true culture, which is life and creation, is replaced by a subculture which can be defined as the consumption of the culture of others, or of the other, that is to say, of the master" (14). Consequently, the peoples of the colonies lack the confidence necessary for creation, and as a result, "the spirit of creation is replaced by the spirit of imitation" (15).

Since the "subculture" of the colonized people does nothing more than copy the values of the dominant culture, it produces no elements that will ever be universalized: "It follows from these considerations that in colonial or neo-colonial countries, the culture of the people cannot flourish, translate into actions, or be realized through numerous and coherent works, and cannot contribute to civilization if we agree once again to call civilization the universalizing dynamic contained in every vigorous culture" ("Société et littérature" 15–16). Césaire states that only when a culture has acquired the "coming to consciousness" that leads a people to think of itself as a nation is it possible for it to industrialize without losing its traditions. For him, this is not yet the case in the Antilles, as he remarks in an interview: "Up until now, any observer in good faith is obligated to note that the coming to consciousness of the people of the Antilles is not yet sufficient" (Kesteloot 198).

In his 1956 speech at the first international congress for black artists and writers, Césaire describes the Japanese as an example of a society that has obtained the state of mind, characterized by a "self-confidence," that makes it possible for them to assimilate borrowed elements while maintaining traditions: "Yes, Japan has managed to mix traditional elements and elements borrowed from Europe and merge them into a new culture that remains a Japanese culture. But this is because Japan is free and has no law but that of its own needs. Let us add moreover that such an amalgamation postulates a psychological condition, historical audacity, self-confidence. Yet it is precisely this that the colonizer, from day one, tries in a thousand different ways to take away from the colonized" (Tsunekawa 123). Césaire writes that Japan, unlike the Antilles, is not a former colony and has thus not been subjected to the colonizers' efforts at dismembering this confidence. In contrast to the psychological state he ascribes to Japan, Césaire describes the mind-set in the Antilles as "the poignant feeling of a lack, of a non-self-fulfillment, in short, of an immense frustration" (5). National liberation will only come about, according to Césaire, once there is a "freeing up of the psychological mechanism which colonialism has caused to seize up" (5), which will in turn provide the conditions necessary for the passage from a "subculture" to a fully developed, autonomous culture.

According to Césaire, the people of the Antilles must liberate themselves from the colonial and neocolonial domination of the French through a national "coming to consciousness," which he believes can be induced through theater and other artistic forms. This will render them capable of both contributing "vigorous" elements, such as technologies, to universal civilization, and assimilating the ones they receive from other cultures, without losing their own traditions. Césaire views his theater as a means of provoking a national consciousness that will lead to the creation of a modernized, industrialized Martinique.

It is very instructive to compare Césaire's approach to mimicry with that of Homi Bhabha. Bhabha's famous discussion of mimicry in *The Location of Culture* describes it as a subversive action that undermines the hierarchy between colonizer and colonized. In particular, imitating authoritative colonial discourse—for instance, the educational system—highlights the ambiguity of that discourse in its very reproduction of it, which is "*almost the same, but not quite*" (Bhabha 86). As a result, Bhabha concludes that "mimicry is at once resemblance and menace" (86). For Césaire, by contrast, imitation always leads to domination of the colonized, relegating them to a secondary existence, a "subculture." But does this spirited critique of imitation preclude all forms of interaction between the metropole and the colony, or postcolony?

In fact, Césaire advocates for the transfer to the former colonies of Western technologies, which constitute for him the primary example of a "universal" element that cannot be ignored by any culture. He writes regarding technology: "It is what explains that traditional cultures today cannot close themselves off, without the risk of dying out, from the introduction of, for example, modern technology, which is actually of European origin, but which has become universal" ("Société et littérature" 11). Thus, technology transfer is not a form of imitation but a necessary adoption of an element of universal culture: an element first developed in Europe but that is a part of humanity's shared patrimony. While European societies will contribute their technologies to universal civilization, according to Césaire, non-European ones will offer their "values": "Universal civilization today cannot renew itself, rebalance itself, save itself from a new form of barbarism without opening itself up to the values contained in nontechnical cultures, which up until now were despised by the West" ("Société et littérature" 11). Césaire never gives any concrete examples of these "values," whether for the Caribbean or other postcolonial cultures. This is again due to his bleak view of the situation there, as a result of a legacy of colonial violence that has removed any "self-confidence" and thus hindered the successful adoption of universal cultural elements, such as modern technologies. This idea that nontechnical cultures will contribute "values" to universal civilization while European ones will provide technologies echoes Senghor's writings about the "Universal Civilization" (discussed in chapter 2), in which he states that "Negro-African" cultures will bring a sensual outlook that will temper the Western, technical viewpoint.

Although in his early writings Césaire often presents an opposition between the primordial state of nature and a modern, technological society, his attitude toward industrialization becomes progressively more favorable throughout his literary and political career, beginning with his turn to theater in the early 1960s. For Césaire, the nontechnological nature of African and Caribbean cultures is not, as it is for Senghor, the result of biologically inherited characteristics; rather, it is the consequence of the particular historical circumstances of colonialism, which destroyed the land and culture of the colonized. The violence of colonization forced colonized peoples to assume the position of "consumers" and not "creators," thus robbing them of the "self-confidence" necessary to develop socially and economically. It was precisely to restore this lost confidence that Césaire began to produce dramas in the 1960s, as part of the "theater of development" movement; he viewed his theater as a means of provoking a national consciousness that would lead to the creation of a modernized, industrialized Martinique. Two plays he wrote and produced with Serreau in the 1960s, *King Christophe* and *A Tempest,* express his vision of such an island, and show his desire to maintain close ties with Europe as a way of ensuring a movement toward modernization that will combat the threat of American hegemony, which he believes to be a greater danger than ongoing ties to Europe. As a politician, Césaire called upon French leaders to provide assistance for the island's economic development, adamantly promoting the transfer to the Caribbean of Western technological innovations, which he identified as part of humanity's patrimony, a fundamental element of universal civilization in the postcolonial era.

CHAPTER TWO

Technics and Poetics in Léopold Sédar Senghor

Césaire is frequently linked to the poet, cultural theorist, and politician Léopold Sédar Senghor, his close friend at the École Normale Supérieure in Paris and cofounder (along with Léon Damas) of the Negritude intellectual movement, which emphasized the uniqueness and significance of black African culture. As a writer, Senghor is best known for his collections of poems and essays, and as a politician, he is most famous for being the first president of Senegal, an office he held from 1960 to 1980.

As with Césaire, literary critics have often portrayed Senghor as the enemy of all forces of progress, including modernization and new inventions. Jacques Louis Hymans writes, for example, that Senghor opposes many of the values of Western civilization, including capitalism, rationalism, and industrialization (31, 57, 191). Similarly, in her study of the concept of Negritude in Senghor's work, Sylvia Washington Bâ writes that he portrays the technological civilization of the West as a nefarious force that stifles true human values (154), stating that for him, the processes of slavery and colonization "culminated in the moral sterility of dehumanized technology" (155). Many African philosophers, including Marcien Towa and Stanislas Adotevi, have vehemently criticized Senghor for assuming a worldview that is contrary to progress and relegates African nations to a state of technological stagnation.[1] Both Towa and Donna V. Jones have labeled him a "revivalist" who wants to bring back African traditions at the cost of scientific and technological progress.[2] Similarly, Abiola Irele writes that Negritude is characterized by a conservatism that is at variance with the exigencies of the moment, including practical issues of socioeconomic and technological development (85).[3]

In this chapter, I propose a reconsideration of the relationship between Negritude and technology, by calling into question this portrayal of Senghor as an antimodern revivalist, through an examination of the representation of technology in his work. Although Senghor's poetry only rarely addresses issues of technology, instead valorizing nature and sensuality, this portrayal is not characteristic of the essays and speeches included in his five-volume collection *Liberté 1–5*. Literary critics, I argue, have overlooked three central aspects of Senghor's work, clearly evident in these writings, which reflect the importance of technology for him. The first is the tremendous influence of the French and German phenomenologists Jean-Paul Sartre and Martin Heidegger on Senghor's thinking about Negritude and technology, especially Heidegger's classic essay "The Question Concerning Technology." The second is the fundamental role Senghor assigns modern technological innovations in his nation-building project and in his utopian vision of a "Universal Civilization," developed through a close reading of Marx. The third is the numerous comparisons Senghor makes between technologies and literary texts, and his portrayal of both as cultural objects fostering positive forms of interaction between Europe and its former colonies.

In my analysis, I will consider some of the following questions: What does Senghor's appropriation of German phenomenology tell us about the origins of Negritude? How does Senghor envision his notion of a Universal Civilization, and how does this relate to his nation-building project? To what extent is there a tension between the representation of technology and nature in his poetry, and their portrayal in his essays and speeches? What does this tell us about Senghor the writer as opposed to Senghor the politician? What are the implications of this reading of Senghor for conceptualizing Negritude?

SENGHOR'S POETRY

Senghor was an extremely prolific poet, producing seven volumes of verse between 1945 and 1988. Although the question of technology is central to the essays of this same period, his poetry is characterized by an almost complete lack of engagement with this issue. The poems generally focus on representing a sensual, emotional mode of being: their language is meant to evoke the sensory perception of the speaking subject, while the rhythm of the words and metric structures reproduce the "rhythm" that Senghor attributes to black African peoples.

Senghor does address technology in several poems. In "Snow upon Paris" from *Chants d'ombre* (Shadow songs) (1945), he describes how the construction of the railway between Dakar and Niger by the French colonists led to the fall of African empires and ruined the traditional way of life: "White hands that fired the shots which brought the empires crumbling . . . / White hands that felled the forest of palm trees once commanding Africa, in the heart of Africa / . . . They cut down the dark forest for railway sleepers / They cut down the forests of Africa to save Civilization, for there was a shortage of human raw-material" (*Selected Poems* 7). Hymans writes that "these same 'white hands' placed the 'long narrow rails'" and that for Senghor, the "rails crossing Senegal symbolized that intrusion of the white man, and his technical civilization, which was both destruction and progress: destruction of the 'Garden of Eden' which existed before colonization, progress into the modern world of machines. Henceforth return to the past was impossible" (3).

Similarly, in "Despair of a Free Volunteer" from *Hosties noires* (Black hosts) (1948), Senghor writes, "For dam-building engineers have not quenched the thirst of souls in the polytechnic villages" (*Selected Poems* 33), suggesting that it is poetry—and not technology—that is needed to satisfy the desires of black African peoples.

Senghor likewise examines technological issues in two key poems from *Éthiopiques* (1956): "To New York" and "Chaka."[4] "To New York" describes the city of Manhattan as a body made of steel that needs the vibrant blood of black Harlem to bring it back to life. New York is described as a cold, industrial place: she has "metallic blue eyes" (*Selected Poems* 78), is full of "skyscrapers" (78), and possesses "muscles of steel" (78). The poet depicts Harlem as the blood that will warm the cold steel arteries of New York, vivifying the city: "I say to New York, let the black blood flow into your blood / cleaning the rust from your steel articulations" (79). In this extended image, Senghor contrasts the vitality of black culture with the surrounding industrialized urban body, which it animates. Here, it seems that black culture has a fundamental role to play in a complex technological society; as we shall see, this corresponds closely to Senghor's vision of a future Universal Civilization in which elements of what he calls "Negro-African" and "Albo-European" culture function in harmony.

The next poem in *Éthiopiques,* "Chaka," about the mythical Zoulou leader by that name, is far less optimistic about technology and development. The poem takes the theatrical form of a dialogue between Chaka and a "white voice." Chaka repeatedly speaks out against modern technology and science, which are portrayed in the poem as instruments of oppression. In the opening song (*chant*) of the poem, Chaka declares, addressing the "white voice": "And you talk about conscience ["*science*" in the original] to me?" (68). Chaka then declares himself to be the valiant killer of science: "Yes, I killed her, while she was telling stories of the blue lands / I killed her yes! my hand did not tremble. / A flash of fine steel in the odorous thicket of her armpit" (68). In a key passage of the poem, Chaka recounts the legend of the moment of colonization: "They are landing with rules and set-squares, with compasses and sextants" (70). He then describes a prophetic vision about colonization: "I saw in a dream all the lands to the four corners of the horizon set under the ruler, the set-square, the compass" (71).

Chaka relates how the landscape of the world is redrawn through the construction of railways, shipyards, ports, and mines: "I saw the lands to the four corners of the horizon under the grid traced by the twofold iron ways" (71). The workers are exploited in this new technological and capitalist order, and have become alienated from their labor: "I saw the people of the South like an anthill of silence / At their work. Work is holy, but work is no longer gesture" (71). Their days are spent working in misery: "Peoples of the South, in the shipyards, the ports and the mines and the mills / And at evening segregated in the kraals of misery. / And the peoples heap up mountains of black gold and red gold—and die of hunger" (71). Chaka seeks to counter this future industrial, colonial civilization with the rhythm and power of the "tam-tam," a traditional African drum. Senghor likewise suggests that poetry can provide a means of opposing this dehumanized condition.

As a poet, Senghor emphasized a natural, sensual mode of being and believed this was what Africans could bring to a Universal Civilization. Although his poetry presents a clearly negative portrayal of technology, as with Césaire, it is important to make a distinction between the use of technology for colonization and the potential benefits of its appropriation in postcolonial society. Like Césaire, Senghor's perspective of what constitutes a positive or a negative use of innovations is largely informed by his reading of Marx, to which we now turn.

SARTRE, SENGHOR, AND THE "TECHNIQUES OF PRODUCTION"

In his essays and speeches from the 1960s to the 1980s, Senghor posits a relationship between race, technology, and a mode of "being-in-the-world" that is greatly influenced by Sartre's essay "Black Orpheus."[5] In the essay, Sartre famously proclaims Negritude to be an "anti-racist" form of racism, and calls it the "anti-thesis" to the colonizer's "thesis" (of the inferiority of the black man) that will eventually lead to a more balanced "synthesis" of the two doctrines. Although this essay has been widely read and commented on, a highly neglected element is Sartre's discussion of technology and its relationship to race, culture, and economic classes.

In "Black Orpheus," Sartre provides a Marxist interpretation of racial difference and explains differences in the white and black proletariats' perceptions of the world in terms of their relationships to modern technologies. Citing the passage from Césaire's *Notebook* that begins, "My negritude is not a stone with its deafness flung out against the clamor of the day," Sartre writes: "Negritude is portrayed in these beautiful lines of verse more as an act than as a frame of mind. But this act is an *inner* determination: it is not a question of *taking* the goods of this world in one's hands and transforming them; it is a question of *existing* in the middle of the world. The relation with the universe remains an *adaptation*. But this adaptation is not technical" (36). According to Sartre, the black man's nontechnical relation with the universe exists in contrast to that of the white man: "For the white man, to possess is to transform. To be sure, the white worker uses instruments which he does not possess. But at least his techniques [*techniques* in the original, which also means "technologies"] are his own: if it is true that the personnel responsible for the major inventions of European industry comes mainly from the middle classes, at least the trades of carpenter, cabinet-maker, potter, seem to the white workers to be a true heritage" (37). "But," he continues, "it is not enough to say that the black worker uses instruments which are lent to him; techniques are also lent to him" (37).

Referring to the passage in Césaire's *Notebook* in which he speaks of technology ("Those who have invented neither powder nor compass / those who have never tamed either steam or electricity / those who have not explored the seas and the sky"), Sartre calls it a "haughty claim of non-technicalness" that "reverses the situation" described above by turning "what could pass as a deficiency" into a "*positive* source of wealth" (37). According to Sartre, the white man's "technical rapport with Nature reveals Nature as simple quantity, inertia, exteriority: nature dies" (37). In contrast, Césaire's approach—which Sartre considers characteristic of Negritude and the black man more generally—constitutes a "haughty refusal to be *homo faber*" (37), such that Nature is given life again.

Sartre writes that although the white laborer does not own the instruments he works with, he owns the "techniques of production" because the intellectuals within his class developed them (37). The white laborer thus finds himself in a position of exploitation, according to Sartre, but still possesses the outlook characteristic of a technological society. The black laborer, for Sartre, owns neither the instruments *nor* the techniques of production and thus holds an agricultural view of the world (38). Since each proletariat must acquire *both* the techniques and instruments of production in order to be free from exploitation, the black proletariat must first acquire the techniques before finding itself in a situation comparable to that of the white one. Sartre sees this as occurring in the near future, since he writes that the rapid industrialization of many European nations makes it possible to foresee a similar fate for Africa (19).

Sartre believes that the assimilation of new technologies will provide black proletariats with the revolutionary means of liberating themselves, but the result will be the loss of the position vis-à-vis technology that made it possible for them to write poetry. In "Black Orpheus," Sartre explicitly associates literary genres with relationships to the "techniques of production": poetry is the mode of expression of an agricultural society, while prose is that of a technological culture. Sartre claims that the white laborer avoids using poetry to express himself because he would like to think of himself as a "technician." As the black proletariat acquires the "techniques of production," Sartre wonders: "Will the source of poetry run dry?" (52). Sartre finds it difficult to conceive of the production of Negritude poetry in a more technological and less agricultural society, since, for him, poetry is the expression of a nontechnological ontology. As we will see, Senghor also appears to associate poetry with a natural, agricultural outlook, and prose with a more rational, technological one.

Senghor, like Sartre, views the black peoples of Africa as a global proletariat that must acquire the technological means of production in order to improve its situation. For him, as for Sartre, a people's ontology is largely determined by a relationship to technology resulting from its position within a global capitalist hierarchy. According to this logic, the common condition of the black peoples of the world—both the black American working in North America, and the African laboring on another continent—lies in their lack of ownership of the "means of production" (science and technology) and their association with the *Lumpenproletariat* (the subproletariat denied any rights). As a result of this condition, the black proletariat possesses, for Senghor, a mode of "being-in-the-world" that differs from the technological outlook attributed to Western society in the modern era.[6]

In *Liberté 1, 2,* and *3,* Senghor divides the peoples of the world into two groups: "Negro-Africans" and "Albo-Europeans." Senghor groups together black Africans and members of the black diaspora as "Negro-Africans" as a result of the subservient relationship they share with the "Great White Men" (*Grand Blancs*) or "Albo-Europeans." The distinction that Senghor makes between these two kinds of peoples is based largely on the degree of development that they exhibit, as evidenced by their mastery—or lack thereof—of science and technology. He uses the term "Negro-Africans" to refer to the blacks of Africa and the diaspora who do not have access to these means of production and thus find themselves in a more subservient position. The term "Albo-Europeans," on the other hand, refers to people living in "developed countries," who occupy a privileged position within a global capitalist hierarchy. The Japanese are an interesting case because, according to Senghor, they have fully assimilated the science and technology of the West: "The only exception concerns the Japanese, named honorary Albo-Europeans since they have assimilated, along with their science, the technology and the management of the 'Great White Men'" (*Liberté 3* 8). Senghor's inclusion of the Japanese in the group of "Albo-Europeans" suggests that for him, the valorization of a culture by the West, as well as its place within the global capitalist hierarchy, is the direct consequence of the degree to which it has assimilated modern science and technology.[7]

Senghor equates science and technology with "property" and the "means of production," stating that the black proletariat has access to neither, due to its place within the hierarchy. Senghor contrasts the "Negro-African" conception of property and work to the capitalist one, which becomes dominant in the "transnational society" of the post–World War II era. Senghor writes that the advent of capitalism in the post–World War II era caused the world to become one large "transnational society": "Since the end of the Second World War, capitalism has reached, in the form of imperialism, its final stage of organic development, with the transnationalization of societies" ("Marxisme et humanisme" 202). This "transnational society" is characterized, for Senghor, by the existence of global capitalist hierarchy, with the "Great White Men" at the top and the black man at the bottom, regardless of the continent he inhabits.

In "Ce que l'homme noir apporte" (What the black man has to offer), Senghor writes that in capitalist society, "property does not essentially repose on work"; but in black society, "work, or perhaps more precisely productive activity, is considered the sole source of property" (*Liberté 1* 29). For Senghor, the black peoples of the world once possessed a similar, nonalienating relationship to labor, which was disrupted by the spread of capitalist social property relations (*Liberté 1* 29). In *Pour une relecture africaine de Marx et Engels* (Toward an African rereading of Marx and Engels), Senghor writes: "in the tropical lands of the New World, like the laborers of Euramerica in the factories and mills of the cities, black Africans will be exploited by the capitalists, alienated, according to the Marxist dialectic, from their labor as they are from the products of their labor" (23).

Senghor advocates a return to the mythical era in which the existence of nonalienating work, and the communal ownership of the means of production, was still possible. In "Ce que l'homme noir apporte," echoing a Marxist, idealist claim, he writes, "Far from alienating us from ourselves, labor must force us to discover and fructify our intellectual wealth" (*Liberté 1* 29). Despite this valorization of a primeval paradise, Senghor, like Marx, considers capitalist imperialism to be a necessary—albeit destructive and alienating—step toward the creation of a utopian Universal Civilization in which work will once again comprise a spiritual "Negro-African" dimension, though it will be performed in conjunction with modern technologies.

Although Senghor insists that the historical condition of black peoples is the primary subject of his analysis, the weakness of his argument suggests that he is in fact presenting a biological explanation for the inferior position of black peoples.[8] Both Sartre and Senghor flagrantly confuse hierarchies: in one case they are discussing a relation between entire nations, and in the other, a relation between various people within a nation. They appear to believe that a black American and a "Negro-African" an ocean away experience a similar mode of "being-in-the-world." Nevertheless, as the member of a wealthy, modernized society, it is difficult to imagine that the black American's relationship to technology is so fundamentally different from that of a white American. The Africans Sartre and Senghor describe, as members of a society not yet fully modernized, most likely have a much more limited access to new innovations than that of a black American. The extent to which Senghor insists on ignoring the differences between the two groups suggests that he feels black peoples possess an inherent inferiority consistently placing them at the bottom of the hierarchy. Senghor appears to believe that the black peoples of the world lack the means of production because they are inherently incapable of developing technologies by themselves and are therefore forced to accept the place assigned to them by those who *are* capable.

SENGHOR AND HEIDEGGER

Senghor's ideas about technology were also profoundly influenced by his reading of Martin Heidegger's "The Question Concerning Technology." Senghor read the German phenomenologists, especially Heidegger, extensively throughout his life and appropriated many of their ideas in his writings on Negritude. In "Senghor and the Germans," János Riesz observes that "Senghor's relationship to Germany and the Germans marks every phase of his life" (25). In "Négritude et Germanité 'I' and 'II'" (Negritude and Germanity "I" and "II") Senghor writes that he was drawn to the German phenomenologists because they described a way of relating to reality that resembled that of African culture, and he identifies himself as a "Negro-African" "who has always paid close attention to the Germans, who has always reacted to contact with their civilization" (*Liberté 3* 11). While interned in a German prisoner-of-war camp from 1940 to 1942, Senghor studied German and spent much of his time reading Heidegger (Bâ 17). Regarding his experience there, he writes: "And living among the Germans, I found what were like echoes of my cries in the night, like vivid expressions of the ineffable ideas and feelings which swirled in my head, in my heart" (*Liberté 3* 13). After he was freed from the camp in 1942, Senghor continued to immerse himself in the reading of German philosophers, including Heidegger: "If, after my discharge and demobilization in 1942, I immersed myself, once again, in the German philosophers, starting with Marx, Engels and Hegel, if, after Sartre, I discovered Heidegger, it is, without any doubt, that I feel, even in the work of the socialist thinkers, this *Wirklichkeitssinn* which is the mark of German genius" (*Liberté 3* 15–16).

In the only analysis of Senghor's appropriation of Heidegger, Sandra Adell writes that Senghor "blindly assumes that Heidegger—through his preoccupation with the relationship between (hu)man, Being, the *logos* and *poësis*—is engaged in a 'modern universal humanism' with its emphasis upon the 'role and action of Man in and upon the world'" (36). Adell argues that when Senghor claims Negritude has "already responded affirmatively" to this form of humanism, he is grossly misreading Heidegger, who "is concerned with what humanism, as it is articulated in twentieth-century discourses, obscures from man: his *essence* and its relation to the *truth* of Being" (37). Adell concludes: "In accord with Heidegger, then, to think Negritude as a humanism is to further impede the questioning of the relation of Being to the essence of (the black) man" (38). According to her, Heidegger's and Senghor's notions of humanism are incompatible, since for Heidegger, humanism is a negative force that blocks the nature of Being from man, and for Senghor, it is a positive entity capable of forming the basis of his utopian Universal Civilization.

Although Adell rightly points to Heidegger's influence on the notion of humanism that Senghor seeks to develop, her critique of Senghor does not explore the full extent of Senghor's use of Heidegger. In fact, a closer reading shows that Senghor advocated the *one* form of humanism accepted by Heidegger. Heidegger makes a clear distinction in his writings between the traditional humanisms he condemns, which assume a technical interpretation of the world and apply it to man, and the new humanism he would like to forge, which is separated from the instrumental view of reality and thus much more in touch with "Being." In his 1947 "Letter on Humanism," Heidegger writes, "every humanism which conceives man other than belonging to 'being' makes him nonhuman: only that humanism is true, which sees man as a function of 'being'" (217). In order to forge this new kind of humanism, according to Heidegger, "we must free ourselves from the technical interpretation of thinking" (218). By associating his project with Heidegger's vision of a new humanism, Senghor is intent on showing that black African culture, due to its nontechnical mode of perceiving reality, is well positioned to realize it.

Heidegger's work in this area, which provides ideas that Senghor appropriates in his articulation of Negritude, is based on Aristotle's *Nichomachean Ethics* and his notion of four modes of causality. In Heidegger's analysis of the *Nichomachean Ethics*, he reviews the four modes of causality: *causa materialis, causa formalis, causa finalis,* and *causa efficiens.* Heidegger writes that of these four modes, the first three, which correspond to *poiesis,* or "creation," have been forgotten in the modern era. The only mode of causality that Aristotle describes that has not been forgotten, according to Heidegger, is the *causa efficiens,* or "efficient cause," which resembles our modern notion of causality. According to Heidegger, the "forgottenness" of the first three modes corresponding to *poiesis,* and the dominance of the *causa efficiens* in the modern era, results in a worldview he calls "Enframing."

Heidegger describes Enframing as a technical perspective according to which objects in the world are considered purely in terms of their potential use value. The worldview of Enframing is characterized by the reduction of reality to an "inventory" that is available for "using up," the perception of the world as "standing reserve." Heidegger believes that the greatest danger of modern technology lies not in the potentially destructive power of machines but in the prevalence of Enframing.

In Senghor's reading of Aristotle's text, he equates the three modes of causality that correspond to *poiesis* with intuitive reason, and the *causa efficiens* with discursive reason. Senghor, like Heidegger, claims that although the ancient Greeks founded Western civilization ("as you know, it is the Ancient Greeks who founded what I call the Albo-European civilization" [*Liberté* 5 128]), their mode of Being and perception of reality differed greatly from that of modern Europe. Senghor says that there is a common misconception that the Greeks founded Western civilization solely on the notion of discursive reason, "on *dianoia*" (*Liberté* 5 128). This is not the case, according to Senghor, because *dianoia,* or discursive reason, is only one of the factors leading to truth that Aristotle mentions in the *Nicomachean Ethics:* "There are, in the soul, three predominant factors which determine action and truth: sensation, intellect and desire. I translated the word *noûs* as 'intellect.' In truth, it is the symbiosis of discursive reason and intuitive reason, of thought and feeling" (*Liberté* 5 128). Senghor substitutes discursive reason for Heidegger's interpretation of the *causa efficiens* in Aristotle: "Far from privileging discursive reason, which, we have just seen, is only one of the four instruments of understanding and action, the Ancient Greeks, in founding the Albo-European civilization, tried to make of it the civilization of the whole world"(*Liberté* 5 128). Much as Heidegger says that "Being" and *poiesis* are suppressed by Enframing in the modern era, Senghor writes that the factors that correspond to intuitive reason, especially feeling and spirit, have been forgotten by the West and that discursive reason has come to dominate.

Senghor appropriates Heidegger's idea about the differences between the modes of "being-in-the-world" of "primitive" cultures and those that have experienced the advent of modern technologies, and he uses it as a basis for his description of the characteristics of black African culture. In both "The Question Concerning Technology" and *Being and Time,* Heidegger proposes two primary modes of *Dasein:* the technological outlook that characterizes societies with modern technologies, in which every object is viewed in terms of its potential instrumentality or use value (what Heidegger calls Enframing); and the viewpoint existing in pretechnological societies, which is best described as an "awareness" of one's place in the world that is in touch with Being. A culture that has not assumed the worldview of Enframing, because it does not possess the modern technologies that destroy nature, is "primitive" in Heideggerean terms. Heidegger draws a distinction between technical instruments like hand tools and the windmill, which incorporate themselves into nature while leaving it intact, and modern technologies, which permanently consume natural resources. While the use of technical instruments does not obscure Being, the emergence of modern technologies leads to the dominance of Enframing as a worldview in the West. A culture that does not possess modern innovations and has thus not assumed the weltanschauung of Enframing possesses a "primitive *Dasein*" in Heideggerean terms and is much more in touch with Being than Western man in the technological era.

Senghor attempts to show that a culture's mode of "being-in-the-world" is primarily determined by the extent to which Enframing has become dominant, as manifested in a culture's attitude toward technology and art. For Heidegger, cultural *Dasein* is reflected in the separation—or lack thereof—of technologies and the arts. Heidegger writes in "The Origin of the Work of Art" that in the weltanschauung characteristic of ancient Greeks or medieval Europeans, art was not considered separate from technical inventions; the classical Greek temple and medieval cathedral, for instance, were, like art, formative to notions of self and reality, due to their place in the everyday life of a culture. In the era of the dominance of technological thinking, however, the nature and potential function of art changes. Heidegger finds that art's marginal place in modern society demonstrates the extent to which the technical perspective has come to dominate and causes him to wonder whether it is technology, and not art, that constitutes the fundamental element in the West's outlook on everything. For him, the separation of art from the technical—as evidenced by the use of *poiesis* to refer only to art, and *techne* to industrial objects—is symptomatic of the dominance of Enframing as a mode of perceiving reality in the modern age.

In cultures with "primitive" *Dasein,* on the other hand, art is integrated into all aspects of living and plays a fundamental role in how a society conceives of itself. According to Heidegger, neither "primitive" cultures nor the ancient Greeks—as pretechnological societies—make a distinction between the modes of production of *techne* and *poiesis.* In "Building, Dwelling, Thinking," Heidegger writes: "To the Greeks *techne* means neither art nor handicraft but rather: to make something appear, within what is present, as this or that, in this way or that way" (*Poetry, Language, Thought* 157). For the Greeks, the term *poiesis* was used to denote both creation by man and an emergence from nature; according to Heidegger, it refers not only to the work of a craftsman artist or poet but also to the rising up of nature (*physis*). In "The Question Concerning Technology" he writes, "The Greeks conceive of *techne,* producing, in terms of letting appear" (35). Heidegger appears to feel a sort of nostalgia for the time when *techne* referred at once to technology and art: "Once there was a time when the bringing-forth of the true into the beautiful was called *techne.* And the *poiesis* of the fine arts was also called *techne*"; "And art was simply called *techne.* It was a single, manifold revealing" (*Technology* 34).

In the essays of *Liberté 1* and *3,* Senghor associates Negritude with the mode of revealing characteristic of cultures untouched by modern technology, such as the ancient Greeks or cultures that are "primitive" in Heideggerean terms, by emphasizing the unity of art and the technical in black African life. He does so at first by highlighting the similarities between the Greek and "Negro-African" conceptions of art. Senghor writes that the ancient Greeks used *poiesis* to refer to all forms of creation and did not distinguish between art and technical creations. In "Pour un dialogue des disciplines et des cultures" (Toward a dialogue of disciplines and cultures) Senghor, like Heidegger in "The Question Concerning Technology," highlights the Greek use of the terms *techne* and *poiesis* to refer to both artistic and scientific endeavors in order to demonstrate the unity of art and the technical in this culture: "It is true that in Greek the word *techne* has meant successively 'manual skill,' 'method,' 'art,' but also 'theoretical knowledge,' 'science'"(*Liberté 5* 125). Senghor then signals the etymological roots of the term "engineer" (*ingénieur*) to illustrate the ideal unity of the arts and sciences at the time of the ancient Greeks: "Etymologically speaking, but especially in the modern sense of the word, the engineer is a man possessed of spirit: a poet, that is to say a creator"(*Liberté 5* 124). When asked during a 1980 interview, "After all these years of action and poetry, which is the word that you love the most?" Senghor responds: "It is the word *poiesis*. It is Aristotle who tells us in *Nicomachean Ethics: poiesis,* it is fabrication, in other words, beyond the word 'poetry,' the word 'creation'"(*Poésie de l'action* 235). Senghor would like to see a return in the West to the Greek notion of *poiesis* and believes that the influence of "Negro-African" culture on Europe can provide the means of doing so.

In his interviews and essays, Senghor frequently emphasizes the unity of the technical and the poetic in black African culture. In another interview, he declares that "poetics is at once an art, a technology and a science" (*Poésie de l'action* 67) and calls the poet a "master of science" (*Poésie de l'action* 67). In "Le musée dynamique" (The dynamic museum), Senghor explains that in black African culture, no separation exists between the work of art and the industrial object—"the work of art is not an industrial product"—and that "technique" is used to refer to practices that produce both artistic and more practical creations (*Liberté 3* 64). In "Fonction et signification du premier Festival mondial des arts nègres" (Function and meaning of the first Global Festival of Black Arts), Senghor writes: "When I speak about *Négritude,* I am speaking about a civilization where art is at once technique and vision, artisanal handicrafts and prophesy" (*Liberté 3* 61).

In "Négritude et modernité ou la Négritude est un humanisme du XXème siècle" (Negritude and modernity or Negritude is a twentieth-century humanism), Senghor writes about the lack of distinction between the technical and the artistic in black African culture: "In this black African civilization, one of whose most characteristic traits is unity in coherence, art is, essentially, a technology" (*Liberté 3* 224). According to Senghor, cultures south of the Sahara perceive no distinction between the technical and artistic domains but view them as part of the same reality: "It is that south of the Sahara, both worlds, the visible and the invisible, the earthly and the spiritual, the technical and the artistic, are merely two sides of the same cloth: of the same reality" (*Liberté 3* 227).

He then declares that African art possesses two primary characteristics. The first is that it is a "total art" because it incorporates all other artistic forms within it. The second is that it is a "technique": "The second characteristic of black African art is to be a technique/technology [*technique*]. Contrary to what Europeans believe, every art—dance and music, song and poem, sculpture and pottery, painting and weaving—is a precise technique/technology [*technique*]" (*Liberté 3* 228). Here Senghor plays on the meaning of *technique* in French, which can mean either a skill ("technique" in English) or "technology." On the one hand, he appears to be referring to skills; on the other hand, the context of the passage, which is inserted into a discussion of the etymology of *techne* (the root of the word "technology") and a rereading of Heidegger's "The Question Concerning Technology" indicates that the French "technique" also denotes technology for him. By showing the lack of distinction between *techne* and *poiesis* in black African culture and illustrating the extent to which art occupies a central place in everyday life, Senghor seeks to show that "Negro-African" culture possesses a mode of "being-in-the-world" that is akin to the cultural weltanschauung Heidegger attributes to societies existing prior to, or without access to, modern technologies: primitive *Dasein*.

For Senghor, as for Heidegger, art is the ultimate expression of a culture's ontology or mode of "being-in-the-world." In "The Age of the World Picture," Heidegger writes that the mimetic standard for judging art that exists in the West is a reflection of the technical worldview, which seeks to master reality by reproducing it exactly. He calls this phenomenon the "world picture," which, he explains, "when understood essentially, does not mean a picture of the world but the world conceived and grasped as picture" (*Technology* 129). According to Heidegger, "the fact that the world becomes picture at all is what distinguishes the essence of the modern age" (*Technology* 130), and the "fundamental event of the modern age is the conquest of the world as picture" (*Technology* 134). Heidegger considers the separation of art and function in European culture, and the predominance of the mimetic standard, in order to argue that this approach to art is the ultimate manifestation of Enframing as the dominant mode of perceiving reality in the West.

Senghor contrasts the ontology expressed in "*art nègre*" to the technological outlook reflected in the mimetic standard of art in the West. Senghor writes in "La Négritude est un humanisme du XXème siècle": "Art, like literature, is always the expression of a certain conception of the world and of life, of a certain philosophy and, firstly, of a certain ontology" (*Liberté 3* 75). According to Senghor, as he writes in the same essay, black African peoples have a particular way of living that is expressed in their art: "Who will deny that the black African peoples, too, have a certain way of understanding life and of living it?" (*Liberté 3* 69). Senghor writes that these differences in ontologies manifest themselves in diverse attitudes toward art. In Africa, according to Senghor, art is not relegated to the margins of society, as Heidegger claims it is in the modern West, but remains an integral part of life: "For, in sub-Saharan Africa, art is not a separate activity: in itself and for itself. It is a social activity, a technique of living and, in fact, an artisanal handicraft" (*Liberté 3* 76). Unlike Western art, African art, according to Senghor, does not seek to master nature by reproducing it, by "photographing" it: "art does not consist in photographing nature, but in taming it" (*Liberté 3* 77). For Senghor, the lesson that "black art" (*art nègre*) has to teach is that art and photography are not the same: "The lesson to be learned from black Africans is that art is not photography" (*Liberté 3* 77–78).

To illustrate the difference between the ancient Greek and black African conceptions of art, on the one hand, and those in the modern West on the other, Senghor uses the example of the Venus de Milo. At the time of its creation, according to Senghor, the statue was a goddess: "Of course, the sculptures of Venus—and that is what the name indicates—once represented a goddess, at the time of the Hellenic fervor" (*Liberté 3* 95). She possessed a ritual function within society: "The Greek statues of Venus were sculpted to assist with fertility, to aid in the actions of the ancestors and of God: they carried charms, they were magical" (*Liberté 3* 95–96). Since the time of the ancient Greeks, however, the perception of this work has changed: "But since then, the goddess has been brought from the heavens down to earth, from the spiritual to the material world" (*Liberté 3* 95). Now, according to Senghor, this spiritual dimension has been forgotten, and the work is viewed in terms of its ability to represent a reality, that of the ancient Greek woman who posed for it: "There is thus a desire to represent a Greek woman and not something else" (*Liberté 3* 95). Consequently, Senghor writes, "The Venus de Milo is, in short, a sculpture-photograph" (*Liberté 3* 95). This is characteristic of what he calls "the art of discursive reason: it imitates nature, it photographs it" (*Liberté 3* 96). Senghor echoes Heidegger's terminology in his description of the Venus de Milo as a "sculpture-photograph"; for Heidegger, the development of modern technologies, like photography, is symptomatic of the mode of revealing in the modern era, in which the world is viewed as an image to be mastered through its reproduction in art.

Senghor thus appropriates Heidegger in a way that allows him to affirm the positive value of African cultural production and, at the same time, underscore the importance of acquiring what he believes African culture lacks: European technology. In order to justify his critique of the West's technical perspective all the while seeking to acquire its inventions, Senghor points to Heidegger's distinction between the instrumental use of technologies (considered by Heidegger to be relatively innocuous) and their "essence" as the "mode of revealing" of Enframing (the real danger, according to Heidegger). In "The Question Concerning Technology," Heidegger writes: "What is dangerous is not technology. There is no demonry of technology, but rather there is the mystery of its essence. The essence of technology, as a destining of revealing, is the danger" (*Technology* 28). Senghor attempts to draw a similar distinction between the use of modern innovations and the dominance of Enframing by showing that he is not against the transfer of machines to the colonies a priori. The primary role that modern technologies should play in a culture, according to Senghor, is the satisfaction of these needs and not the determination of the nature of things: "I believe, more seriously, that the role of technicians is not to make us understand the nature of things, but to help us first satisfy our 'animal needs,' the *sine qua non* of all spiritual development" (*Liberté 3* 42). In advocating a transfer of technologies from the West to the colonies, Senghor seeks to allow African culture to take advantage of the utility of modern inventions, without assuming the framework of Enframing.

This contradiction, far from suggesting a misinterpretation of Heidegger, actually displays a profound internalization of his discourse. Senghor reads Heidegger so closely that some of the problems and contradictions that arise in "The Question Concerning Technology" manifest themselves in his own appropriation of the work. Heidegger never fully describes, for instance, whether Enframing brought modern technologies into existence, or the advent of these technologies produced the dominance of Enframing as a way of viewing reality. Similarly, Senghor does not explain whether the West's instrumental view of reality provided it with the means of developing new innovations, or whether it was the development of the inventions themselves that produced the total dominance of the technical perspective. In his discussion of black African culture, Senghor also fails to specify whether its spiritual, intuitive mode of perceiving reality resulted in a lack of technological development, or whether it was the inaccessibility of modern innovations that engendered this emotional state of being.

The absence of an adequate explanation in Senghor's writings of why the West developed technologies while Africa did not suggests that Senghor believes that this discrepancy is due to the inherent inferiority of black peoples. Although Senghor appropriates the basic principles of French and German phenomenology in order to describe differences in cultural modes of "being-in-the-world," he fails to provide an adequate explanation of their origins. This failure to problematize the origins of the discrepancy between the technical and primitive *Daseins* suggests that he has internalized a notion of inequality between the races that is primarily based on differences in their propensities toward technological development. Senghor's thinking on technology thus reflects the essentialism in his writings, since it implies that the origins of the positions of Europeans and Africans in the global capitalist hierarchy lie in a biological inequality between the capacities of white and black peoples to develop modern technologies.

Senghor insists that the acquisition of innovations by black African peoples is the fundamental means of instigating economic and social development in the former colonies. Following Heidegger, he believes that it is possible to obtain technologies without appropriating the perspective of Enframing, through the creation of a new humanism based on Being. For him, technological innovations will provide the means of establishing both the African socialist nation and the Universal Civilization of the future, which he conceives of as modernized and industrialized societies in which the book—as an invention at the crossroads between the intuitive and the technical—plays a fundamental role.

For both Senghor and Heidegger, literature—which they associate with *poiesis*—provides the means of combating the dangers of Enframing, because it constitutes the primary means by which a people expresses its particular *Dasein* or cultural "being-in-the-world." Senghor equates this cultural *Dasein* with Negritude, while Heidegger emphasizes the fundamental role of the *Volk* (which he equated with the collective German people) in creating a viewpoint capable of countering the technological mind-set of Enframing.

According to Heidegger, the *Volk* could provide the means of overcoming the dominance of Enframing, by conceptualizing Being as something different from the "present-at-hand" (an instrumental view of reality). In his 1953 *Introduction to Metaphysics*, Heidegger makes it clear that he believes that the German people are the only one capable of realizing this goal. In Heidegger's 1933 speech "The Self-Assertion of the German University," he praised the historical mission of the *Volk* and invoked "the power that most deeply preserves the people's strengths, which are tied to earth and blood" (475).

In his essays on Hölderlin, written in the 1930s, Heidegger attempts to restore the connection between the ancient Greeks and the Germans—much as Senghor tries to link ancient Greece, modern Germany, and black African cultures—in order to revitalize the idea of an original "German essence." Heidegger believed that Hölderlin had offered to the Germans a program (spiritual reappropriation of the homeland) through which they would be able to discover their essence (Farías 271). Heidegger considers the Germans a nation of poetry and thought, just as Senghor describes black African culture as dominated by *poiesis*. Heidegger's praise of the "essence" of the German people echoes Senghor's description of a "black soul" (*âme nègre*) as the essence of Negritude in the essays of *Liberté 1–5*.

Heidegger believed that the Nazi Party had found a means of breaking free of the oppressive mind-set of Enframing by utilizing technology in an instrumental fashion, while emphasizing the importance of the *Volk*. In his *Introduction to Metaphysics*, Heidegger writes that National Socialism strove for "a match between a planetary-determined technology and modern man" and claims that this political movement provides the only possible means of establishing "a satisfying relationship with technology" (Farías 227). In his 1966 interview with *Der Spiegel* (published posthumously), Heidegger insists that his engagement with Nazism be considered in light of his struggle to find a means of confronting the newly emerging reign of modern technology: "It should have become more evident in the last thirty years that the global movement of modern technology is a force whose scope in determining history can hardly be overestimated. It is a decisive question for me today how any political system can be assigned to the current technological age—and if so, which system? I do not have an answer to this question. I am not convinced that it is democracy" (324). In this same interview, Heidegger states that he does not see democracy as being "in actual engagement with the technological world" and disagrees with the assumption that humans control technology: "There still stands the presupposition that humans have control over the essence of technology. In my opinion, this is not possible. The essence of technology is not something that humans can master by themselves" (324). In the *Der Spiegel* interview, Heidegger cites America and Russia as countries where the widespread use of modern technology has led to a detrimental mind-set.

Senghor's Negritude, which provides him with the means of countering discursive reason, is analogous to the Heideggerian principle of the *Volk*. Just as Heidegger believed that National Socialism would counter Enframing by glorifying the *Volk*, Senghor's African Socialism embraced the idea that Negritude would unite with the technological mode of Being of the West, to create the ideal, utopian Universal Civilization. In the essays of *Liberté 1–5*, Senghor claims that German, Greek, and black African cultures possess the same intuitive "being-in-the-world" and that the presence of these cultures in his Universal Civilization will serve to counter the discursive reason brought by technological civilizations. Both Heidegger and Senghor write favorably about the instrumental functions of modern technology, all the while condemning the mind-set (Enframing for Heidegger, discursive reason for Senghor) that it provokes; they affirm that the intuitive "being-in-the-world" of their cultures will counter the negative effects of the dominance of technology.

Senghor's African Socialism was developed through the appropriation of ideas from a thinker who himself participated in National Socialism, which suggests some troubling parallels between the politics of these two thinkers. Both Heidegger and Senghor present the "being-in-world" of their respective cultures as the means of escaping the tyranny of the technological age demonstrated in the notion of Enframing. Both seek a form of humanism more attuned to "Being"—but their response is to create "humanisms" grounded in the culture of a particular people and race. In his writings, Heidegger explicitly denounces the racial aspects of National Socialism, yet he replaces the biological discourse of the movement with his own racially charged notion of "German *Dasein*." This strategic move by Heidegger is reflected in Senghor's own rhetoric: although Senghor repeatedly denies the biological component of Negritude, adamantly defending himself against accusations of essentialism, he presents the existence of a "black soul" as the foundation of Negritude. In his quest for a humanism to serve as a basis for his utopian Universal Civilization, Senghor thus commits some of the same mistakes as Heidegger. Senghor's choice of which aspects of Heidegger's thinking to appropriate—and which to ignore—reflects his own attempts to justify his politics of African Socialism, which sought to promote development in Senegal through technology transfer from Europe, all the while emphasizing the importance of safeguarding Negritude culture.

TECHNOLOGY, NATION BUILDING, AND THE UNIVERSAL CIVILIZATION

Senghor continually praises the utility of modern Western technologies in his essays and interviews and adamantly advocates the transfer of modern technologies from the metropole to the colonies. For Senghor, the worldwide diffusion of technological innovations developed in the West—including the book, which he classifies into this group—will play a fundamental role in the construction of both the African nation and the Universal Civilization that he envisions. He believes that the transfer of modern Western technologies to the former colonies constitutes the sole means by which they can rise from their subservient position within a global hierarchy.

In his approach to technology transfer, Senghor is dependent on Oswald Spengler's analysis in *Man and Technics,*[9] while reversing its valorization. Spengler was a German philosopher who was highly influential in Europe in the early 1920s, primarily as a result of his *Decline of the West,* which claims that history is a series of cycles in which one civilization dominates and then declines; he predicted the imminent decline of western European domination. In *Man and Technics,* Spengler warns against the dangers of allowing certain races to gain access to Western technologies. He writes that the machine is "the most cunning of all weapons against nature that is at all possible" (19), calling the transfer of Western technologies to the non-West an extremely dangerous historical phenomenon, because it will allow "the colored races" to overtake the West. Once non-Western economies acquire technological innovations, the developed West will lose its economic hegemony.

While the diffusion of technology in the non-Western world is nefarious for Spengler, Senghor considers it the primary means by which the former colonies will develop into nations capable of challenging the hegemony of the West. Senghor thus writes about the need to promote economic development and progress in the colonies through the acquisition of European technologies. In "Fonction et signification du premier Festival mondial des arts nègres," he ponders: "How could we, as Black Africans, reject the scientific and technical discoveries of the peoples of Europe and North America, thanks to which man can be seen transforming himself, along with nature?" (*Liberté 3* 62). Although he frequently praises the arts and literature, Senghor states that they cannot found the "new City of Negritude" alone: "We cannot build the new City of Négritude on literary and artistic values alone, this city must reflect our economic and social evolution by integrating, in an active assimilation, Europe's scientific advancements" (*Liberté 1* 85).

In addition to modern technology, Senghor believes that the acquisition of a "national style" is necessary for the establishment of a nation. In the speech "Pour une tapisserie sénégalaise" (Toward a Senegalese tapestry), he declares, "We must find a national style and modern technologies that correspond to our contemporary moment" (*Liberté 3* 103). In "Plan de développement économique et social" (Plan for economic and social development), Senghor outlines his vision of a technologically advanced, African Socialist nation, in which modern agricultural technologies have been assimilated and a large percentage of the student population attends technical schools.

This vision of African Socialism depicted by Senghor entails an idyllic union of the latest technologies and most cultivated arts. He believes that the acquisition of modern Western innovations promotes cultural development by providing a means of satisfying the material needs of the population. In two instances in *Liberté 3*, Senghor paraphrases the famous passage from *The German Ideology* in which Marx declares the satisfaction of material needs to be the prerequisite for the development of the arts in a society; according to Senghor, Marx clearly states that it is first necessary to satisfy "animal needs"—food, shelter, clothing—and that it is only once these needs have been met that man can engage in his generic activity, which is to "create works of beauty" (172, 218). In "Le Brésil dans l'Amérique latine" (Brazil in Latin America), Senghor describes the relationship he perceives between the development of technologies and art in a culture. For him, they are one and the same, and he uses Brazil as evidence that the most technologically advanced civilizations are the most advanced in terms of the arts as well. According to Senghor, the development of both industry and art plays a fundamental role in the transformation of a "developing country" into a "developed" one (*Liberté 3* 27–30), much as Césaire says that the theater can turn former colonies into modernized nations.

As Irving Leonard Markovitz shows in *Léopold Sédar Senghor and the Politics of Negritude*, Senghor's ideas about the role of technology in nation building were reflected in his politics. In his analysis of Senghor's postindependence politics, Markovitz describes the time of Senghor's presidency of Senegal as the period of the "ideology of technology" (213). Markovitz writes that the acquisition or transfer of technologies from the metropole during this time constituted the fundamental means of convincing the proletariat that progress was possible (217). Senghor's theory of socialism bases itself on the idea that "the lot of the peasantry is improved neither by taking wealth from a dominant class nor by eliminating this class as a 'fetter on the productive forces,' but by economic development made possible by the universal realization that it is possible, as well as increased technical efficiency" (Markovitz 218). This explains Senghor's major advocacy of scientific education and research, since "science is of great importance to Senghor in his political maturity, for it holds out the promise of rapid, painless economic development" (Markovitz 224).

Senghor also used new technologies, according to Markovitz, to justify the ongoing ties to the metropole after independence: "He argued that conditions of scarcity and technological backwardness in Africa necessitated continued strong ties between *métropole* and dependency" (234). In this sense, his assessement of the situation resembles that of Césaire, who advocated maintaining close ties to France in the name of technology transfer and development. Although Markovitz describes Senghor as fearful of the "problems of machine civilization" (129), he admits that "in the final analysis, Senghor does not frown upon modern machine-based technology; rather, he views it as essential to progress" (129).

The assimilation of the latest discoveries in science and technologies clearly forms an integral part of Senghor's African Socialism. Senghor frequently emphasizes that Western innovations cannot be developed in Africa; they must be acquired abroad. Since this idea implies that "Negro-Africans" are incapable of developing modern technologies on their own, for Senghor, the economic improvement of the colonies requires the acquisition of innovations and transfer of knowledge from the West. Herein lies the great paradox of Senghor's nation-building project: much like Césaire, but for different reasons, he believes that African peoples must actually strengthen their ties to the metropole in order to acquire the innovations and scientific knowledge that will allow them to develop economically and thus become more autonomous and independent.

For Senghor, the acquisition of these modern technological innovations and scientific knowledge from the West will provide the primary means of establishing his utopian vision of a Universal Civilization, which will ultimately be an industrialized, technological society. In the introduction to *Liberté 3: Négritude et civilisation de l'Universel* (Negritude and Universal Civilization), Senghor describes the multicultural, mixed, and universal civilization that he says will be "the communal work of all races, of all the different civilizations" (*Liberté 3* 8). This civilization is synonymous with the new humanism he envisions for the twenty-first century: "I am not speaking of a 'universal civilization,' which would only be the Euramerican one, spanning the globe. I am speaking of a new humanism which will be the symbiosis of the complementary values of all ethnicities and all nations" (*Liberté 3* 430–431). According to Senghor, such a civilization existed on the shores of the Mediterranean Sea several thousand years ago: "This civilization of cultural hybridity, after flourishing on the shores of the Mediterranean, from the Egyptian civilization to the Arab civilization via the Greco-Roman world, was broken up and scattered into closed societies throughout the Middle Ages" (*Liberté 3* 9).

For Senghor, the development of new innovations plays a fundamental role in the edification of the Universal Civilization. He writes that at the time of the Renaissance, new inventions and exploratory voyages allowed the creation of such a civilization to regain some momentum by returning to its Mediterranean roots (*Liberté 3* 9). This phenomenon also occurred at the beginning of the twentieth century, when technological innovation produced a similar resurgence in the creation of this mythical, multicultural civilization: "Since the beginning of the twentieth century, due to the accelerated development of sciences and technologies, notably means of transportation and communication, populations are becoming better and better acquainted with one another and are increasing every kind of exchange between them, progressively developing the Universal Civilization" (*Liberté 3* 430). According to Senghor, this continues to occur today, since the improvement of technologies of communication and transportation will accelerate the process of edifying the Universal Civilization even more, by bringing cultures increasingly into contact with one another: "Today, thanks to the improvement and proliferation of means of communication, the world is getting smaller, men are being brought closer together" (*Liberté 3* 241).

Significantly, even though Senghor describes the Universal Civilization as a mix of cultural ideologies, the civilization produced by the exchange of knowledge between peoples will be a technological one: "The civilization of the twenty-first century—for which today's civilization is paving the way—will surely be *super-industrial*, that is, technological" (*Liberté 3* 241). The modernized character of such a civilization suggests that each culture will not play an equal part; ultimately, it will be the West that will dominate, primarily because of its technological superiority. This is an important contrast with Césaire's notion of a universal civilization, described in chapter 1, in which each society will contribute its own "vigorous elements," whether technological or otherwise, to a larger cultural commonwealth; Césaire appears to believe more strongly in a balanced contribution of several societies, based on the elements that they can provide, than does Senghor.

LITERATURE AS COMMUNICATIONS TECHNOLOGY

The constant comparisons between the technical and the artistic, as well as the previous discussion of the perceived unity between *techne* and *poiesis* in black culture (discussed earlier in this chapter) suggest that for Senghor, the most significant technological innovations imported from the West in order to found the Universal Civilization are not only those of transportation and communication but also the French language, writing, and the book. In his essays, Senghor frequently compares writers and technicians, language and instruments, and describes the book as a technology. The privileged position of the literary text—on both sides of the dichotomy between a technological and a sensual mode of being—assigns it a key role in Senghor's visions of an African socialist nation and Universal Civilization.

Senghor's use of technical metaphors to describe the influence of French authors on black francophone poets is suggestive of the general relationship he perceives between the two. In "Poésie française et poésie négro-africaine" (French poetry and Negro-African poetry), he describes the writing of poetry as a combination of technical skills and inner inspiration. According to Senghor, the artist, like the scientist, shows order in chaos by throwing a sort of grid on reality that allows one to see it more clearly: "His superiority is that the net of metaphors that he casts, the fabric from which he remakes reality, because it is rhythmic images, illuminates, by giving it a meaning, reality, which is nothing more, at first, I repeat, than a dull and dark chaos" (*Liberté 3* 25). Language, for the artist, provides him with the means of doing so, since it constitutes a "panoply of instruments" that allows him to fully express himself: "In truth, the artist acts like a mathematician with his variables, in order to grasp reality in its entirety" (*Liberté 3* 25). Senghor claims that just as poets use science for inspiration, scientists study the methodology of artists to sharpen their own "gift of invention": "What is less known is that scientists are beginning to study the methods of the poet, of the artist, as the surest means of sharpening in themselves the gift of invention" (*Liberté 3* 43).

Perhaps most significantly, Senghor characterizes the French poet as a technician: "The French poet is, firstly, a technician, who has fully explored his verbal world, who has weighed and tested all of this tools. He is a master of language before being a master of speech" (*Liberté 3* 24). He portrays black poets writing in French as workers who have acquired from their French counterparts the technical instruments required to create poetry. For Senghor, Césaire represents the prime example of this phenomenon: "Black poets of the French language have learned their lesson well, the best of whom, like Aimé Césaire, are products of the French university system" (*Liberté 3* 24). For Senghor, poetry involves the expression of an "inner inspiration" (the Negritude sensibility) through the technical instruments of the West: the French language and writing. In his Universal Civilization, he believes that the French writers will furnish the "technicity" for the creation of poetry, while the black African poets (*poètes nègres*) will provide the "inner inspiration."

In "La semaine du livre" (The week of the book), Senghor describes the book as a technology of communication capable of bridging distances and allowing faraway peoples to interact with one another. The book, therefore, is able to transmit thoughts, ideas, and technical knowledge across cultures: "Thus able to stop time without fixing thought, without depriving it of its nuances or paralyzing its movement, the book remains the privileged tool of intellectual exchange, that is to say, the exchange of ideas and technical knowledge" (*Liberté 3* 321).[10] Senghor goes on to say that the book, much like photography or recording devices, has the ability to expand our notion of reality to include the far corners of the earth: "Whereas the camera describes and the microphone reproduces, the book prolongs the event, puts it in perspective and in prospective, increases its depth and size to the dimension of global understanding. It is totality" (*Liberté 3* 320–21). He even writes that as a technology of communication, the book is superior to many other Western innovations, because it offers a more totalizing perspective: "The written word transcends the most recent communication technologies, like the audio-visual, which tend to be overestimated these days" (*Liberté 3* 320). He ends this essay by calling the book "the surest technology for the diffusion of knowledge" (*Liberté 3* 323) and an "art-invention" (*Liberté 3* 326). For Senghor, it is precisely the book's status as both art and invention, as well as its capacity to hold within it a more profound, intuitive perspective of the world, that accords it a privileged place with regard to new technologies.

As a product of a Western innovation—the printing press—that is capable of expressing an African sensibility through language, Senghor considers the book to be the ideal technical instrument for the creation of his utopian Universal Civilization, at the crossroads of the "Negro-African" and "Albo-European" modes of being, between the technical and the intuitive. According to Senghor, the book constitutes the perfect technology of communication for promoting national development and founding the Universal Civilization. This is in part because the survival and development of African languages in the modern world requires their reification in a written form (*Liberté 3* 321). Senghor writes that the book must occupy an important place in any plans for national development (*Liberté 3* 321). The acquisition of the technique of writing is also a necessary step for entering into modernity for Senghor (*Liberté 3* 321). So is the creation of a literate population, according to his plan for educational reform: "Literacy for our masses, we know, is a necessity of the twentieth century, which must not be delayed" (*Liberté 3* 321). "Education for children and literacy for adults," Senghor writes, "are one of the conditions for economic and social development" (*Liberté 3* 321). "In this day and age," he continues, "there is no better means than the book to allow us to reach our full potential" (*Liberté 3* 322), and he calls for "an industry of the book" (*Liberté 3* 322).

Senghor's discussion of the creative process in "Poésie française et poésie négro-africaine" and "La semaine du livre" suggests that he believes that black writers cannot produce literary texts without first acquiring technical instruments—the French language and writing—from French writers. Senghor never acknowledges the existence of any technical elements in African culture that could be used for the creation of literature, nor does he seem open to the possibility that a literary text could be anything other than a book written in French. In contrast to later francophone authors, such as Amadou Hampâté Bâ, he seems to have relatively less interest in African oral traditions, possibly because he did not consider them to be literature within his narrow definition of the term.

Just as Senghor's analysis of the role of Western technologies in African development implies that the former colonies cannot modernize without technological innovations imported from Europe, his discussion of black francophone poets suggests that they must rely on their colonizers to provide the tools necessary for building a postcolonial culture, in this case African Socialism. Much as Senghor writes that (paradoxically) the former colonies must acquire innovations from the West in order to become more independent, he considers the French language, writing, and the book to constitute the primary weapons that the colonized will use to fight the colonizers. As he writes in his introduction regarding the influence of French literature on his work: "I tried to take the weapons from the hands of the colonizers for the defense and illustration of Negritude" (*Liberté 3* 58), and "we have chosen the weapons of the colonizer in order to turn them against him" (*Liberté 1* 19).

Although in his poetry Senghor valorizes a sensual mode of being while condemning industrial society, he writes very favorably about technology in his speeches and essays. In order to illustrate the relationship he perceives between race, technology, and the mode of "being-in-the-world" of different cultural groups, Senghor sets up a complex framework that draws heavily from his readings of Marx, Sartre, and Heidegger. For Senghor, the history of oppression shared by black peoples is a result of their proletariat status in a global capitalist hierarchy. As long as they occupy this place and do not have access to the "means of production"—mainly science and technology—they will continue to possess the mode of "being-in-the-world" of a nontechnological society. Like Césaire, Senghor insists that the acquisition of innovations by black peoples is the fundamental means of instigating economic and social development in the former colonies. Following Heidegger, Senghor believes that it is possible to obtain technologies without appropriating the perspective of Enframing, through the creation of a new humanism based on Being. For him, technological innovations will provide the means of establishing both the African Socialist nation and the Universal Civilization of the future, which he conceives of as modernized and industrialized societies in which the book—as an invention at the crossroads between the intuitive and the technical—plays a fundamental role.

Senghor's failure to provide a convincing reason for why certain cultures developed modern innovations before others implies his essentialist assumption that certain races are more predisposed genetically toward technological development than others. Although the West successfully modernized without appropriating the spiritual dimension of African cultures, Senghor seems to believe that the black peoples of the world are incapable of producing new innovations without the Western assistance that he adamantly supports. In this sense, he differs from Césaire, who condemns colonization for halting the already-existent processes of technological progress and modernization in the Caribbean and West Africa, thus leading to underdevelopment (*Discourse on Colonialism*). Although the moment of colonization is profoundly traumatic for Césaire, there is no sense of that in Senghor's writings. In line with Marx's writings about colonization in India, Senghor appears to believe that colonialism, like capitalism, is a necessary step for progress and modernization in Africa due to the technology transfer that it instigates.

A final puzzle in the interpretation of Senghor's work is the relationship between his literary production and political program. While Césaire's speeches and literary works (as we have seen) show a remarkably unified perspective on the advantages of technology transfer to postcolonial Caribbean societies, Senghor's political writings and essays stand in stark contrast to his poetic works, which valorize nature and have little to say about technology or modernization. On the one hand, the coexistence of natural and technological perspectives in Senghor's writings could be said to characterize him as a living embodiment of the poet/technician, who seeks to bring Senegal closer to the Universal Civilization by combining its African and European elements in his literary corpus and persona. Although this utopian, transnational vision of Senghor was largely based on technology, as I have argued, it was also his hope that African peoples would reinvigorate it with a natural, poetic inspiration that the industrialized West had lost. So while Senghor the poet retained the African landscape as muse, Senghor the politician worked arduously to imbue the country with modern technology. Since Senghor's image as a cultivated poet and "man of letters" was a crucial aspect of his image as a politician, and evidently of his electoral success, the valorization of nature in his poetry no doubt served a political function. By praising a presumably "natural" and "African" way of life, Senghor may have sought to gain the support of a segment of the population that was without access to modern technologies and that approached their use with ambivalence, all the while pursuing a politics that led to the creation of an elite, technocratic class.

In the following two chapters, I explore this ambivalent perspective regarding modern technologies, characteristic of the lower-status members of society in Algeria during the War of Independence and in postindependence West African countries. In order to achieve a better sense of the attitudes toward technology and development across these societies (and among men and women), I now turn to the work of Frantz Fanon.

CHAPTER THREE

Radios and Revolution in Frantz Fanon

Much like Césaire and Senghor, Frantz Fanon has at times been classified as a revivalist who seeks to resuscitate past traditions. As a result, his ideas about modern technology remain a largely neglected aspect of his thinking. As Nigel Gibson has shown in his seminal study, the vast majority of scholarship on Fanon has focused on his portrayal of violence in revolution in *The Wretched of the Earth*,[1] his psychoanalytic deconstruction of racism in *Black Skin, White Masks*,[2] or his influence on African American culture.[3] Fanon's views on technology—especially as expressed in his journalistic writings and several chapters of *The Wretched of the Earth*—illuminate these major themes, given its essential role in anticolonial struggles and decolonization.

In this chapter, I examine the question of technology in Fanon's work, beginning with *Black Skin, White Masks* (1952) and his essays from *Toward the African Revolution* (1952–61) and *A Dying Colonialism* (1956–57), many written originally for newspapers; and continuing with his classic work on decolonization, *The Wretched of the Earth* (1961). In my readings of these texts I seek to address the following questions: What does Fanon consider to be the necessary conditions for a society to appropriate and invent technologies? What is the relationship between Fanon's psychoanalytic deconstruction of racism in *Black Skin, White Masks* and his opinions on modernization and technological development? How does Fanon's adherence to the FLN (Front de Libération Nationale, Algeria's dominant revolutionary party) relate to his views on technology? What is the correlation (if any) between Fanon's perspective on technology and his views on violence in revolution as expressed in *The Wretched of the Earth?*

Ultimately, I argue that far from rejecting new technologies, Fanon had a profound faith in their ability to transform societies. His view of technology and its key role in liberation reveals the extent to which he was concerned with not only physical but also psychological violence; his quest for revolution thus also strove to combat and reappropriate certain discourses, including the colonialist discourse on technology. Through his writings, he sought to provoke an awakening of consciousness in the formerly colonized that would allow them to accept these technologies—whether originating in Europe or elsewhere—and even embrace their revolutionary potential. Fanon believed that technological development was a necessary element in both the struggle for decolonization and the process of nation building following independence.

FANON AS OPPONENT OF MODERNITY

Scholars have long interpreted Fanon's virulent attack against colonization as a stark rejection of all elements of Western culture. Ato Sekyi-Otu states that Fanon is best known as a xenophobic cultural nationalist inimical to "the whole heritage of Europe" (181) and "one who turned with neoprimitivist revulsion against the city, against technology, and against all that is modern" (157). In her noted chapter in *Feminism without Illusions: A Critique of Individualism,* Elizabeth Fox-Genovese concludes that Fanon argued that all colonized people must "destroy the elevators, machines, and all the products of Western technology" (185). Nguyen Nghe also asserts that Fanon rejects modern technologies for originating in the West, and criticizes him for doing so (205–13).

In his well-known study *New Theories of Revolution* (1972), Jack Woodis groups Fanon with Debray and Marcuse, asserting that all three of them lament urbanization and technological advances (397).[4] Woodis claims that Fanon's sympathy for the tribal chiefs in Algeria translates into an advocacy of traditional society as the basis of national culture, in opposition to modern Western ideas; he concludes that Fanon wants to turn his back not only on European socialist thought but also industrial and technological development (35). Similarly, in *The Postcolonial Unconscious,* Neil Lazarus writes that Fanon saw modern practices as contrary to the Algerians' traditional way of life (172–73). In *Black Soul and White Artifact,* Jock McCulloch likewise suggests that Fanon defends traditions against modernity, when he asserts that Fanon equates "national" and "pre-colonial" culture (60) and views "traditional culture as a springboard for revolutionary action" (61).[5]

Believing that Fanon positions himself on the side of tradition over modernity, many critics have taken him to be a staunch defender of the kind of worldview promoted by the Negritude movement, despite his concerted efforts to disavow it.[6] For example, McCulloch identifies a shift in Fanon's attitude toward Negritude between 1952 and 1961 and claims that he became increasingly sympathetic with the movement with the passing of time (36). McCulloch goes on to conclude that Fanon's supposed embrace of Negritude led to his glorification of the peasant class in *The Wretched of the Earth,* stating that Fanon views their traditional culture as forming the basis for not only the Revolution but the postindependence national culture as well (61).

In this chapter, I explore some of these misconceptions about Fanon's work as a way to introduce his views on technology and revolution. Fanon's emphasis on the role that the *fellah* (the indigent agricultural class) will play in the Revolution, his critique of capitalist exploitation of the urban proletariat, and his adamant rejection of colonization have all led many scholars to assume a complete opposition to technology in his work; but in reality, quite the opposite is true. As I will show in this chapter, in his writings on the Algerian War, not only *The Wretched of the Earth* but also his journalistic essays for the newspaper *El Moudjahid* (collected in *Toward an African Revolution* and *A Dying Colonialism*), Fanon strongly advocates, even glorifies modernization through technological development. In these writings, he puts forth a significant and coherent theory about modernization through technology that closely relates to his analyses of racism, revolution, and modernity, including his psychoanalysis of racial complexes in *Black Skin, White Masks* and his call to arms for the liberation of all colonized peoples in *The Wretched of the Earth.*

BLACK SKIN, WHITE MASKS

Although it does not explicitly address issues of technology and modernization, *Black Skin, White Masks* (1952)—the sociological and psychoanalytic study of racism and dehumanization that first made Fanon famous—sets the stage for the analysis of decolonization in his writings on Algeria by presenting ideas, such as that of the "white mask," that will take on a collective dimension in *The Wretched of the Earth.*

Fanon's explicitly stated goal in *Black Skin, White Masks* is to unmask the illusions that the colonizer has established over the colonized and thus to debunk them. These illusions together form what Fanon calls the "white mask" of French culture, an image that is repeatedly applied to language, culture, and the visual realm, and indeed constitutes the main argument of the book. Fanon explains how the Antillean views the world according to this mask—as a result of his/her immersion in French language and culture—such that it defines his worldview. When the Antillean looks at himself in the mirror, still wearing this mask, and sees that his own skin is black, he experiences a crisis, the result of an ego split between the French culture that surrounds him and devalues his skin color, and the body he possesses.[7] As he writes in the introduction to *Black Skin, White Masks,* by describing the condition of the Antillean he hopes to "unmask" it, such that his black skin is perceived more clearly. Fanon considers his writing to enact a kind of psychotherapy performed on the reader, who perceives the existence of the white mask, seeing it clearly for perhaps the first time. As the process of unmasking unfolds, the reader's consciousness is raised, and he acquires a newly found self-confidence.

One of the primary illusions Fanon hopes to unmask, of course, is the presumed cultural and intellectual superiority of the white colonizer, including the notion of the "civilizing mission": that Europeans were inherently more technologically advanced than non-Europeans and thus had a "duty" to share their knowledge with other peoples by colonizing them. The Antillean in Martinique as well as the Arab in Algeria finds himself surrounded by a culture—that of the French colonizer—that greatly values technology; this technological perspective constitutes the "white mask" that Fanon describes. Similarly, when the colonized looks at his own culture from the perspective of this mask, a splitting of the ego also occurs, since he believes in progress and technology but perceives his own culture as backward, traditional, and antitechnological. Far from positioning himself against technology and modernization, as has been asserted, Fanon views the notion that the colonized are backward and that they adamantly defend their traditions against modernity as part of the colonially imposed "white mask" that must be destroyed in order to pave the way for progress in newly independent nations after the Revolution. Just as Fanon seeks to combat the negative associations with black skin by revealing them to be illusions, he strives to debunk the notion that black peoples are inherently protradition and antitechnological by shedding light on the "white mask" of French culture.

Fanon considered this awakening of consciousness to be a necessary condition for modernization and viewed his own writing as a part of this process. The reading process is meant to train his readers to think of themselves as a society that could become just as modern and technological as the West. This, in turn, prepares them for the struggle ahead in the Revolution and the acceptance of technologies that will help rebuild the new nations in the era of decolonization.

FANON'S JOURNALISTIC WRITINGS

Fanon approaches questions of Western technology, science, and modernity in his unduly neglected journalistic writings about the war in Algeria. In three essays in particular, "Racism and Culture" (1956), as well as "This Is the Voice of Algeria" (1957) and "Medicine and Colonialism" (1959) (both originally written for the FLN newspaper *El Moudjahid* and collected in *A Dying Colonialism*), Fanon strongly urges the acceptance of technology, science, and modernity as universally positive elements that will lead to progress in an independent Algeria and all former colonies.

In "Racism and Culture" (a speech before a congress of artists and intellectuals at the Sorbonne in Paris anthologized in *Toward the African Revolution*), Fanon addresses technological development in his critique of colonial theories about the relationship between race and culture, especially the notion that certain societies "lack culture" altogether. Fanon begins this essay with a critique of the notion of "civilizing mission," stating with characteristic irony: "The technical, generally advanced, development of the social group that has thus appeared enables it to set up an organized domination" (31). As a result of this discourse, the language, dress, and technologies of the colonized are devalorized (33). Fanon asserts that the minimal technology transfer and industrialization that is practiced in colonized countries serves as a means of "camouflaging" the exploitation of the colonized, which is a consequence of racism, but which is presented as a result of the colonizer's technological superiority (35). He states that once the colonized has appropriated the colonizer's technologies, he/she will more fully perceive this underlying racism (39).

Fanon openly mocks those who declare that there exists a contradiction between technological development and the presumably "emotional" base that characterizes the cultures of the colonized. Speaking in a highly sarcastic tone, he writes: "There is an hiatus, a distance between intellectual development, technical appropriation, highly differentiated modes of thinking and of logic, on the one hand, and a 'simple, pure,' emotional basis on the other" (42). Fanon is particularly spiteful about the notion that the colonized have a mode of intellect that is less logical and rational and therefore less conducive to appropriating modern technologies. In this sense, he is critiquing not only French ethnographers and historians but also African philosophers and Negritude writers such as Léopold Sédar Senghor, who famously asserted, "Reason is hellenic, as emotion is Black" (*Liberté I,* 24).[8]

Fanon is also critical of the colonized who react to this oppressive ideology by turning toward tradition and rejecting all elements of modernity: "Rediscovering tradition, living it as a defense mechanism, as a symbol of purity, of salvation, the 'decultured' individual leaves the impression that the mediation takes vengeance by substantializing itself" (42). He considers this attitude to be "archaic," paradoxical, and contrary to progress: "Arab doctors sleep on the ground, spit all over the place, etc. . . . Negro intellectuals consult a sorcerer before making a decision, etc. . . . The past, becoming henceforth a constellation of values, becomes confused with the Truth" (42–43). Fanon believes that in order to fight against all forms of exploitation and alienation, the indigenous people must rid themselves of this mentality (43), a position to which he will return in *The Wretched of the Earth,* when he criticizes the national bourgeoisie for its backward-looking vision.

In "Racism and Culture," Fanon writes that by appropriating modern technologies, the colonized are finally able to perceive the racism of the colonizer, since they become aware of the value of their own intellect and realize that it is no less than that of their oppressor, while experiencing a rise in self-esteem and consciousness. This process debunks the myth of the "civilizing mission," which claims that it is the duty of technologically superior peoples (a.k.a. Europeans) to conquer less-developed ones (Africans, Asians), who presumably have no way of making progress without this "assistance."

In another essay from *El Moudjahid,* anthologized in *Toward the African Revolution,* "French Intellectuals and Democrats and the African Revolution" (1957), Fanon vehemently criticizes the condescending, infantilizing discourse of the "civilizing mission," including the supposedly revolutionary parties that advocate maintaining close ties with

France in the name of technological progress (80, 87). He writes that all of this is done in the name of a "technocratic paternalism" (88). Increasingly sarcastic, he asserts that advocates of this ongoing colonialism ask themselves, "After breaking all links with France . . . what will you do?" (88), and are unable to imagine any technological development independent of contact with the metropole: "You need technicians, currency, machines" (88). Their image of an independent Algeria without France is a barren, underdeveloped land: "a catastrophic prospect of an Algeria consumed by the desert, infested by marshes, and ravaged by disease" (88). In *The Wretched of the Earth,* Fanon will extend this critique further, arguing that these ties to France actually thwart progress rather than promote it.

In "This Is the Voice of Algeria" (1957), an essay published in the FLN newspaper *El Moudjahid* a year after the speech "Racism and Culture," Fanon presents what is perhaps his most explicit statement on technology in colonization and revolution through his analysis of the changes in the attitudes of the indigenous and Arab population toward the radio in Algeria, from before the war to after its outbreak.[9] In the first half of the essay, he describes the initial attitudes of the Arab people toward the radio. Before the war, according to Fanon, radios could only be used to listen to stations such as Radio-Alger, which was owned and controlled by Europeans and expressed, above all, colonial society and its values (55). Fanon states that before 1945, 95 percent of radios were owned by Europeans, and the few owned by Algerians were possessed by the bourgeois elite (53). Although Fanon acknowledges that "sharp economic stratification" in large part explains this gap (53), he emphasizes that it does not fully explain it, since hundreds of Algerian families possessed a standard of living that would have allowed them to own a radio, yet chose not to buy one (53).

Fanon then describes the way in which ethnographers and sociologists have explained Algerians' refusal to buy and listen to radios, criticizing their portrayal of the indigenous Arab population of Algeria as backward, tied to tradition, and therefore inherently unaccepting of science, technology, and medicine. He calls into question the presumably scientific and rational methods of ethnographers (although he does not cite specific studies), declaring that there is no clear evidence of organized resistance to technology or practices of "counter-acculturation," despite what some of them may describe (53). Fanon then takes on a highly ironic tone and, speaking from the point of view of the colonizer, describes the reasons given by ethnographers and white colonizers to explain Algerian families' reticence to acquire a radio. One is the content of radio programs, whose erotic and burlesque allusions presumably make it uncomfortable for the families to listen to the broadcasts together, which is why service officials began signaling which programs could be comfortably listened to in a familial setting. Fanon expresses the colonizer's viewpoint: "The ever possible eventuality of laughing in the presence of the head of the family or the elder brother, of listening in common to amorous words or terms of levity, obviously acts as a deterrent to the distribution of radios [*télé sans frontières*—TV without borders] in native Algerian society" (54). He then describes (likewise with great irony) the conclusions of the French: "Here then, at a certain explicit level, the apprehension of a fact: receiving sets are not readily adopted by Algerian society. By and large, it refuses this technique [technology] which threatens its stability and traditional types of sociability" (54). According to Fanon, the French claim that radio is rejected because, as a modern technology, it challenges the stability of the traditional mode of life led by most Algerians. Increasingly sarcastic, Fanon continues by declaring that the radio programs, according to the Europeans, do not correspond with the strict, patriarchal hierarchy, almost feudal in nature, and the numerous prohibitions of the Algerian family (54).

In his book-length study of radio culture, *Radio: Essays in Bad Reception,* John Mowitt performs a reading of Fanon's "This Is the Voice of Algeria," grossly misinterpreting it by stating that Fanon believes that the Algerians initially refuse radios because they conflict with their traditional culture. Fanon does in fact state precisely this in his essay but using a highly *sarcastic* tone meant to mock French ethnographers who make this claim. Unfortunately, Mowitt takes these ideas at face value, failing to hear the irony in Fanon's voice. Elaborating on why the Algerians initially refused the radio, according to Fanon, Mowitt writes that it was "a power perceived to be capable of calling into question or otherwise undermining traditional values" (91). Finally, Mowitt states that when the Algerians finally decide to accept the radio, it is in part because they no longer perceive it as "modern."[10] These conclusions are evidently based on a literal reading of Fanon's highly ironic statements, as well as the frequently made assumption that he rejects all marks of modernity.

In Fanon's stringent critique of French ethnographers, he is referring to the writings of those stationed in Algeria, including Bourdieu,[11] who wrote about the presumed disjunction between traditional Algerian society and modernity.[12] In Bourdieu's own ethnographic studies of Algerian peasants, *Travail et travailleurs en Algérie* (Work and workers in Algeria) (1963) and most notably *Sociologie de l'Algérie* (Sociology of Algeria) (1958), as well as his extensive photography, he focuses on describing the traditional practices of the Kabyle population in the villages he visited and explores how these are affected by the advent of colonialism. Whereas Fanon generally insists on the separation between the time before the beginning of the Algerian conflict (1940s and 1950s) and the period that follows, Bourdieu considers the divide as occurring before and after *colonization* (1830). While Fanon emphasizes the effect of the war on practices and analyzes attitudes toward modernity more generally, Bourdieu seeks to illustrate the different ways in which colonialism has disrupted the traditions of the inhabitants of the small villages he observed. In doing so, Bourdieu sometimes appears to go back more than a hundred years, idealizing the time before the initial arrival of French colonizers in 1830; "Bourdieu argued that almost from the moment the French set foot in Algeria, they had profoundly and irremediably disrupted the traditional socioeconomic organization" (Goodman 15). Fanon, on the other hand, never idealizes the precolonial past and instead promotes the postcolonial future, when the Algerian people will be free of oppression. In fact, he is highly critical of such idealizations of the past, whether by French ethnographers or Negritude writers.

Bourdieu presented traditional Algerian society as very delicate, a system disrupted by the slightest intrusion from colonialism and/or modernity, and whose structure was collapsing due to the unwelcome contact with the outside world from which it was previously isolated, including not only the French colonial presence but also modern elements such as photography.[13] He constantly portrays peasants as irremediably torn between a traditional and modern habitus, "in a permanent state of social liminality" or what he calls a "split habitus" (*habitus clivé*).[14] In his book cowritten with Abdelmalek Sayad, *Le déracinement: La crise de l'agriculture traditionnelle en Algérie* (Uprooting) (1964), Bourdieu suggests that Algerians are incapable of adapting to certain elements of modernity, due to the highly traditional nature of their lifestyle: "The peasant only lives rooted to the land, the land where he was born, the land to which his habits and his memories tie him. Uprooted, there is a good chance that he will die as a peasant, that the passion that makes the peasant a peasant will die within him" (115). On Bourdieu's position regarding the Algerian peasant class, Jane Goodman astutely remarks: "Yet although Bourdieu criticized the French Left for its utopian view of the revolutionary potential of Algerian peasants, his ethnography of rupture is predicated on an equally untenable myth: that a precolonial Algerian society had existed in relative equilibrium prior to the imposition of colonialism" (20). Bourdieu felt his project was urgent, due to "his distinct sense that 'traditional' Kabyle culture was in danger of disappearing" (Goodman 22).

In his "Le paysan et la photographie" (The peasant and photography) Bourdieu analyzes the diffusion of a modern technology, photography, into the "peasant milieu," arguing that there is a disjunct between "precapitalist" (traditional) and "rationalized" (modern) economic systems. His particular focus is on the social uses and meaning of photography in early 1960s Béarn peasant society, where it was first introduced for recording special occasions, such as weddings. In general, the use of cameras was strictly limited, since taking pictures was considered a luxury (169). Bourdieu argues that the type of pose assumed for photographs was frowned upon for implying a kind of hubris in the subject. Photography was also strongly associated with urbanity, which was regarded so negatively: "Associated with city life, the practice of photography is understood as a manifestation of the desire to play at being a city-dweller" (170). Extending his analysis further, Bourdieu states that all technological innovations—including photography—are always viewed with suspicion in this agricultural society, as an affront to the tradition that must be so staunchly defended (169). Although the Béarn society he analyzes is found in the south of France, his notion of a divide between a traditional and modern habitus applies to his writings on Algeria, in which he discusses the incompatibility of traditional and modern cultures. For Bourdieu, all Béarnais and Algerians—whether intellectuals, peasants, or urban workers—are caught between two worlds: modernity and tradition. Bourdieu argues that opposition between modernity and tradition leads to "hysteresis," a term he uses to describe the process by which behaviors learned in one field (rural/traditional) impede adaptation to another (urban/modern). In other words, Bourdieu claims that Algerians were held back by a traditional habitus, which was incompatible with the adoption of modern practices.

Fanon's views are in clear opposition to Bourdieu, as if they are a response to him:[15] he emphasizes the malleability and adaptability of Algerian peasant societies, who only reject the colonial order due to its outrageous violence rather than an inherent resistance to all change, including technological. In "This Is the Voice of Algeria," Fanon embarks on disproving such theories by signaling the changes in the attitudes toward the radio that take place during the war of independence (55).

According to Fanon, it is the colonial situation that has caused the colonized to reject anything that is associated with the colonizer, regardless of its potential use or utility, rather than an inherent inability on the part of the colonized to accept these aspects of modernity. He begins by examining what the radio meant to different social classes. For the wealthier *pieds noirs* (settlers of European origin), a clear minority in Algeria, acquiring the radio (among other technologies such as a refrigerator and an automobile) provided a means of feeling like they belonged to the "Western petty bourgeoisie" (*petite bourgeoisie occidentale*) (55). For those living in the countryside, the radio made them feel more connected to urban areas. In the case of the colonizers, the radio provided a means of feeling "civilized," as well as a sense of security and serenity; this was particularly true for the agricultural settlers living in rural areas and greatly outnumbered by the Arab population. Fanon writes that the radio programs were used to disseminate the colonial discourse in a way that allowed the listeners to feel certain of their own destiny as colonizers, and rightful place in the country (55); on a daily basis, Radio-Alger would remind the settlers not to mix with others and to safeguard their own "superior" culture (56).

Fanon contrasts this attitude with the lack of interest among Algerian families in buying a radio, even when such a purchase was well within their means. He provides a reason for this hesitation: "The radio in occupied Algeria, is a technique [technology] in the hands of the occupier which, within the framework of colonial domination, corresponds to no vital need in so far as the 'native' is concerned" (56). Fanon thus emphasizes that in the colonial context, the Arab has no use for a radio since it does nothing more than project the words and ideology of the colonizer. In this context science and technology are never perceived by the Arab as neutral but instead are given a negative evaluation. In the mind of the Arab, Fanon writes, they are always placed within the context of the colonial situation, where everything is either extremely positive or negative (56–57). The idea that the radio is extremely negative, as part of the colonizer's world, is reinforced, according to Fanon, by the almost exclusive use of it by the colonizer as a means of transmitting information. This situation changed as a result of the conflict in Algeria, whose most immediate origins Fanon (like many historians) places in 1945, with the massacres of Sétif.[16] According to Fanon, forty-five thousand died during the massacre and subsequent retaliation against the Arab population (the same figure given by the FLN, although the real number is still in question), provoking an awakening in the colonial world:

"The awakening of the colonial world and the progressive liberation of peoples long held in subjugation involved Algeria in a process which reached beyond her and of which, at the same time, she became a part" (58). Fanon asserts that this awakening corresponded with the first widespread introduction of radios in Algeria, which happened at the same moment when new national radio stations were broadcast from Syria, Egypt, and Libya (57). Suddenly, Radio-Alger became one station among many, with the typical Algerian listening exclusively to foreign stations, according to Fanon: European stores, realizing that Algerians were more likely to buy radios from Algerian merchants, began using these as intermediaries.

The most significant change in the attitude of Algerians toward the radio occurred in early 1950s with the first skirmishes in Tunisia and Morocco that eventually led to the independence of these protectorates. Fanon argues that these skirmishes produced a desire on the part of Algerians to find their own sources of information, since they felt that they had to oppose the information disseminated by the colonizer with their own set of truths. More precisely, he places the turning point in 1956, when the Revolutionary message was institutionalized through the creation of the "Voice of Free Algeria" (66), a radio station reporting on the Algerian conflict in French, which caused the stock of radios to become depleted within twenty days. Given the lack of electricity in most of the country, the demand grew for communal posts, that is, locations where Algerians would go and listen to one radio together, leading to a more collective perspective on the struggle for liberation.

Fanon writes that suddenly, "almost magically . . . the technical instrument of the radio receiver lost its identity as an enemy object" (67). The radio is a weapon, one that was first part of the colonizer's arsenal but is now a means of resistance. Fanon describes how the French, perceiving the power of this new technology, do their best to prevent its use among the Arab population; they prohibit the sale of radios—much as they had already done with weapons such as firearms—and continually try to block the signals of the nationalist radio stations broadcasting from abroad. This triggered the "battle of the airwaves" (*guerre des ondes*), which entailed Algerians fighting to hear any kind of signal—even if incomprehensible—as the French army desperately tried to block it; for Fanon, this was as significant as the struggles in the Casbah. In fact, although much has been made of Fanon's portrayal of violence in *The Wretched of the Earth* (a text I will consider later in this chapter), in "This Is the Voice of Algeria," he presciently emphasizes the psychological warfare involved in the dissemination of information.[17]

From a psychoanalytic perspective, initially the radio was a kind of "bad object": "Before 1954, in the psycho-pathological realm, the radio was an evil object, anxiogenic and accursed" (72). This notion corresponds to Melanie Klein's formulation of "good" and "bad" objects, following object relations theories originating with Sigmund Freud.[18] According to this notion, the division between "good object" and "bad object" represents a separation between the comforting and the unpleasant, which the mind seeks to expel. According to Fanon, for white colonialism, the bad object is the black race, which makes the black man an "object that provokes anxiety" (*objet anxiogène*) (*Black Skin, White Masks* 123). He also suggests that the reverse process occurs for the colonized in Algeria: all elements of the colonizer's culture (the West/Europe) are equated with the "bad objects/parts" for the colonized, while those opposing these are the "good objects/parts." Applying this analysis to the collective Algerian psyche, Fanon suggests that the radio begins as a bad object and eventually becomes a good object.[19]

Fanon's use of an explicitly psychoanalytic vocabulary for race in "This Is the Voice of Algeria" relates this analysis to his treatment of racism in *Black Skin, White Masks* (1952). In this collection of essays, Fanon, a trained psychologist, describes how in the colonial context—in this case, the Antilles under French domination—everything even remotely pertaining to the colonizer's culture becomes a phobia; everyday objects provoke horror and fear. Fanon describes a phobic reaction as one that is, by definition, irrational and excessive in nature. In a proper phobic reaction, one endows the object with the evil attributes of a malefic power, as is the case with the radio, which Fanon calls "an accursed object" (*un objet maudit*). And yet, according to object relations theories, phobias are generally accompanied by a secret desire for the forbidden object. This corresponds to Fanon's treatment of bad objects in *Black Skin, White Masks,* which suggests that there is not only a fear that accompanies their presence but also a secret and suppressed desire that draws one toward them. This analysis, extended to the radio, suggests that the Arab population, at the same time that it loathed the radio, secretly longed to possess it, a fantasy that became reality when control of the radio waves shifted and they began acquiring radios to listen to prorevolutionary broadcasts from Cairo, and newscasts from posts in Syria, Morocco, and Egypt.

Once they had heard the radio broadcasts, the listeners, in turn, became their own transmitters, by relaying what they believed was said; Fanon writes, "Every Algerian, for his part, broadcast and transmitted the new language" (71). Fanon's choice of words, especially "emit and transmit" is very deliberate: he suggests that the transmission of information via word-of-mouth (or in this case, the interpretation of sounds said to be information) works alongside the radio to produce fully the sophisticated system of communication that allowed all sectors of the Arab population to hear and participate in the creation of the Voice of Algeria (71).

Fanon frequently uses radio-like terminology to refer to the oral system of communication developed in the Arab population, describing it as a kind of technology. Fanon writes that the general illiteracy of the Arab population makes it indifferent to written texts and particularly responsive to the oral form of communication represented by the radio. He states that after the beginning of the war in 1954, the pejorative expression of the "Arab telephone," (*téléphone arabe*), used to explain how information spread quickly through word-of-mouth (much like the "grapevine" in English), takes on an almost "scientific" connotation (62). Later on both Europeans and Algerians will refer to this process, according to Fanon, as a mysterious communications technology: "a remote broadcast technology which vaguely recalls the system of signaling, of *tam tam,* as is found in certain regions of Africa" (61). Fanon suggests that the Arab population, including the *fellah,* has already developed a means of spreading knowledge throughout large distances orally; he compares this process, as well as the use of tam-tam drums in francophone West Africa to transmit signals, to a communications technology such as the telephone or the radio.

Similarly, Fanon adopts anthropomorphic discourse to refer to the radio, when he says it emits "protective, complicit" voices and invokes its therapeutic qualities by calling it a "protective organ against anxiety" (73). By characterizing it in this way, Fanon implies that the radio takes on an almost ritual-like quality, that it becomes a "fetish object" warding off the demons of colonization, which, paradoxically, has its origins in the colonizer's culture. He writes that, ironically, foreign technology engenders liberation: "The foreign technique [technology], which had been 'digested' in connection with the national struggle, had become a fighting instrument for the people and a protective organ against anxiety" (73). For Fanon, the radio and the Arabs' system of orality are one and the same technology: a "machinic assemblage" of the organic and the inorganic, in the Deleuzian and Guattarian sense of the term.[20]

In their adherence to this modern technology, Fanon considers the Algerian people to have skipped some of the stages of development undergone in European nations, which transitioned from one technology to the next. Since most of the Arab population was illiterate, Fanon suggests that newspaper and print culture were to some extent "skipped over" in the passage from oral transmission to the use of communications technologies. Similarly, the lack of electricity in most of the country caused the fixed forms of radio (which had to be plugged into an outlet) to be "skipped over" in favor of the more recently developed portable posts, at which people would gather together to listen to the radio. He writes, "The Algerian, in fact, gives the impression of finding short cuts and of achieving the most modern forms of news-communication without passing through the intermediary stages" (67). Paradoxically, Fanon's essay suggests that the *fellah* (the most traditional, indigent, and rural social class) is perhaps the most open to modern communications technologies, such as the radio, due to its use of orality as a means of relaying information. This flies in the face of the claims of French ethnographers such as Bourdieu, who claim that this class is too uneducated and traditional to be capable of accepting modern technologies.[21]

Notably, in his analysis of how information spread among the Arab population in Algeria before the radio, Fanon suggests that oral traditions, far from causing Algerians to reject new communications technologies such as the radio, actually facilitate their acceptance. Fanon insists that the important role of orality in Arab culture actually *promotes* the use of the radio rather than *impedes* it. In fact, Fanon describes how village communities, which were already accustomed to spreading information via word-of-mouth, and slightly altering it, continued to do so once radios were propagated; the only difference was that now the radio, as opposed to a person, became the initial source of information. Thus, in contrast to the conclusions of Bourdieu and the French ethnographers whom Fanon mocks at the beginning of his essay, Fanon presents extensive arguments that traditional culture can actually *promote* the appropriation of modern technologies—once they are detached from their associations with the colonizers. Through his analysis of this link between orality and the radio in this 1957 essay, Fanon makes a case for the revolutionary power of the *fellah*—the lowly social class that he will later argue in *The Wretched of the Earth* is the key to the Revolution—by stating, paradoxically, that their traditional culture and oral traditions actually make them *more* open to modern technologies of communication.

Fanon emphasizes that the radio-listening process was more focused on knowing that a widespread movement existed, not only in Algeria but abroad, than on actually acquiring concrete knowledge of events; the sense of a broader community encouraged the people to continue their struggle. In other words, the process of radio-listening created the sense of a broader "imagined community" of Algerians—to use the terminology of Benedict Anderson's classic study on the nation[22]—who were following the events, and whose members believed in the liberation, much as listening to Radio-Alger had made French colonizers feel more at home. In fact, Fanon believes that the radio, like other technologies, is a key element in identity formation and the creation of "imagined communities" of listeners, which constitute the future Algerian nation in embryonic form. He also signals that a similar process occurred during World War II with the "free radio stations," which allowed peoples occupied by the Germans to maintain a sense of nationality. By comparing the plight of the Algerians under the French to that of the French under the Germans, and highlighting the similarities in the role of the radio in both situations, Fanon simultaneously emphasizes the injustice of the colonial situation to a French reader and presents this communications technology as a universal instrument of liberation that all peoples should have the opportunity to acquire.

Fanon's extensive discussion of the radio in "This Is the Voice of Algeria" is a natural entrée for other topics of great importance to him, such as the French language and science, technology, and modernization more generally. He makes explicit comparisons between modern technological innovations and the French language, which he calls an "instrument" and "communications technology." Fanon goes on to say that the transformation in attitudes he observes with the radio also occurs with the French language: "The French language, a language of occupation, a vehicle of the oppressing power, seemed doomed for eternity to judge the Algerian in a pejorative way" (73). Indeed, when the pro-FLN radio station "Fighting Algeria" (l'Algérie combattante) transmitted its broadcasts in *French,* this shattered the associations of the French language with humiliation and oppression. Fanon writes that the entire attitude of the Algerian people to the French language changed to their considering it an instrument of liberation, even declaring it to be "exorcised" of its demons (74). Paradoxically, Fanon attributes the spread of French throughout Algeria to the Revolution rather than to colonization (73).[23] Fanon, as a French speaker who feels solidarity with other peoples colonized by the French, emphasizes that through the Revolution, the French language, like the radio, becomes a universal instrument of liberation detached from its particular cultural origins. This is no doubt also a way for Fanon to explain and justify his own involvement with the independence movement as a member of the FLN who wrote and spoke exclusively in French, as opposed to Arabic, which he was never able to learn adequately.[24]

This discussion of the French language in turn connects Fanon's analysis of the radio to his theories about cultural immersion in *Black Skin, White Masks.* In this text, Fanon writes passionately about how the Antilleans' immersion in French culture—including the French language and a particular mode of being-in-the-world—causes them to view their own Antillean culture extremely negatively; this is the so-called "white mask" he describes, the French perspective that the Antilleans (and the colonized more generally) assume when perceiving their own "black skin."[25] In the chapter "The Lived Experience of the Black Man," Fanon argues that white culture depersonalizes the black man by considering him an object among other objects, lacking subjectivity. Fanon describes how a young white boy, seeing a black man, says to his mother, "Look! A black man!," referring to him in the third person and thus rendering him an object lacking subjectivity. According to Fanon, white culture makes the black man "invisible"; it establishes a phenomenology of invisibility.[26] This is precisely the process of dehumanization, depersonalization that occurs through the radio when it is in the hands of the colonizer. Radio stations such as Radio-Alger, by speaking constantly from the perspective of the colonizer and to the colonizers, render the colonized invisible; by referring to him in the third person, they produce a constant reiteration of the exclamation, "Look! A black man!" But in the hands of the Algerian people, according to Fanon, the radio is transformed into a means of gaining subjectivity and of becoming manifest; and acquiring visibility leads to an awakening of consciousness. Fanon thus suggests that the appropriation of modern technologies by the colonized during the Revolution provides a means of allowing them to break free from this perspective.

Fanon frequently emphasizes that the radio is a representative technology for him and that the changes in attitude he describes with regard to the radio apply to all modern technologies. In fact, for Fanon, science, technology, and medicine together form a set of knowledge and instruments that are initially associated with the colonizer but that can come to play an important role in everyday life for the colonized—not to mention the Liberation—once they are embraced and dissociated from these initial colonial associations. He strongly believes that colonization has inflicted nefarious forms of psychological and even physical violence not only by failing to provide adequate access to technology, medicine, and science but also by provoking negative reactions to all aspects of modern life, which are automatically associated with the colonizer. Nevertheless, Fanon's writings on Algeria suggest that the colonized will experience a catharsis in the Revolutionary struggle, provoking an awakening of consciousness that will allow them to assert their own subjectivity and undo the negative associations with objects of modernity, thus paving the way for creativity, discovery, and original inventions, and finally entrance into a global community.

Fanon extends his analysis even further in "Medicine and Colonialism," by explicitly comparing changing attitudes toward technologies such as the radio to the perception of medicine, a discipline in which he was trained in France, and of which he was a practitioner. In this journalistic piece—as in "This Is the Voice of Algeria" and "Racism and Culture"—Fanon criticizes ethnographers once again for declaring the colonized backward and inherently unaccepting of technology and science, and disproves their theories by illustrating the changing attitudes of the indigenous Arab population toward Western medicine before and during the Revolution. Fanon views technology and medicine as one and the same; throughout "Medicine and Colonialism," he makes numerous comparisons between them, frequently referring to new medical practices as "the new technique/technology" (*la nouvelle technique*) and doctors as "technicians" (*techniciens*) (112). This suggests that by discussing the case of medicine—as with radio—he is really describing a situation that concerns all aspects of Western modernity.

Indeed, many of the observations that Fanon made about radio also apply to his discussion of medicine. Although Algerians first rejected modern medicine due to its associations with the colonizer, after the beginning of the Revolution it becomes widely accepted and plays a fundamental role in the Revolutionary struggle. Fanon states that there is no evidence that the Arab people are inherently against modern medicine because it conflicts with their traditional culture; this argument is made by ethnographers who fail to understand that anything associated with the colonizer is automatically viewed negatively. In fact, he writes that the negative associations with medicine resulting from the colonial situation are one of its most tragic consequences (102).

At the beginning of the essay, Fanon openly advocates the transfer of science, technology, and medicine from one culture to another, if it is done in a positive way: "In all objectivity and in all humanity, it is a good thing that a technically advanced country benefits from its knowledge and the discoveries of its scientists" (102). He declares that there are disciplines and practices that are simply good from an objective standpoint: "When the discipline considered concerns man's health, when its very principle is to ease pain, it is clear that no negative reaction can be justified" (102). Although this may seem obvious, Fanon writes that the colonial situation is such that this logic is broken, since everything associated with the colonizer is automatically rejected (102). The colonized mixes together all aspects of modernity (103), and, feeling like a prisoner of the colonial system, rejects them all, regardless of whether or not they might lead to progress: "He rejected doctors, school-teachers, engineers, parachutists, all in one lump" (103). When a doctor, even one of Arab origin, comes to treat patients, he is accompanied by French police officers, and his visit is preceded by a rounding up of the population by the police (102). Consequently, every doctor's consultation is approached as a confrontation on the part of the colonized (102). He is often trained in a French system and obtains his medicine from French stores. In such a situation, it becomes very difficult for the Arab population to separate the treatment from the colonizer. Fanon believes that in the colonial situation, going to see the doctor, the administration, the police sergeant, or the mayor are identical actions. This leads to a rejection of the most positive and profitable things for the population, according to Fanon.

Fanon further criticizes those who believe that the indigenous person's reluctance to trust a European doctor should be attributed to an attachment to traditional medical practices or desire to consult witch doctors or healers (106). He defends the indigenous, declaring it natural to favor traditional practices out of habit and to be skeptical of new ones. Nevertheless, Fanon writes that in numerous cases, the colonized, having gone to the doctor, nevertheless undergoes the traditional treatment of his/her group for political reasons, and claims that it was the latter that cured him/her as opposed to the Western medicine (111).

Fanon writes that the skepticism toward Western science, technology, and medicine extends to any member of a colonized group who acquires these aspects of modernity from the colonizer (112). On the one hand, such a person constitutes proof that any other member of the group could acquire this knowledge: "For the group, in fact, the native technician is living proof that any one of its members is capable of being an engineer, a lawyer or a doctor" (112). On the other, it represents evidence of a split in the group: "The native doctor is a Europeanized, westernized doctor, and in certain circumstances he is considered to be no longer a part of the dominated society" (113). Fanon calls the indigenous doctor a "technician" rejected by his/her own group, and criticizes the way that Algerians continue to view science, technology, and medicine as strictly European, often preferring to see European doctors over Algerian ones because they consider the colonizers to be "the true possessors of the techniques" (113). This skepticism is abruptly changed by the struggle for liberation; medicines, much like radios, become weapons in this war. Suddenly, the conflict brings the problem of public sanitation to the forefront, and medicines and technicians become indispensable (122). The Algerian doctor is reintegrated into the group and embraced as one of its own: "He was no longer 'the' doctor, but 'our' doctor, 'our' technician" (123). From this point on, according to Fanon, the Algerian people embraces medical technology, which is no longer associated with the colonizer: "The people henceforth demanded and practiced a technique stripped of its foreign characteristics" (123). People want to cure themselves and others, and to understand the explanations of doctors; and their beliefs in superstitions begin to unravel (124). Suddenly, every element of the colonized's culture that appeared to be part of its very essence and that ethnographers used to explain the rejection of all aspects of modernity, is shaken by the actions of revolutionaries (124–25).

At the end of the essay, Fanon compares the nation to a sick body, one that he no doubt feels must be cared for using modern medicine: "Once the body of the nation begins to live again in a coherent and dynamic way, everything becomes possible" (125–26). He thus ends the essay with a call to arms, so to speak, for the colonized to assimilate the beneficial fruits of modernity: "The people who take their destiny into their own hands assimilate the most modern forms of technology at an extraordinary rate" (126). For Fanon, the people's ability to accept and assimilate new technologies is directly related to its relative level of self-esteem, so to speak, its willingness to take up its own destiny, much like what Césaire wrote about the need for a people to have a certain "self-confidence" in order to modernize.[27]

Indeed, for Fanon, the Revolution itself is inextricably connected to the assimilation of technology: he calls it a "purging," in which the peasantry frees itself completely from the mentality that all aspects of modernity—science, technology, and medicine—are negative because they originate in the colonizer's culture. Fanon strongly believes that once the lower classes extricate themselves from this mind-set, the Revolution will change everything, which will in turn lay the foundation for a national culture and lead to technological development; that is, as long as this development is kept out of the hands of the national bourgeoisie.

THE WRETCHED OF THE EARTH

While Fanon's essays on radio and medicine examine changes in culture during the Algerian War by focusing on the reception of particular elements of Western modernity (for instance, radio), in *The Wretched of the Earth* (1961) Fanon expands his outlook, discussing the forces at work in the Revolution more broadly, including the vital role he assigns modernization and technological progress in both the process of achieving independence and the postindependence national culture he envisions. Standing the discourse of the "civilizing mission" on its head, *The Wretched of the Earth* equates colonization with backwardness, and liberation with modernization and technological progress. According to Fanon, not only do the French foster a lack of development in Algeria by causing the native population to reject all aspects of modernity as part of a regime of oppression, but they also transfer almost no technologies or industry to the colonies, for the sake of maintaining an economy of extraction, which involves constantly pillaging resources and exploiting the Arab population.[28] Consequently, Fanon believes that no technological progress can occur without a complete reversal, namely the Revolution followed by a longer process of decolonization. Throughout *The Wretched of the Earth,* Fanon develops an extended argument about the role of technology in the Revolution and its aftermath; while this has been mostly overlooked by scholars, it is closely related to his better-known ideas about colonization and revolution, including the revolutionary potential of the *fellah,* the dangers of an unenlightened national bourgeoisie, and the need to establish a postindependence national culture.

Critics have often emphasized the role of revolutionary violence for Fanon. In his foreword to the English translation of *The Wretched of the Earth,* Homi Bhabha argues that Jean-Paul Sartre's preface to the text has led to reductive readings of Fanon that overemphasize the importance of violence in his doctrine. Indeed, Fanon does frequently emphasize the physical force involved in maintaining colonial rule, which he believes can only be countered with similar physical aggression. Nevertheless, by focusing so intently on this aspect of Fanon's work, critics have greatly overlooked his emphasis on psychological forms of domination—such as the discourse of Radio-Alger and the ideology of the "civilizing mission"—as well as his surprisingly astute and prescient theories about technology, modernization, modernity, and processes of globalization.

In the preface to *The Wretched of the Earth,* Sartre draws attention to the importance of technology and modernization in Fanon's text, an understudied element of Sartre's essay. Sartre's analysis here echoes "Black Orpheus," his celebrated preface to the *Anthologie de la nouvelle poésie nègre et malgache de la langue française* (Anthology of black and Malagasy poetry of French expression) (1948), in which he writes about the black colonized's need to appropriate the white colonizer's instruments and techniques of production.[29] In the preface to *The Wretched of the Earth,* Sartre compares the colonial system to feudalism, writing, "The colony is planted with settlers and exploited at the same time" (10–11). He links the lack of development in the colonies to the emergence of the peasantry as the most revolutionary class: "For in those countries where colonialism has deliberately held up development, the peasantry, when it rises, quickly stands out as the revolutionary class" (11). Since colonialism has deliberately thwarted development,[30] according to Sartre and also Fanon, the *fellah* finds itself in a position of desperation, making it the most radical of classes. Sartre, a member of the French Communist Party, writes that the national revolution will necessarily be socialist (20); and, like Senghor and Fanon, he views technological development as a fundamental component of postrevolutionary socialism.[31]

In the first chapter of *The Wretched of the Earth,* "On Violence," Fanon emphasizes the stark division between worlds that occurs in the colonial situation: "The colonial world is a world divided into compartments" (37); it "is a world cut in two. The dividing line, the frontiers are shown by barracks and police stations" (38). In these two worlds, the city with its abundant food, coal, and lights represents the space of the colonizers, while the village, characterized by famine, the life of the colonized. Fanon argues that since the presumed "superiority" of the white world is imposed and maintained through perpetual violence, the colonial system can be overturned only by similarly violent forces. In subsequent chapters of *The Wretched of the Earth,* Fanon's focus shifts from physical violence to the need to create a national culture, one that will ultimately be modern and technological. As in his earlier essays, he also emphasizes psychological forms of oppression—that is, the ideologies propagated by the colonizer—as well as the colonized's ability to overturn these by appropriating the colonizer's own instruments, including the French language.

Fanon associates colonization with not only the French but also the national bourgeoisie: wealthy, elite Algerians whom he characterizes as backward, antitechnological, and unwilling to promote progress. This virulent critique of the national bourgeoisie forms a fundamental part of his theory in *The Wretched of the Earth* about revolution and modernization in postindependence Algeria. According to Fanon, as the landed elite, the national bourgeoisie asserts power and control by maintaining the agricultural order, as does the colonizer. The national bourgeoisie is thus unwilling to lead the nation on the path to development, as well as being incapable of doing so because it lacks expertise: "Neither financiers nor industrial magnates are to be found within this national middle class. The national bourgeoisie of underdeveloped countries is not engaged in production, nor in invention, nor building, nor labor. . . . The psychology of the national bourgeoisie is that of the businessman, not that of a captain of industry" (149–50). Fanon even goes so far as to suggest that in a sense the bourgeoisie may be worse than the colonizers, because they lack the technical skills and investment capital possessed by the bourgeoisie from the mother country.[32] Never truly against the colonial order, they will do nothing more than replace the colonizers at the head of enterprises: "Since the middle class has neither sufficient material nor intellectual resources (by intellectual resources we mean engineers and technicians), it limits its claims to the taking over of business offices and commercial houses formerly occupied by the settlers" (152). The economy of extraction and exploitation will continue under their leadership, according to Fanon: "Not a single industry is set up in the country. We go on sending out raw materials; we go on being Europe's small farmers, who specialize in unfinished products" (151–52). In fact, Fanon believes that this bourgeoisie will maintain strong ties to the colonizers and establish nothing more than a precarious tourist industry meant to serve the exotic tastes of the Western elite. Under their rule, there will be no development, no modernization, according to Fanon.

He also characterizes the national bourgeoisie as backward and turning toward the past. As in his essay on the radio, Fanons thus argues that the peasantry, not the Algerian urban elite, is the most inclined to appropriate technologies. Furthermore, he passionately insists that the *fellah* must find a way to modernize independently of both the colonizer and the national bourgeoisie: "If the Revolution is able to initiate economic growth, elevating the peasants beyond their current state of indigence, then they will support it," he writes. "And, by implication, if acquiring technologies allows the peasants to improve their situation (as in the case of the radio), they will embrace these as well" (152). According to Fanon, it is precisely the lack of economic development (in addition to physical violence) that allows the colonizer to maintain the colonized's state of degradation. In general, Fanon seeks to counter the elitism associated with technology, emphasizing that all peoples have a fundamental right to possess modern technological developments.

Given these challenges and opportunities outlined by Fanon, he presents the FLN (Front de Libération Nationale) as a grassroots, pro-modernization political party that will promote technological transfer and foster invention among the lower classes. In his view, the FLN had already worked to undo the economy of extraction established by the colonial elite: "In these liberated districts which are at the same time excluded from the old trade routes we have had to modify production, which formerly looked only toward the towns and toward export" (192). He also claims that the FLN has increased the amount of agricultural production that directly benefits the Arab population, which remains unaware of these benefits (192). Although they lack the necessary technicians, Fanon believes that members of the FLN are actually more capable of promoting development than the colonizers: "This coordination was decided upon by the FLN and it was they who set up the system of communications. We did not have any technicians or planners coming from big Western universities" (192). While Fanon may have ultimately been wrong in promoting the FLN as a modernizing force, so distinct from the national bourgeoisie that he despised, his depiction of this party reflects his notion of an ideal revolutionary movement.

Technology and modernization will play a large role not only in the Revolution but also in the postindependence national culture that Fanon says will emerge after the Liberation, which he describes extensively in the chapter from *The Wretched of the Earth* titled "On National Culture." He emphasizes that the basis of this culture will be the Revolution itself—that is, the very process by which the Algerian people gained independence—and that it will be characterized by rapid modernization. Fanon believes that the violence involved in the Revolution constitutes an enormous act of purification, purging the population of the degradation of the colonial situation; it is a cathartic process, a tremendous act of consciousness-raising whereby the *fellah*, the lowly agricultural peasant class, will gain the confidence and esteem necessary to embrace technology.

In this chapter, Fanon famously presents three phases in the development of a national culture that are highly relevant to his views on technology and modernization. In the first phase, characterized by mere imitation, the native intellectual mimics the colonizer's culture, as a means of demonstrating that he/she has fully assimilated it. Fanon describes this as an "unqualified assimilation," which he views very negatively: "At the very moment when the native intellectual is anxiously trying to create a cultural work he fails to realize that he is utilizing techniques and language which are borrowed from the stranger in his country" (223). Indeed, Fanon considers this mode of production a failed attempt at creating a national culture: "The native artist who wishes at whatever cost to create a national work of art shuts himself up in a stereotyped reproduction of details" (224).

In Fanon's second phase of national-culture building, the native is shaken by the dominance of the occupier's culture and decides to remember the culture that he/she possessed before colonization: "The native is disturbed; he decides to remember what he is" (222). This period involves recuperating childhood memories, legends, and a general turning toward the past and tradition. Although this is the stage so often embraced by francophone writers,[33] Fanon is highly critical of artists and intellectuals who turn to the past for inspiration, since he believes that doing so only maintains the backwardness resulting from the colonial order. He also vehemently attacks the national bourgeoisie and other movements (including presumably revolutionary ones) that seek to use the past as a basis for postrevolutionary national culture by reviving traditional folklore, music, etc. For Fanon, Negritude is one such movement, and in *The Wretched of the Earth*, he greatly criticizes the writings and ideas of his fellow Martinican and former mentor Césaire.[34]

Fanon considers a return to traditional culture futile because he believes that modern technology has already greatly transformed the colonized's worldview, "reorganized the people's brains" (210), whether they realize it or not. According to Fanon, for an artist to deny this transformation by turning toward the past simply causes him/her to be disconnected from the reality of the nation, such that his/her work cannot be considered "authentic." Ultimately, Fanon saw the Revolution not as a turn toward a precolonial past but as an opening up toward modernity and modernization leading to an integration of the new nation into a global culture. As Nigel Gibson observes: "Fanon claimed that the end of colonialism would be truly expressed in the reformation and recreation of a vibrant national culture which had its basis in revolutionary transformation rather than ethnic identity, with a future constructed by all who wanted to play a positive part" (13). Radio and technology would no doubt form part of this new national culture.

In the third phase, which Fanon calls the "fighting phase" (*de combat*), the colonized intellectual, who once tried to become one of the people, will now "shake" them, acting as an "awakener of the people" (*réveilleur de peuple*): "Finally in the third phase, which is called the fighting phase, the native, after having tried to lose himself in the people and with the people, will on the contrary shake the people" (222). In this stage, the intellectual encourages the people to write and create as a means of liberating themselves. This is by far the most productive phase of the establishment of a national culture for Fanon, and the only one that involves creativity and invention. Extending Fanon's analysis to technology (which he does not do explicitly in this part of the text), this stage could be said to mark the moment when the intellectual will inspire the people to appropriate and invent new technologies.

Notably, Fanon does not appear to view the transfer of technologies from Europe as a form of "imitation" corresponding to the first phase but rather as an appropriation that involves creation and therefore forms part of the third stage. This is evidenced in his essay on the radio, in which he states that the difficulty in making out the language that was transmitted transformed listening into a creative process, whereby the listener (here, the colonized) invented what he/she thought had been said, and then repeated it to others, eventually establishing a narrative. Fanon greatly emphasizes that listening was a creative endeavor in order to illustrate the extent to which the Algerian people were taking an active role in the Revolution in their everyday lives, and that their listening to the radio signals from Cairo was a means of showing resistance to the occupiers. Nevertheless, although Fanon does consider the use of radios by the Arab population to be a form of appropriation and not imitation, he emphasizes that the colonized peoples must eventually develop their own technologies.

For Fanon, modernization as imposed by foreign (colonial) cultures is unacceptable; it must be invented within a national culture, becoming one of its essential components. This requires a great deal of self-awareness among the masses, who must be prepared to accept all aspects of modernity as distinct from the colonizer's culture. "If the building of a bridge does not enrich the awareness of those who work on it," Fanon writes, "then that bridge ought not to be built and the citizens can go on swimming across the river or going by boat" (200–201). While Fanon notes that new technologies have already changed the minds of the people, technological development must occur in a way that enriches their consciousness, not in a top-down manner from the colonizer: "The bridge should not be 'parachuted down' from above; it should not be imposed by a *deus ex machina* upon the social scene; on the contrary it should come from the muscles and the brains of the citizens" (201).[35] Fanon's choice of the word "parachuted" (*parachuter*) here is highly significant: it is, of course, a reference to the *parachutistes*, French soldiers who were airdropped into Algiers during the war, the very symbol of colonial oppression. Fanon thus suggests that the transfer of technologies from abroad, without the use of the colonized's "brains and brawn" to develop them, is merely a continuation of French occupation and rule; he views technology as a potential means of domination, if the instruments are developed elsewhere and simply transferred.

Fanon envisages a new form of modernity based on discovery and invention by the (formerly) colonized, and thus fundamentally different from the Western exploitative version: "If we want humanity to advance a step further, if we want to bring it up to a different level than that which Europe has shown it, then we must invent and we must make discoveries" (315). In *Fanon's Dialectic of Experience,* Ato Sekyi-Otu explores this perspective: "Fanon holds out the possibility that the body of 'intellectual and technical capital' which the national bourgeoisie had 'snatched' from imperial institutions of knowledge will, in the hands of the dissident intelligentsia, be the meeting place for this 'conversation of discovery'" (184). He gives the following definitions of what "appropriation" means for Fanon: "the enterprise of transforming into one's own tradition of possibilities an imposed order of practices and thereby overcoming their violence" (184); and "the process by which the impositions of colonial modernity—in the form of the artifacts of instrumental reason and the institutions of communicative action—are salvaged from their original violence" (185).

Fanon does acknowledge that it may be necessary for foreigners to assist in the process of development, at least at first, but he emphasizes the need for technology to be assimilated into the citizen's mind-set: "Certainly, there may well be need of engineers and architects, sometimes completely foreign engineers and architects; but the local party leaders should be always present, so that new techniques can make their way into the cerebral desert of the citizen, so that the bridge in whole and in part can be taken up and conceived, and the responsibility for it assumed by the citizen" (201). In a striking image, he states that the skilled colonized must find a way to embed themselves not in diagrams and statistics but in the body of the people (187). In this way, the peasants will participate in the process of appropriating foreign technology for their own specific needs, thereby making it part of the national culture. Gibson summarizes Fanon's position as follows: "The notion of appropriating and 'taking over' modern techniques does not mean that the movement is indebted to the colonial system" (133). For Fanon, decolonization is the first, and necessary, step toward modernization.

In sum, Fanon is against the simple transfer of technologies from one place to another (what Daniel Headrick calls the "geographic relocation" of instruments), without its "cultural diffusion" (the dissemination of the technical knowledge and techniques used to produce them).[36] Fanon emphasizes that only a cultural diffusion of technologies will lead to development and believes that modern technologies should ultimately be both invented and constructed by the citizens. This can only occur for him by raising the consciousness of citizens, especially young people, a process in which communications technology, such as the radio, plays a central role. Fanon considers the resulting awakening of consciousness essential to both liberation and the subsequent development of a national culture. In *The Wretched of the Earth,* Fanon emphasizes that the Revolution will result in a profound psychological freedom, resulting from the appropriation of technologies and the elimination of all negative associations with aspects of modernity.

For Fanon, the process of appropriating modern technologies empowers all social classes, who grow in esteem, intellect, and self-sufficiency with every instrument acquired. Technological progress will also make the population wealthier overall, lessening the gap between the *fellah* and the colonizers and national bourgeoisie, therefore allowing the Algerian people to be more free and united. Once the lower classes cease rejecting technologies because they are associated with the colonizer, the country will modernize. The Revolution itself is a fundamental part of this process since it provokes a "purging" that entails the peasantry freeing itself from an anti-modern mentality.

In Fanon's writings on Algeria, the psychoanalysis of race that he first presented in *Black Skin, White Masks* takes on a collective dimension. In his essays such as "This Is the Voice of Algeria" and in *The Wretched of the Earth,* the sickness, the trauma to be uncovered is that of colonization, including its physical and psychological violence. His journalistic writings, especially "This Is the Voice of Algeria," explain the initial rejection of modern technologies (in this case, radio) by the colonized from a psychological perspective and emphasize how this attitude begins to change with the Revolution. Fanon emphasizes that there was never an organized refusal of Western technology, medicine, and science on the part of the Arab population, and that far from being incompatible with traditional practices, these aspects of modernity were often complemented and reinforced by local beliefs. Paradoxically, he asserts that it is the war of liberation that more fully and effectively integrates Western medicine and technology into the daily lives of numerous Algerians. This claim, just like the ones made about the radio and the French language, suggests that for Fanon, the revolutionary struggle is the primary impetus for the spread of technology in Algeria, *not* colonization, as the colonizer—who promotes the ideology of the "civilizing mission"—has led everyone to believe. In *The Wretched of the Earth,* Fanon continues this argument by further describing the revolutionary awakening of consciousness that will lead to a fully modernized national culture. Although initially the *fellah* have no access to technologies, while the urban working class rejects them as a part of European culture, Fanon believes that the Revolution is associated with a change in mentality that will cause all of these classes to embrace technologies. He adamantly equates colonization with backwardness and lack of development; technological progress belongs to the Revolution and postwar national culture he hopes to achieve.

In his discussions of science, technology, and medicine, Fanon focuses on the fundamental importance of creating a sense of "imagined community" and "national culture" in order for true liberation to occur. In postindependence Algeria, new technologies must be developed from within and transferred from Europe and elsewhere only when necessary. According to Fanon, a key form of colonial violence promoting backwardness in Algeria and the colonies is precisely the elimination of mutually beneficial relations between these countries and the rest of the world; technological progress in Algeria will be accompanied by its entry into a larger global community. More broadly, technology and modernization will undergird the postindependence "national culture" that Fanon envisions not only for Algeria but for other nations as well. Fanon, a native of Martinique who studied in France, practicing medicine and journalism in Algeria, believed that the Revolution originating in Algeria would become truly global in nature. At the end of *The Wretched of the Earth,* Fanon, who also traveled to Ghana to spread his revolutionary message, declares that Africa must develop using invention and technology.

Fanon shares with many other authors in my study the idea that literature itself, especially with regard to its portrayal of technology, serves a social function, by preparing the population to modernize. A journalist who published in newspapers, he wrote the essays of *Toward the African Revolution, A Dying Colonialism,* and *The Wretched of the Earth* for a broad audience. Fanon believed that an awakening of consciousness was a necessary condition for modernization and viewed his writing as a part of this process. The reading process, like psychoanalytic therapy (for instance in *Black Skin, White Masks*), is meant to train the readers to think of themselves as a society that could become just as modern and technological as the West. His writings, like Césaire's theater and Sembène's novels and films, are meant to raise consciousness and thus prepare the public/population to modernize.

Fanon may have died before the advent of the Internet, but he was ultimately an extremely prescient theorist of globalization. In a telling sentence from *The Wretched of the Earth,* Fanon writes that the awakening of the people will not happen in "one stroke" (*un seul coup*) because the communications systems are not yet developed enough: "The awakening of the whole people will not come about all at once . . . first because the means of communication and transmission are only beginning to be developed" (193). The unstated implication is, of course, that a highly developed system of communications—for instance, the Internet—*could* provoke such a simultaneous awakening. The recent events of the "Arab Spring," in which protesters used online social networking tools to organize, appear to prove Fanon right on this point.[37] Fanon was very much aware of the extent to which the medium technology affects communication, and almost everything he writes about radio could be applied to the Internet. He emphasizes the process by which a technology initially perceived as a source of oppression can become an instrument of liberation. The battles ensuing in cyberspace, as the Egyptian government tried to restrict access to the Internet and people struggled to maintain contact through satellite connections, mirror how Algerians fought to listen to the radio stations broadcast from Cairo, whose wavelengths were frequently blocked by the French. Fanon also shows how certain cultures perform a strategic appropriation of particular technologies; for instance, the Arabs of colonial Algeria adopted the radio because it was useful to them but no doubt rejected other technologies from the colonizer's culture. Similarly, while Facebook and the Internet were dissociated from the West for participants in the Arab Spring, these same protesters in Cairo raised the canisters of tear gas that had been thrown at them by Mubarak's military before the cameras to show that they read "Made in USA," thus strategically associating certain military tools and technologies with the West (in this case, the United States), but not others.

In the following chapter, I consider how another author writing in the 1950s, Ousmane Sembène, portrays the potential role of technology in African revolutions and independence movements, including the appropriation of innovations such as the railway, and use of media (radio, television and film) for consciousness-raising.

CHAPTER FOUR

Machines and Media in Ousmane Sembène

In the first three chapters of this book, I examined the representation of technology in the works of Negritude and Fanon's writings on Algeria. In the next two chapters, I explore sub-Saharan African works of different genres, the novel and film (in the case of Sembène), focusing on the transition between the colonial period and independence. Much like the texts analyzed in the previous chapters, these works portray modernization and the transfer of Western technologies as essential components of nation building, economic development, and even social progress.

The focus of this chapter, Ousmane Sembène (1923–2007), was a Senegalese writer and director known as the "father of African film." He was born in Ziguinchor, Casamance, to a Muslim Wolof family and educated in Islamic and French schools. A man of many trades, he worked as a fisherman (with his father), a manual laborer in Dakar, a *tirailleur sénégalais* (black African soldier) for the French military during World War I, a factory worker for Citroën in Paris, a docker in Marseille, and a union leader and Communist Party member in both Marseille and Dakar. But it was ultimately writing and filmmaking that became his primary profession, one that he viewed much as he did the other jobs he had practiced. Sembène was always famously at odds with Léopold Sédar Senghor, who censored many of his films, including *Xala* (1973), which includes a character who is a mocking caricature of the first Senegalese president.

The question of technology is central to Sembène's work throughout his entire career as a writer and filmmaker, although this topic has been largely overlooked by critics. Sembène is highly critical of the colonizers and colonial system at the same time that he denounces retrograde practices and advocates a push toward the modern. Many of his works, whether novels or films, present characters confronting the questions: Should technology be rejected as part of the colonizer's culture or accepted, even embraced, as part of a new modernity? And what role should modern technologies play in postindependence societies?

Sembène's work exhibits an evolving notion of the utility of modern technologies that is inextricably linked to his ideas about language, including the use of French as a lingua franca and the ability of film to bypass both the written form and former colonizer's tongue. *God's Bits of Wood* (generally considered his novelistic masterpiece) confronts issues of technology transfer directly through the depiction of a railway line. The novel presents the different discourses surrounding this European technology brought to Africa, such as the elders who consider it an evil by association with the colonizers, and the younger generation who value the machine as an equalizer capable of eliminating hierarchies. Much of what Sembène writes about the railway—which is portrayed as a democratizing, liberatory force—can be applied to film for him, the medium to which he turns after the publication of this novel in 1960.

Sembène's cinematic output continues the exploration of technology begun in *God's Bits of Wood* by first portraying technological innovations as fetishized objects, then later as liberating media. His work suggests that while some innovations, such as the railway in *God's Bits of Wood*, can be used to decrease inequalities, technology fetishism serves only to increase them. The 1973 film *Xala* (The curse) shows how in postindependence Senegal, the African bourgeoisie (as represented by the ridiculous protagonist, El Hadji) has rendered technologies useless by having them serve as markers of social status rather than as objects capable of promoting economic growth in a way that might decrease tremendous disparities in wealth (represented by the crippled beggars). While *Xala* demonstrates the uselessness of fetishized technology, Sembène's last film, *Moolaadé*, showcases the power of the media to enact social change, since the radios that the women of the village listen to give them the strength to rebel against the traditional practice of female genital mutilation. In this film, as in other works by Sembène, the portrayal of technology provides a metadiscourse for describing the role that his own artistic works will play in promoting modernization, development, and social progress.

Ô PAYS, MON BEAU PEUPLE!

Sembène's first novel, *Le docker noir* (*Black Docker*) (1956), examines the racism faced by an African immigrant working on the docks of Marseille. His second, *Ô pays, mon beau peuple!* (Oh country, my people!) (1957), marks his first profound engagement with the question of modernization in postcolonial Africa, which will later become the focus of much of his work. David Murphy writes that these pre-independence novels "are infused with the optimism of the independence movement, and they attempt to deal with some of the issues facing an increasingly urbanized and industrialized Africa" (*Imagining Alternatives* 27).

Ô pays, mon beau peuple! tells the story of a black farmer, Oumar Faye, who returns to his native Casamance after studying agriculture and engineering in France, bringing along his new wife, Isabelle (a white French woman). Upon his arrival, Faye stirs up controversy among the villagers by proposing to use modern agricultural practices to increase crop productivity and ease the reliance on fishing. The narrative recounts Faye's many unsuccessful attempts to integrate himself and his wife into the family and social milieu of his native Senegal. Facing vehement opposition from both the colonial regime and the leaders of traditional African society, Oumar is eventually murdered, an act that symbolizes the refusal of many to adopt the practices he promotes. Nevertheless, his vision of progress does not die with him but rather lives on in the minds of his people.

Ô pays, mon beau peuple! asserts the notion—also found later in the novel *God's Bits of Wood* and the film *Moolaadé*—that in order for modernization and technological development to proceed in Africa, the impetus must come from the outside, even if the desire to sustain this development should emerge from African cultures. The novel illustrates the schism that divides Africans between the progressives who favor technology transfer, modernization, and contact with the West, and the traditionalists who reject all aspects of European culture and modernity; a schism that subsumes attitudes toward race. In fact, it is the primary conflict represented in the novel, rather than one between colonizers and the colonized, or black Africans and white settlers.

Throughout *Ô pays, mon beau peuple!*, Sembène stages a series of conversations between progressives and traditionalists, two groups that represent the opposite sides of a debate about African nations in the era of independence. The progressives consist mostly of the young people referred to as "the buddies" (*les copains*), including Dr. Agbo and Agnès, as well as the protagonist, Oumar Faye. The "buddies" are much more open to Faye's ideas and willing to accept the potential value of knowledge and instruments originating in European cultures. The traditionalists, on the other hand, reject anything even remotely associated with the West. Dieng and Diagne, for instance, are reactionaries who criticize Oumar for marrying a French woman and refuse to believe that anything positive can emerge from contact with the colonizers' culture. While less extreme than these two characters, Moussa emphasizes the importance of maintaining village traditions, which he views as incompatible with the modern vision that Faye proposes. On several occasions, Faye is accused of being a traitor to his race, since he advocates progress for Africans. Yet the "buddies," especially Faye, often emphasize that embracing modernity does not require abandoning ancestral traditions. In fact, this is one of the novel's central themes: that traditional practices from Africa and modern technologies originating in the West are inherently neither positive nor negative but should be examined critically in order to establish their potential purpose and utility. Although he advocates modernization, Faye is not against carrying on traditions but rather advocates an ideal synthesis of the two ways of life.

As in other works by Sembène (*God's Bits of Wood, Moolaadé*), a favorable attitude toward technological progress and modernity is equated with fighting for social progress, since the characters who are most open to adopting modern Western innovations are likewise the most willing to fight for the rights of women and most opposed to institutions like polygamy. The reactionary Diagne not only rejects Faye's proposals but also has strong opinions about the dangers of educating women: "A woman's place is in the home. . . . As soon as they are educated, we are under-valued. My daughter will not go to school. . . . And to learn what? That her ancestors are Gaulois? We know that they were blond and blue-eyed, and she looks like a sack of coal" (105). Diagne equates women's education with insidious Westernization and thus rejects it outright, just as he refuses to even consider Faye's proposals for modernizing agricultural practices, since he has been a fisherman his whole life. Dr. Agbo, representing the progressives' viewpoint, voices his strong disagreement with Diagne: "You mix everything up. Accepting progress doesn't mean that you turn your back on your ancestors. But there are some things that we should no longer practice" (105). Dr. Agbo and other progressive characters also accept modern medicine and are critical of the use of fetishism and witchcraft to deal with illnesses. Their critique echoes Fanon's declarations in "Medicine and Colonialism," as well as those made by other characters in postindependence African novels, such as the works of Olympe Bhêly-Quénum and Aké Loba that are the subject of the next chapter.

Overall, *Ô pays, mon beau peuple!* sets the stage for the examination of technology in Sembène's later works by presenting a debate between progressives and traditionalists that illustrates some of the central issues involved: the potential role of technology in combating poverty and hunger, the association of technologies with the colonizer, and the problem of reconciling modern practices such as medicine with traditional beliefs.

THE RAILWAY MACHINE IN *GOD'S BITS OF WOOD*

Although Sembène's first two novels were met with critical acclaim and established him as a major literary figure, it is *God's Bits of Wood,* published in 1960, which is his most famous novel by far and generally considered his masterpiece. Sembène recounts the 1947 strike of African workers employed along the Dakar–Niger railway line, which he witnessed firsthand as a union organizer. The novel takes place in three different settings: Dakar, Thiès, and Bamako, the major cities along the railway line in Senegal and Mali. The story begins as the workers gather for a vote to determine whether they should join the others who have already begun to strike. Sembène then describes in great detail the long and arduous strike, which causes all aspects of society to be called into question: the authority of the elders, the role of women, religious beliefs, and the use of the French language. Although most characters in *God's Bits of Wood* are identified primarily with the larger collectivities to which they belong, one individual stands out: Bakayoko, a young worker and leader of the labor movement, who is an avid reader of French literature and a passionate speaker. In the end, the workers acquire their demands, and victory is declared.

Despite the setting of the novel, the portrayal of the African workers' revolt against their colonizers is as much about the independence movements of the 1950s as the historical events of 1947. The epic work was written between 1957 and 1958, the year of the referendum that granted Senegal autonomy from France, and published in 1960, when it and many other African countries (including Côte d'Ivoire and the two Congos) obtained full independence.[1] *God's Bits of Wood* is thus a landmark in francophone literature; it represents a shift from the anticolonial novels of the 1950s, which focused on issues of race and the evils of colonization, to the postindependence novels, with their emphasis on questions of modernity and technological progress in the new republics. Although Sembène still criticizes colonialism and racism by representing a great act of resistance against the injustices of this system, he also examines the role of Western technologies in the newly independent African nations through the motif of the railway.

Most of the criticism on *God's Bits of Wood* has focused on either the overtly Marxist thematic of the strike, including the realist style reminiscent of Émile Zola's *Germinal*;[2] Sembène's portrayal of a collective "coming to consciousness" (awakening) of the people in the story;[3] or the central role of women in the formation of this collective consciousness, including their role in the victory that comes at the end.[4] In "Smoke of the Savannah: Traveling Modernity in Sembène Ousmane's *God's Bits of Wood*," Marian Aguiar takes a slightly different approach by examining how modernity "travels through" different collectivities in order to be realized in the postcolonial context (284–305). Unlike other critics, Aguiar addresses the question of technology, concluding that Sembène's novel presents an ambiguous picture of the machine. According to her, Sembène believes that modern technologies' initial ties to the colonial era render their use problematic for Africans, a conclusion about the novel that I will refute in this chapter. Moreover, Aguiar's analysis does not discuss the primary significance of the machine motif in the novel, namely as an extensive metaphor for the instruments and ideas brought to Africa from the West, including written laws, literature, and the book, which can either be appropriated by the formerly colonized or rejected by them.

In the following analysis, I consider some outstanding questions raised by the novel concerning technology in the postcolony: Why does Sembène, in a novel about Senegalese independence, choose to focus so much on the figure of the machine and the technology of the railway line? What is the role of technology in the collective "coming to consciousness" and by extension the culture of independence that Sembène is advocating for Senegal and Africa more generally? How does technology function as a metaphor and metonymy for the role that instruments and materials brought to the colonies from Europe can play in African life?

In the first section, I chart the construction of three kinds of discourses surrounding the machine in *God's Bits of Wood*, each corresponding to particular groups of people with different attitudes with regard to technology. In the second, I examine the relationship between technology and another recurring theme in the novel: the need to find a mode of communication between members of different cultures, and the potential role of language and writing in the process of liberation. The third section examines the relevance of Sembène's novel to the era in which it was written, the late 1950s, especially to the creation of an independent, modernized, and technological society in Senegal and West Africa more generally.

In *God's Bits of Wood,* the "machine," as the railway line and the trains that run on it are called in the novel,[5] is described from three different perspectives; each perspective corresponds to the view of the relationship between colonialism and modern Western technology—as represented by the railway—held by an important group. The attitude of every group with regard to technology is determined by a number of cultural factors, including religious beliefs, age, and race.[6]

The first perspective views technology as an extremely positive force in Africa and strictly associates its development with European colonialism. This discourse reflects the ideals of the "civilizing mission": technology is perceived as a gift brought by the colonizers to Africa from Europe. This is, of course, the ideology that was traditionally used by imperial powers to justify violent colonization as a necessary evil for the advancement of colonized peoples. In the novel, this discourse first takes the form of a discussion among the white colonizers, who criticize the African workers for striking. In a key scene, the bosses sit around and discuss the "ingratitude" of the colonized, to whom they believe to have brought progress. For instance, Victor, one of the French bosses, gives a speech to his "young neighbor" that illustrates the infantilizing gaze directed toward the African workers: "'You'll see,' he said to his young neighbor, 'you have to learn how to forget. Twenty years ago there was nothing here but an arid wilderness. We built this city. Now they have hospitals, schools, and trains, but if we ever leave they're finished—the brush will take it all back. There wouldn't be anything left'" (166). Victor's speech presents a vivid image of technology versus nature; he claims that without the efforts of the colonizers, nature would take over. He portrays the colonized people as a group incapable of countering the forces of nature (portrayed extremely negatively) without help from the Europeans, denoted by the "we" of the statement.

The enunciation of such a discourse by the white owners of the railway line is not surprising, but one of Sembène's great innovations in the novel is to show the extent to which the words of another group, the

Muslim leaders or "spiritual guides," resemble those of the colonizers. They are against the strike and try to convince the young workers to accept their situation as God's will. For them, the traditional caste system, the economic disparity between the workers and the bosses, and the inequalities of colonialism more generally are all the result of the will of God and therefore should be accepted as such. They launch a massive campaign of antistrike propaganda, which the narrator describes as a danger and an obstacle to the workers' movement: "A demoralization campaign against the strikers and, in particular, their wives had been undertaken by the 'spiritual guides,' the imams and the priests of the different sects" (318). The Muslim leaders disseminate their message about the strike and technology by placing it in the form of a sermon given after prayers: "After the prayers and religious services all over the city, there would be a sermon whose theme was always the same: 'By ourselves, we are incapable of creating any sort of useful object, not even a needle; and yet you want to strike against the *toubabs* [white settlers] who have brought us all of these things? It is madness!'" (206). The leaders present their antistrike propaganda after the Friday prayers in order to invoke their authority and convince the workers that continuing the strike means turning their backs not only on their bosses but also on their own leaders, religion (Islam), and even on God, since it was his will that caused the *toubabs* to come in the first place.

The sermon continues: "You would do better to be thanking God for having brought them among us and bettering our lives with the benefits of their civilization and their science" (206). One of the religious leaders, Mabigué, gives a speech: "It is not our part in life to resist the will of heaven. I know that life is often hard, but that should not cause us to turn our backs on God. He has assigned a rank, a place, and a certain role to every man, and it is blasphemous to think of changing His design. The *toubabs* are here because that is the will of God. Strength is a gift of God, and Allah has given it to them" (44–45). Much as the white colonizers described technology as a gift brought to Africa by the Europeans, the religious leaders view technology as a positive force brought to their people, whom they believe to be incapable of developing modern technologies on their own. The passage on the antistrike campaign emphasizes the difficulties faced by the workers continuing the strike: they face opposition not only from the white owners of the railway line but also from their own religious leaders. By juxtaposing the discourse of the white colonizers with that of the spiritual leaders in a way that shows the similarities between the two, Sembène satirizes the speeches of the spiritual guides, emphasizing their abuse of power and their submissiveness to colonial authority.

The second discourse takes the form of oral traditions recounted by the elders to the young workers. This discourse is the antithesis of the "civilizing mission": although technology is also considered to be inextricably linked with colonialism, the machine is associated with the violence of colonization, and its absence with an idyllic past that preceded the arrival of the Europeans. Since the railway line was built at the beginning of the twentieth century, and the novel takes place in 1947, the elders remember its construction and the hardships created by it; they view the railway line primarily as a means for the colonizers to exploit the Africans who work for them.

For the elders, there are two eras: the time before the arrival of the trains, which is described as an idyllic, fertile past; and the subsequent period, which is equated with famine and hardship. They portray the time before the construction of the railway line as a privileged past in which people lived harmoniously with nature. The narrator describes this, from the point of view of the young workers, as the "age their elders had told them about, when all of Africa was just a garden for food" (32). The primary representative of this viewpoint is Mamadou Keïta, also called Fa Keïta, a greatly respected elder affectionately known as "the Old Man," who views the railway line as an instrument used by the colonizers to exploit African workers. In one of the opening scenes of the novel, Fa Keïta makes a speech before the workers on the day of the strike vote, in which he recounts the early days, when he witnessed the establishment of the railway line at Koulikoro: "He spoke slowly, but precisely, evoking the laying of the first rails. At that time he had not yet been born, but later he had seen the completion of the railroad at Koulikoro. Then he spoke of the epidemics, of the famines, and of the seizure of tribal lands by the company" (8). Fa Keïta transforms the arrival of the railway into a legend, assuming the role of the griot, a class of wise elders in West Africa who know traditional songs, tell stories, and are authorities on the local histories of their region.

Fa Keïta elsewhere associates the changes brought by the railway with the emergence of a new order: "A long time ago, . . . before any of you were born, everything that happened happened within a framework, an order that was our own, and the existence of that order was of great importance in our lives" (94). For Fa Keïta, the old order pertains to the African peoples, since he describes it as "ours," whereas the new order is "theirs." He says that now, everything has changed: "Today, no such framework exists. There are no castes among people, no difference in the quality of grain or of the bread that is made from the grain; there are no weavers, no artisans in metal, no makers of fine shoes" (94). According to him, not only has the caste system changed, but so also has the form of knowledge represented by the griots and other traditional professions. He believes that it is the machine that has changed everything: "I think it is the machine which has grounded everything together this way and brought everything to a single level" (94). When the young workers decide to hold a trial to decide the fate of a strikebreaker—an idea taken from a book written by the "white settlers"—the Old Man warns of the dangers of imitating the colonizers too much: "If you imitate the hirelings of your masters, you will become like them, hirelings and barbarians" (95).

Although Fa Keïta would be considered an authoritative figure under traditional village governance, the young workers completely ignore what he says and continue to debate the strike as if he had never spoken, talking about the need to revolt against their masters and the liberating power of the machine. These workers are presented to some extent as a mob that won't listen to reason; nevertheless, Keïta's speech is portrayed as out of touch with the reality of modern times and the issues at hand. Rather than trying to apply his wisdom to advocate a form of action, he tells a story of the past and says simply: "I did not say that I was against the strike. I said only that a decision of this importance has never before been taken here, and that we must think about it carefully" (10).

The portrayal of the perspective of the elders in *God's Bits of Wood* is meant to satirize the Negritude movement, which Sembène criticized extensively. For Sembène, upholding the ideals of Negritude is contrary to progress; in a speech given at the 1963 Congress for Cultural Freedom, Sembène declared that Negritude "neither feeds the hungry nor builds roads" (Moore 57). Sembène believes that Negritude (as well as other idealizations of a mythical African past) is out of touch with the times and is not a constructive vision for Africa, since it is impossible to go back to a precolonial past. The novel suggests that authoritative figures such as Fa Keïta need to adapt their message to modernity.

Several passages from *God's Bits of Wood* emphasize the futility of the elders' wish to return to a mythical precolonial era and the need to progress beyond it. The machine is presented as having irreversibly changed the country's landscape. Although the griots evoke a mythical past in which Africa was a fertile garden, the arrival of the colonizers has altered the perception of the natural environment. Thus, at the beginning of the strike, with the disappearance of the smoke they are so used to seeing on the savannah, the workers exclaim: "When the smoke from the trains no longer drifted above the savannah, they realized that an age had ended—an age their elders had told them about, when all of Africa was just a garden for food" (32). Now those times are over, and the era of the machine has emerged.

The narrator, speaking in the indirect style, notes the perspective of the young workers, who realize that the landscape has changed with the arrival of the machine, on which they are now dependent for their very existence: "Now the machine ruled over their lands, and when they forced every machine within a thousand miles to halt they became conscious of their strength, but conscious also of their dependence" (32). Here, the "machine," or railway, serves as a metonymy for the way in which European colonizers brought new technologies to the colonies and then created a dependence on them by structuring the entire economy around their use. In the case of French West Africa (l'Association Occidentale Française), the economy was developed to ship agricultural products on trains from the inner land to the coasts, where they could be shipped to Europe, thus establishing the "economy of extraction" described by Daniel Headrick, a process that is recounted in *God's Bits of Wood.*

The agricultural workers, for instance, are furious about the strike, because they are unable to ship and sell goods without the trains. One of the farmers confronts Tiémoko: "Do you think the trains belong to you? They don't—no more than they did to your fathers—but you decide to stop working, just like that, without thinking about other people. And yet you workmen, of all people, should be satisfied with what you have. You don't have to worry about drought or rain or taxes, and you don't have any expenses. Why should you prevent these farmers from going where they want to go?" (83). This exchange shows that the strike affects not only the European owners of the railway but African workers as well. Although the strike is presented primarily as a movement against the colonizers, they are not the only ones affected, since the entire economy has become dependent on the railway line.

While the first two discourses reflect traditional attitudes about the relationship between colonialism and technology, the third, developed by the younger workers who grew up around the railway, constitutes one of Sembène's great innovations in African literature: it not only dissociates the machines from the colonizers who brought them to Africa but also views them extremely positively, as a liberating force. African culture can thus appropriate technology to contribute to its own common good. Furthermore, the portrayal of the railway by the young workers undergoes a series of transformations throughout the novel, which reflect the evolving attitude of African society toward technology, and its relationship to the colonizers.

At first the younger workers also perceive the trains as a European possession and feel proud to have "put an end" to them: "In the beginning the men had announced pridefully that they had 'put an end to the smoke of the savannah'" (76). This is a reflection of their conflicting emotions about the machine: they feel guilty about their favorable attitude toward technology, which they still associate with the colonizers, who are perceived to have a greater knowledge about it: "a dulled fear mixed with hate for this machine that the white men could turn off whenever they wanted" (108).

And yet, they were born after the railway line had been constructed and therefore have grown up around the trains and feel that they form part of their home environment. Soon after the strike has begun, they experience nostalgia for when the trains ran every day: "Now they remembered the time when not a day had passed without the sight of that smoke, rising above the fields, the houses, and the trees of the brush. They remembered when not a night had run its course without the sight of the flickering colored lanterns of the teams at work in the marshaling yards, or the sounds of steel against steel, of the shock of buffer against buffer as the cars came together, and of the far-off whistling of the locomotives" (76). The narrator describes the railway in poetic, even romantic, terms, portraying its aesthetic interaction with the nature (the smoke "rising above the fields") in order to demonstrate the sentiment that the workers feel for it. Nevertheless, since the workers still strongly associate the railway with the colonizers who exploit them, they are embarrassed to show their nostalgia for the train in front of others: "All that had been their life. They thought of it constantly now, but they kept their thoughts jealously to themselves, even as they spied on each other, as if they were afraid that their secret thoughts might somehow become known" (76).

In their speeches to the workers, Tiémoko and Bakayoko, two leaders of the strike, consistently describe the machines as existing outside of racial distinctions and therefore as useful for the fight for equality and justice. In a speech delivered before the strike vote, and immediately following that of Keïta about the evils of the machine, Tiémoko declares: "Only the engines that we run tell the truth—and they don't know the difference between a white man and a black" (8). The "truth" that they tell is the equal value of the African workers' labor, and therefore their right to be paid as much as white workers, the primary demand of the strikers. Since the train functions the same with the workers of either race, it demonstrates the equality between them. Tiémoko therefore associates the machine with an objective truth and justice. Indeed, the workers feel a communion with the machine that is stronger than the divisions with their employers, which can now be overcome: "For a moment, the passage of the locomotive would calm the torment in their hearts, because their fellowship with the machine was deep and strong; stronger than the barriers which separated them from their employers, stronger even than the obstacle which until now had been insurmountable—the color of their skin" (77). The workers also view the machine as their common good, a uniting force, capable of liberating them from their oppressors by turning them into a collectivity.

The machine is ultimately associated with the creation of a new, more egalitarian society for the workers. At the beginning of the strike, the narrator describes their hope to be reborn as new individuals:[7] "Something was being born inside them, as if the past and the future were coupling to breed a new kind of man" (76). The workers feel as if the wind is whispering one of Bakayoko's favorite phrases: "The kind of man we were is dead, and our only hope for a new life lies in the machine, which knows neither a language nor a race" (76). Thus, the naturalist discourse of the elders is subverted; the African environment itself echoes the new creation, the utopian society, which technology is capable of bringing on.

For the young workers, the machine becomes a new sort of religion and culture that replaces the old ones, including Islam. In a notable passage, when a worker enters into the train-repair shop, the machines there are described as gods: "The massive diesels, their copper still gleaming, were formed in solid ranks, standing clean and powerful, and remote as gods" (136). He compares the place to a temple: "This building was their temple, and the acrid odor of hot oil their incense" (136). As a pagan sanctuary, the workshop is clearly opposed to Islam, the religion espoused by the majority of West Africans.

Although the colonizers own the railway line, the workers feel as if the trains belong to them, that they have appropriated them through their labor. In a key passage, the narrator writes: "Even in the midst of their confusion, however, they were conscious that the machine was the source of their common welfare, and they sensed that the frustration they felt in these dark days was also common to them all" (76). Indeed, as Sembène recounts the events that take place in the cities along the line, Dakar, Thiès, and Bamako, it becomes evident that the strike leads to the formation of a proletariat, a collectivity along the railway line, which constitutes an example of an "imagined community" or "contact zone" (to borrow Anderson's and Pratt's terminology) created through a technology. To declare symbolic ownership over this property, they have their own name for the train, "the smoke of the savannah," which refers to the region in which the train runs rather than the place in which the technology was created.

Although there is a great diversity of peoples in this area (the Mali Federation, covering the area known today as Senegal and Mali), the technology of the railway line brings them all together as they find common cause in the fight against the white owners of the machines. The novel highlights some of the divisions that existed, for instance, between the Bambara and the Wolof ethnic groups before they came together as a group against the white colonizers. In one of the opening passages of the novel, the narrator describes the apathy that Niakoro, the mother of Ibrahima Bakayoko, feels toward the Senegalese, whom she refers to as the "Ouolof people" (because most speak Wolof), calling them "the slaves" (2). For her, uniting with these people in the strike is a mistake, since she views them all as liars; the narrator portrays her thoughts on the matter: "Slaves, and sons of slaves, they are nothing but liars—will the Bambaras never learn that?" (2). By the end of the novel, such divisions no longer have the same importance, since the victory is claimed by all the African peoples who participated in the strike together.

In summary, the technology of the railway, the "machine," is portrayed as a force capable of eliminating the inequalities between Africans and Europeans on the one hand, and within African society on the other: the difference in pay between the African workers and their white counterparts; the new class distinction between the workers (who are in the process of forming a politically active proletariat) and their bosses (the bourgeoisie); and the hierarchies of the traditional caste system, which the Islamic leaders seek to maintain. In *God's Bits of Wood,* the different discourses surrounding the issue of Western technology intersect to produce an ideology according to which the machine is portrayed as a useful, politically neutral instrument that can be appropriated by African peoples.

These three different discourses surrounding the idea of the "machine" address not only the link between colonialism and technology but also the question of language: the elders who see Western technologies as nefarious are also against learning French and reading books; in contrast, the younger generation makes great efforts to improve their French and educate themselves, all the while fighting for the right to communicate officially in African languages, especially Wolof, used by the vast majority of the population in Senegal. More generally, *God's Bits of Wood* emphasizes the central importance of language, writing, and books for inspiring ideas and communicating between cultures. And the use of the French language and writing is inextricably linked to the question of technology, since the characters in the novel identify technologies of writing as European inventions and debate the legitimacy of using them to further their own political and economic goals.

In *God's Bits of Wood,* the question of reading and writing is related to the confrontation of two systems of authority and knowledge. The first is the traditional source of knowledge and authority, the wisdom of the elders, especially Niakoro and Fa Keïta. The discourse against the machines, which associates them with the traumatic and violent arrival of the colonizers, takes the form of oral legends passed on by the older, wiser men to the younger ones, who instead turn to books and literature in French. For instance Ab'jibid'ji, the industrious young daughter of Bakayoko, studies from *Mamadou et Bineta,* a book for children to learn to read French. N'Deye enthusiastically reads all the books given to her at school; Tiémoko finds the idea of holding a European-style trial for Diara, who breaks the strike, in a book from Bakayoko's library; and Bakayoko finds inspiration for the strike as a broader political movement in André Malraux's *The Human Condition.*

This generational conflict over French writing and culture is also visible in confrontations between female relatives. In a key scene at the beginning of the novel, Niakoro argues with her granddaughter Ab'jibid'ji about the use of French. According to Niakoro, long ago, the young never did anything without the consent of the old, but now everything has changed. The narrator, speaking in the free indirect style from the point of view of Niakoro, shows that she is upset because no one has consulted her about the strike: "In her time the young people undertook nothing without the advice of their elders, but now, alone, they were deciding on a strike. Did they even know what would happen?" (2). Similarly, Fa Keïta's speech before the strike vote is completely ignored by them, as is his warning against holding a European-style trial. It would seem that the elders no longer exert any power over the young, not even over their own children.

The elders, including female elders, are not only against the strike but often discourage the younger generation from reading books and learning French. Niakoro angrily questions Ab'jibid'ji: "What use is the white man's language [French] to a woman? To be a good mother you have no need of that" (4). In the novel, French is often called *le toubabou* by some of the characters, since for them it cannot be viewed separately from the people who speak it, the "*toubabs,*" or "white men";[8] in other words, language itself is associated with the colonizing force. Niakoro assigns to Ab'jibid'ji the exclusive role of wife and mother (which she will reject) and therefore concludes that learning French for her would be useless. She calls those who want to learn French "uprooted" people, as if they have been forcibly separated from the African landscape. When Ab'jibid'ji lets a word of French, "*alors,*" slip out at the end of a phrase while speaking to her in Wolof, Niakoro becomes extremely angry. She screams, "*Aloss, Aloss!,*" mocking her, and then chastises her for showing a lack of respect: "You speak to me, to your father's mother, and you say '*aloss*'" (5). She continues her tirade: "The white men say '*aloss*' when they call their dogs, and my granddaughter talks to me in the same way!" (5). For Niakoro, it is impossible to dissociate the French language from the colonizers, such that she believes that speaking to someone in French necessarily constitutes an act of oppression.

For Tiémoko, printed French books also contain a number of useful ideas for spreading justice within colonial society. He reads a book about French law and draws from it ideas about how to change the legal system of his people. The book inspires him to hold a European-style trial for strikebreakers; when he suggests that this trial be held, he confidently invokes the book's authority ("Everything we need is in this book" [87]). The elders greatly oppose this idea because it runs counter to their own customary legal system and comes from a source "written by the *toubabs*" (87). Tiémoko then draws an analogy with technology, stating that neither laws nor machines belong to a single race: "And the machines were built by the *toubabs!* The book belongs to Ibrahima Bakayoko, and right here, in front of you, I have heard him say that neither the laws nor the machines belong to any one race!" (87). For Tiémoko the book holds an objective truth independent of language, race, and culture; it is "scientific": "It is not an unbreakable set of rules, it's . . . it's a way of thinking ["scientific book" in the original version]" (87). During the strike, Tiémoko realizes the importance of educating himself: "He needed to read, to learn, to educate himself. At home, he would engage in real orgies of reading" (164).

Sembène uses the question of language to make the broader point that the appropriation of European languages must be done in a critical manner that takes into account their problematic origins, especially through the highly satirical characterization of N'Deye. N'Deye accepts everything that she learns in school or reads in French literature: "For N'Deye there was no questioning the truth of anything she learned at school" (111). She doesn't even bother reading books by African authors because she doesn't feel they have anything to teach her (58). For N'Deye, reading necessarily entails adopting a European context, which is why she initially develops an extremely Western conception of love (although this changes at the end of the novel). In contrast, Tiémoko and Bakayoko are presented as ideal readers because they take ideas and turn them into action. Moreover, they are able to separate the ideas from the original French context in which they are presented and appropriate them for African use. Overall, the novel suggests that books—like machines—can be dissociated from their European origins and made to serve a positive, even liberating purpose.

By highlighting the use of African languages or French, the text underscores its own problematic nature. It is written in French, but the use of French by colonial bosses in the novel is often associated with pretentiousness or a refusal to communicate with the African workers effectively, since very few of the characters in the novel speak French, and fewer still are capable of reading and writing the language. On the one hand, it adopts a European literary form—the novel—that is made possible by a Western technological innovation, the printing press; in other words, it is an object constructed using the colonizers' materials. On the other hand, the characters, as the narrator repeatedly reminds us, usually speak in Bambara or Wolof, and they are the ones who construct the narrative: it is the narrative of their revolt against the white Europeans.

For Sembène, unlike the elders he describes, writing and expressing himself in French does not necessarily present a problem because it is the language of the colonizer; as we have seen in this chapter, *God's Bits of Wood* suggests it is possible to detach the colonizers' instruments from their origins. The use of French as a mode of expression is primarily a problem because of the number of West Africans who speak it, and therefore communication is impeded with the main public he would like to address. The question of the book's audience is also problematic: is it learned French critics or the African people Sembène is trying to unite? This ambiguity is evident in the frequent use of words in Bambara, which are footnoted and translated at the bottom of the page; as some of these words are repeated, the reader gradually internalizes their meaning.

In *God's Bits of Wood*, Sembène does not focus on a mythical African past or on recording oral histories but rather tells the story of African peoples moving forward through collective bargaining, making progress toward the future through the strength of their labor. This novel asserts that progress made in the country is not the result of a top-down system of modernization but of grassroots movements of resistance and organization. The workers view the machines as their own not because someone has handed them over to them but because they have appropriated them through their own hard labor.

Although *God's Bits of Wood* was written a few months before Senegal officially obtained independence from France, and the events take place a decade earlier, it expresses Sembène's vision of an independent, modernized, and technological Africa. The sense of accomplishment at the end of the story, as well as the opening statement asserting that it led to progress for Africa—"Since then, Africa has made progress" (1)—suggest that the strike accomplished much more than the acquisition of higher pay and improved working conditions. Given the number of people who died, the victorious tone at the end of the novel, especially in the epilogue, would otherwise be inexplicable. And indeed the narrator of *God's Bits of Wood* situates the workers' strike in a long line of acts of resistance that have led to greater political freedoms. The intertextuality with Zola's novels *Germinal* and *The Human Beast* places the novel within a French literary tradition that recounts such acts of resistance. Similarly, the allusion to André Malraux's *Man's Fate* (1933), which describes the 1927 Shanghai revolution, evokes a comparison between the events of that novel and those of *God's Bits of Wood*. This allusion emphasizes the political nature of the strike, suggesting that it is a force capable not only of causing the white owners of the machines to concede but also of overturning colonial government. Unlike the two movements referenced in the works by French authors, the strike in *God's Bits of Wood* is successful; the intertextuality is therefore a means of emphasizing the magnitude of the feat accomplished by the African workers.

God's Bits of Wood presents the strike of 1947–48 as the first of a series of acts of resistance that culminated in Senegal's independence in 1960. This is first done through the statement at the beginning of the work, which seeks to link it with the historical strike that took place between October 10, 1947, and March 19, 1948. This statement not only links the strike to progress made after it but attempts to debunk the idea that this progress is the result of either European influences or the work of African politicians: "The men and women who, from the tenth of October, 1947, to the nineteenth of March, 1948, took part in this struggle for a better way of life owe nothing to anyone: neither to any 'civilizing mission' nor to any parliament or parliamentarian. Their example was not in vain. Since then, Africa has made progress" (1). Sembène immediately seeks to discredit two main ideas: that progress in Africa comes from the West; and that Senegalese independence in 1960 was the result of carefully crafted diplomatic relations between the leaders of Léopold Sédar Senghor's political party and the French government. In the 1950s, Senghor's Bloc Démocratique Sénégalais (Senegalese Democratic Group) (founded in 1948) dominated politics in Senegal, such that Senghor took credit when the nation became independent in 1960. His party also claimed to be the force behind modernization in Senegal in the early 1960s.

The enormous struggle presented in the novel is meant to show that the victory in the strike, as in independence, did not occur through simple diplomacy and negotiation. There are discussions between the white leaders and the African workers, but the success of the strike is the consequence not just of diplomacy but also of the difficult times the workers endured. Sembène gives no credit to Senghor's government for assisting in technological development; criticizing his country's leadership in a 2005 interview, he says, "When it comes to scientific and cultural development they don't want to touch it" (Interview, *Socialist Worker*). Sembène claims to be against Senghor more as a politician than as a writer and intellectual. In a 1979 interview he states: "If Senghor were simply a professor, we might be friends. . . . Senghor represents a power which, in my opinion, has brought us nothing. I am not against him as an individual. It is the leader that I oppose because I feel that he is implementing a bad policy for the country for the profit of those who use it" ("Entretiens" 74). Sembène is highly critical of Negritude, especially as a state ideology, and believes it to be contrary to progress. In a 1979 interview, when asked about Negritude, he responds: "Negritude? I don't know anything about it! I don't even want to talk about it. My worth is not tied to the color of my skin. And the worth of African culture is not tied to certain fantasies or to repressed complexes in the presence of the ideals of Greek beauty" ("Entretiens" 74). Sembène also greatly criticizes Senghor for not speaking Wolof well enough and always addressing the nation in French; Sembène, like Bakayoko in *God's*

Bits of Wood, who addresses the group of workers in Wolof, is a major proponent of using African languages. As he has stated repeatedly in interviews, he believes that Wolof, which is spoken by the vast majority (80 percent) of the Senegalese population, should be the official language of Senegal.

Although Sembène claims that progress does not come from the West, he is strongly in favor of importing European technologies and views it as one of the primary reasons that French should still be studied in schools. In a 1979 interview, he states: "The French language is, first of all, a valuable tool, mainly for accessing the technology of industrialized countries" ("Entretiens" 73).

TECHNOLOGY FETISHISM AND MEDIA IN SEMBÈNE'S CINEMA

The difficult question of how to appropriate language and literature in *God's Bits of Wood* reflects Sembène's own frustration with finding a mode of artistic expression capable of reaching his intended audience: Africans. Shortly after its publication in 1960, Sembène went to Moscow to study filmmaking at the Gorki Studios, producing his first film, *Borom Sarret,* in 1963.[9] He then embarked on a prolific career in filmmaking that saw the production of numerous award-winning films, such as *Black Girl, Emitai, Ceddo, The Money Order, Xala,* and *Moolaadé,* that examine the realities faced by Africans in the postcolonial era.

Sembène sought to use the medium of film to reach a wider audience in Africa, much as Césaire turned to theater (which he viewed as a technology) to spread his vision of Negritude and promote consciousness-raising throughout the Caribbean and Africa. For Sembène, film provided a means of resolving some of the dilemmas he faced when writing in French (and expressed in *God's Bits of Wood*), since it allowed him to bypass written media entirely; this was crucial given the high rates of illiteracy throughout Africa. Through the medium of film, Sembène could now present characters speaking in Wolof, as well as in French, which so many Africans understand even if they cannot read it. In fact, Sembène would often distribute the same film in different languages: for instance, *The Money Order* has versions in French and Wolof; and his last film, *Moolaadé,* was dubbed into six African languages and screened throughout sub-Saharan Africa.

The representation of the railway in *God's Bits of Wood* provides an analogy for how Sembène came to view the cinematic medium: as a technology capable of eliminating hierarchies and promoting equality. In fact, Sembène appears to share with Walter Benjamin the idea that film has the potential to liberate and democratize. Although Benjamin writes about the function of film at the turn of the twentieth century in Europe, much of what he says is applicable to the role of film in Africa in the postindependence era. In his famous essay "The Work of Art in the Age of Mechanical Reproduction," Benjamin describes mechanical reproductions, including film, as the democratization of art forms. For Benjamin, film represents the ultimate destruction of the "aura" because it has no original but exists only in the state of its reproductions. This essay emphasizes how new technologies change a society's perception of the world by causing works of art to be interpreted as objects in the time and place of the viewer. Film, in particular, changed Western modes of perceiving reality by presenting a uniquely vivid copy of the world. This process occurs later in Africa than it did in the West, since the advent of cinema comes later, largely as a result of Sembène's works. Sembène seeks to use film to change the way the audience (which for him is African) perceives its current reality.

According to Benjamin, film, unlike painting, presents an object for simultaneous collective experience. Sembène believes his audience can become a collectivity, much like the groups of women and others portrayed in his films. Film also provides Sembène with the ability to profoundly explore the quotidian and acquire a new perspective toward it. Benjamin identifies three revolutionary effects film has on its audience: it helps them to understand experience in industrialized, urbanized societies, which is often turbulent and in flux; it frees them from the mystification of high culture, such that they may adopt a more critical view toward their own societies and elites; and it eliminates the authoritarian distance between a work of art and the masses. For Sembène, film is precisely this: a means of bringing the work of art closer to the spectator, especially the African one, by demystifying it and stripping it of its "aura," thus eliminating the distance between art and the masses. Moreover, Benjamin and Sembène share the opinion that cinema can provide a forum for political engagement and discussion leading to social progress: Benjamin expresses this idea in "The Author as Producer" (1934), and Sembène has called film an "evening school" that can replace traditional gatherings around a storyteller ("Man Is Culture" 9).

Sembène's turn to film also corresponded with his new approach toward questions of technology. Two films in particular illustrate Sembène's ideas with regard to the arrival of modern Western technologies into African communities: his biting satire on the postindependence African bourgeoisie, *Xala* (The curse) (1973), often considered his cinematic masterpiece; and *Moolaadé* (Protection) (2004), his vivid depiction of the horrors and controversies surrounding female genital mutilation. In his interviews about these films, as well as in the works themselves, Sembène offers a coherent perspective on the ideal function of technological innovations in postcolonial Africa: not as fetishized markers of wealth, status, and Western contacts that ultimately increase economic inequality but as powerful instruments capable of countering inequality and enacting social change.

XALA

Sembène's film *Xala* premiered a year after the publication of his novel by the same name. A biting satire on the African bourgeoisie, the film takes place in an unspecified African nation shortly after independence. In the opening scene, following a declaration of independence, a group of African leaders accept suitcases full of money from French "advisors" who sit ominously behind them in all their meetings. The film follows the story of El Hadji, who uses the money he acquires through questionable means—by accepting suitcases from the "advisors" and selling one hundred tons of rice that were supposed to feed the people—to take on a third wife. On his wedding night, and for several weeks afterward, he finds himself unable to consummate his marriage to this younger wife due to the *xala,* or curse, that has been cast upon him (*xala* means "sexual impotence" in Wolof). The story, which is at times comical, follows El Hadji as he desperately tries to rid himself of the curse. At the end, as a last resort, he allows a group of crippled beggars to spit on him, the very people whom he cheated by taking money that was ultimately cursed.

Throughout the film, El Hadji's battle against the curse is linked to his fetishistic relationship to Western technologies. David Harvey defines technology fetishism as "the habit humans have of endowing real or imagined objects or entities with self-contained, mysterious, and even magical power to move and shape the world in distinctive ways" (3). According to Harvey, "the fetish arises because we endow technologies—mere things—with powers" (3). El Hadji's relationship to technological innovations constitutes a form of "commodity fetishism": objects are attributed a value that goes beyond their "exchange-value," the labor that produced them, or their practical utility. This is because he values these innovations more for what they represent—status, wealth, and a connection to European culture—than what they are worth in a practical sense.

El Hadji frequently invokes his relationship to technology as a means of emphasizing his social and economic status. In one of the film's opening sequences, a long panoramic shot shows all the gifts that El Hadji has bestowed upon his third wife as a dowry. These include a small blue car with a red ribbon wrapped around it, a television set, and a box full of gold. As soon as he arrives home, he runs his hands over the blue car, which is never actually driven, only kissed and caressed. The television set likewise remains wrapped up as a gift, a status symbol, and is never actually watched. When El Hadji enters into an office in which they are running an air conditioner, he says that he's used to it, implying that he is accustomed to European comforts, as a way of bragging about his wealth.

El Hadji drives a white Mercedes Benz that serves as a preeminent symbol of European technology and culture. His chauffeur is always wiping the exterior of the car down with a cloth and pouring Evian into the radiator. The fact that El Hadji will allow only Evian to be poured into the radiator reflects his problematic relationship to technology. As any decent mechanic could tell him, the use of this special imported water will do nothing to aid the running of the car; it serves, rather, as a sort of ritual purification of the machine. Notably, when El Hadji goes to visit the marabout Sérigne Marada (a witch doctor) in a desperate attempt to persuade him to lift the curse, he is forced to travel by horse and carriage, since the marabout lives in a remote village inaccessible by roads. The image of El Hadji riding over the mud in the cart, cracking the whip at the horses, serves as stark contrast to his comfortable means of urban transportation. El Hadji must abandon his luxurious automobile and leave the city in order to have the curse lifted (which it is, if only temporarily) because his technology fetishism is itself one of the things causing it in the first place.

Two guards eventually confiscate El Hadji's Mercedes as a result of his unpaid debts. These guards—who are not very attuned to modern Western technologies—take the keys but are forced to push the car away since they do not know how to drive it. This image suggests the total fetishization of the Mercedes, which is no longer used as a mode of transportation but is transformed into a socioeconomic status symbol. This symbol—like that of other fetishized commodities—divides African culture between the "haves" and the "have nots," a process that occurs increasingly as the characters become more and more obsessed with the possession of objects (especially technological ones).

Sembène's own statements in interviews confirm the key, positive role of technology in his works. Mocking those who fetishize technologies, he asserts: "I never see an engineer dancing in front of his machine" (*Busch and Annas* 29). In other words, for the engineer, the machine is functional; it is her creation and therefore does not possess any mystical qualities. Sembène suggests that in order for development to occur, technology must be demystified and used to serve a practical function. He also offers an allegorical interpretation of El Hadji's three wives, Awa, Oumi, and Rama, who "feature Africa at various stages of its development" (*Busch and Annas* 161). The first wife, Awa, is traditional: she dresses in African robes, accepts her husband's authority, and resigns herself to him having multiple wives, even if she does not like it. Oumi, on the other hand, is the modern, Westernized woman. She dresses in provocative dresses and wears heels and makeup. She has a strong personality, rebuking her husband for not paying enough attention to her, and openly saying about her sexuality, "I am always ready." Oumi does not approve of El Hadji taking on a third wife and eventually leaves him, taking her Western commodities (which she fetishizes just as much as her husband) with her.

Rama, who is the daughter of the first wife, represents an ideal synthesis of the traditional and modern ways represented by Awa and Oumi. On the one hand, she values tradition, as evidenced by her African clothing and insistence on speaking in Wolof even when her father addresses her in French. On the other hand, she is open enough to modernity to ride a moped (in the novel it is a Fiat automobile) and decorate her room with posters of black liberation leaders. The moped (or Fiat) is significant because it shows the practical use of a technology rather than its fetishistic function as a status symbol: a moped does not showcase the rider's wealth and status but is an efficient means of traveling around the city. Françoise Pfaff writes that Rama is "not attracted by luxurious automotive machines of the Western world" ("Women in *Xala*" 29). Unlike El Hadji, who drinks only Evian, she refuses to drink imported bottled water because she is opposed to what it represents. According to Pfaff, "she only uses the aspects of Western culture that can serve in daily life—education, modern technology—and does not confer imported goods the same fetishistic quality as her father" ("Women in *Xala*" 29). In short, Rama exemplifies a relationship to technology that is functional and productive as opposed to fetishistic like her father's; she sees cars and television sets much as the young workers in *God's Bits of Wood* view the railway line. For Pfaff, Rama "embodies Sembène's wishes for a modern and truly independent Africa" ("Women in *Xala*" 29).[10]

Laura Mulvey has analyzed the different discourses on fetishism present in *Xala.* She writes that "the film shows an African ruling elite accepting and appropriating the fetishisms of European capitalism" (123). According to Mulvey, "the film is about the function, within that economy, of fetishised objects as signifiers of unequal exchange" (123). She argues that Sembène relativizes the discourses about fetishism by showing the extent to which it exists in many cultures, but in different forms. Although the idea of an "uncivilized" African fetishism played an important part in the European justification of colonialism, in *Xala,* according to David Murphy, "Sembène dismisses the notions of backwardness attached to fetishism: all cultures are seen to have their own rituals and fetishes" (*Imagining Alternatives* 122). Summarizing Sembène's viewpoint, Murphy writes, "The neo-colonial bourgeoisie depends on an amalgam of Western technical/commodity fetishism and African, 'supernatural' fetishism" (*Imagining Alternatives* 122).

Sembène believes that fetishism exists in many cultures and should not be interpreted as a sign of primitivism. In "Man Is Culture" he states, "Much has been said and written about the fetishism of Blacks, their animism, their superstition, as if similarities did not exist in the history of the Greeks. All people practice fetishism. They all have objects which give a concrete form to their beliefs" (2). In a 1974 interview, he delineates the two types of fetishism portrayed in *Xala:*

> The contradiction lies in the fact that contemporary African society is torn between two types of fetishism: firstly, the fetishism of European techniques ["technologies" in original version], and the profound conviction of this privileged class that it can do nothing without Europe's agreement and the advice of its specialists ["technicians" in original version]; on the other hand, there is the fetishism of the marabout, without whose advice any undertaking is doomed to failure. In this situation, genuine human success has nothing to do with the capabilities of Africans, but is rather the result of a happy mixture of the blessings of the European specialist ["technician" in original version] and the *marabout.* (Murphy, *Imagining Alternatives* 108)

For Sembène, the African bourgeoisie—represented by El Hadji—is far from both European technology and African spirituality. In both cases, leaders create false illusions about the objects fetishized: "European specialists ["technological advisers" in original version] are no more credible than the *marabouts*. Having recourse to both is merely the expression of the same impotence" (Murphy, *Imagining Alternatives* 108).

The narrative of *Xala* ultimately suggests that when technology is fetishized, it becomes a means of perpetuating and reinforcing the inequalities present in both traditional African society and European colonialism and capitalism. As inert objects used as symbols of status and wealth, the cars and television sets of *Xala* do little to enact the kind of liberation associated with the railway in *God's Bits of Wood* and with the film genre in Benjamin's writings. However, Sembène's critique of commodity fetishism in the film (in part through the character of Rama) suggests the possibility of a more productive relationship to technology, one that is prominently exhibited in the last film of his career: *Moolaadé*.

MOOLAADÉ

Toward the end of his life, Sembène planned to produce a trilogy about heroism in daily life. He completed the first two films, *Faat Kiné* (2000) and *Moolaadé* (2004), but was unable to begin work on the third, *The Brotherhood of Rats*, before his death in 2007. Both *Faat Kiné* and *Moolaadé* approach questions of modernity, albeit from sharply different perspectives. *Faat Kiné* follows the story of a single mother who owns a gas station in Dakar and whose children set her up with her future husband. *Moolaadé* takes place in a rural setting and recounts the rebellion of a group of women against the traditional practice of female genital mutilation, a rebellion largely inspired by their radio-listening. This section will examine the representation of communications technologies, including television and the radio, in *Moolaadé*, in order to show the crucial role that Sembène assigns the media in fighting for social progress.

The story of *Moolaadé* takes place over the course of one or two days when six girls, four to nine years old, are to be circumcised. Right before the ceremony is to be performed, they run away and seek refuge with Collé, one of the women of the village. They go to her because they know that seven years earlier, she refused to have her daughter, Amsatou, cut. When asking for Collé's help, the girls invoke the *moolaadé*, a longstanding tradition by which a weaker person may seek protection from a stronger one. We soon hear that two other girls who were about to be circumcised have disappeared and later learn that they have drowned themselves in a well to escape the ceremony. As the conflict continues, Ibrahima, the son of the village elder, arrives from Paris, bringing suitcases full of goods. Ibrahima is engaged to Amsatou, but when his father tells him that he disapproves of the union because she is a *bilakoro* (meaning she has not been cut), he agrees to marry his cousin instead. As the narrative progresses, the village is torn between those who support Collé and those who oppose her, culminating in a scene in which Ciré (Collé's husband) publicly beats her in an attempt to make her utter the word that will end the *moolaadé* protecting the girls. During this scene, a woman takes her daughter Diattou (who had sought refuge with Collé) away to be cut, and the girl eventually bleeds to death as a result of the procedure. As her mother mourns her death, the women gather together and decide to rebel against the men and the Salindana (the group of women who perform excision). Chanting in unison, they declare that no more girls will be cut.

Although the film stages a confrontation between older and newer belief systems, the representation of the opposition between tradition and modernity is far from simplistic. As Sembène points out in a 2004 interview, the conflict is not only between the traditional practice of excision and the progressive ideas heard on the radios but between two traditions: "The first tradition is female circumcision. It dates back before Christ before Mohammed. That tradition has been used to perpetuate the subjugation of women"; "The other tradition [*moolaadé*], also as old as humankind, is the right to protect the weak," "the right to asylum and protection and society's demand that the girls submit to excision" (Porton and Rapfogel 21). "When these two values meet . . . cross, multiply, and collide, they become symbolic of society" (Porton and Rapfogel 21). Moreover, Sembène argues that although "the men justify excision by referring to Islamic tradition," the relationship between the practice of cutting and tradition is tenuous at best, since no one can remember its precise origins, and there is nothing in the Qu'ran referring to it. The film highlights this contradiction in the village's traditions, which include both cutting the girls (presented as a violation of human rights) and their right to seek protection from harm.[11]

Although the complexity of Sembène's characterization makes it impossible to equate certain characters with tradition, and others with modernity, two male characters do clearly represent Westernization and modernity: the primary merchant of the village, known as "Mercenaire," and Ibrahima. Although they do not seem all that progressive at first, by the end of the story they take the side of the rebellious women and fight with them to eliminate excision.

Mercenaire is a representative of free market capitalism, globalization, and social progress, including women's rights. In the opening scene, which illustrates the arrival of Western influences to rural Africa, he rides into the village on his bike, pulling a cart behind him, and sets up a makeshift shop in front of the anthill and mosque. Mercenaire wears Western-style clothing (shorts and T-shirt), speaks French, and flirts with all the women. He travels from village to village selling overpriced goods—including stale bread, razors, and the batteries that power the women's radios—that the villagers have no access to otherwise. When Ibrahima accuses him of scamming the villagers by overcharging for bread, Mercenaire defends himself by saying that he must be compensated for the cost of transporting the goods: "You have visited Europe and you know what globalization and free market mean." As the only merchant in the village, Mercenaire enjoys a near-monopoly and is fully cognizant of the forces of free market capitalism.

Mercenaire is also a representative of globalization and social progress. He sells the women the batteries that power their radios, which he most likely sold to them as well. At his stand, posters present vivid images of the world outside the village. And his nickname, meaning "mercenary" in French, was acquired after he led a rebellion of soldiers seeking fair pay. Although he successfully obtained better pay for the soldiers, the incident led to his discharge from the military. As he explains (in French) to Ibrahima, he was referred to as "mercenaire" in the French press coverage of the rebellion, which is how he acquired his nickname.

As the story unfolds, Mercenaire emerges as a defender of women's rights and unlikely mouthpiece for the filmmaker. At first he is presented as a tireless flirt and womanizer who flatters the women of the village in an effort to bed them. Later on, however, he becomes an ally in the women's battle against excision. When Collé's husband, Ciré, publicly whips her in front of the villagers, it is Mercenaire who intervenes and stops the violence. He is later chased out of the village, hunted down, and murdered as punishment for opposing the elder men, turning him into a kind of martyr for women's rights.

Ibrahima is also a complex character who evolves throughout the story, eventually representing progress and change in the village. Mercenaire, who has spent a great deal of time abroad, assumes that Ibrahima's stay in Paris has caused him to adopt more Western ways. When

Ibrahima, whom Mercenaire knows to be engaged to Amsatou, comes by his stand, Mercenaire subtly places a box of condoms on the counter that reads, "Prudence." Mercenaire is aware that Amsatou has not been cut, meaning that in her marriage to Ibrahima, they can enjoy a sexual relationship involving pleasure. She will presumably escape the pain that the excised women experience during intercourse, as graphically depicted in a scene that presents a flashback of Collé biting her finger until it bleeds while her husband pants on top of her, interspersed with images of a girl screaming in pain while being excised by the Salindana. The implication of the box of condoms that Mercenaire tries to sell to Ibrahima (eventually giving him one for free for his wedding night) is that he will enjoy a relationship with his wife in which sex is not simply a means of reproduction. In short, Mercenaire appears to believe that Ibrahima has chosen Amsatou precisely *because* she has not been cut, since he thinks Ibrahima is an enlightened Parisian seeking such a relationship.

During the conversation, however, it becomes clear that Ibrahima is not nearly as enlightened as Mercenaire had assumed. When Ibrahima declares that he will wed his eleven-year-old cousin instead of Amsatou because the younger girl has been cut, Mercenaire does not hesitate to voice his disapproval: "You, your father and your uncle are nothing but pedophiles!" Mercenaire's use of the term "pedophiles" here is very significant, since he is invoking French terminology and laws in an African context. Mercenaire even accuses Ibrahima of criminal behavior: "You, your dad and uncle should be jailed for being pedophiles." Thus, Mercenaire emerges as a defender for the rights of women and children.

At first, Ibrahima is conflicted about how to negotiate his own beliefs and values while respecting the wishes of his father, the village elder. On the one hand, Ibrahima, much like Mercenaire, represents Westernization, modernization, globalization, and the media. His arrival to the village parallels Mercenaire's in the opening scene: he drives a truck, while Mercenaire rode a bike; he comes with a television set, while Mercenaire brings batteries and radios; and his suitcases full of goods are shared with the villagers, much as Mercenaire distributes the goods that he sells. And this is not the first time that Ibrahima brings technologies to the village: the women thank him for having brought the water pump that improved their daily lives.

In a scene shortly after his arrival, we see Ibrahima sitting under a canopy with his father, mother, and uncle, as RFI (Radio France Internationale) blares on the radio. He is fidgeting with some wires in order to connect his television. He soon learns about the women's rebellion and the confiscation of their radios: "Before your arrival, things happened, elders confiscated all the women's radios." He is then told he won't be allowed to set up the television set, because it will have an even worse influence than the radio. Stunned, Ibrahima responds: "Why deny [the women] radios and TVs? Uncle, you can no longer silence these media. Today, everywhere in the world, radio and TV are parts of life. We cannot cut ourselves off from the progress in the world." When Ibrahima's father then tells him that he must marry his cousin instead of Amsatou, because she has not been cut, he responds: "Father, I still do honor and respect you, but my marriage is my own business." His father associates his son's disrespect with the television: "If you do not obey, I disinherit you. Take your television out of here." Since the elders view television and radio as the root of all subversive ideas, they believe that burning them will stop the forces of change, despite Ibrahima's statement that they are inevitable.

Ibrahima exhibits very conflicted feelings about tradition and modernity: on the one hand, as a young man living abroad who watches television and listens to the radio, he believes in a certain degree of individualism (for instance, that he should be able to choose his own wife); on the other, at first he does not seem willing to give up the status and privileges of being the village elder's son (which means he will one day rule). After initially stating he will not marry his cousin, Ibrahima later gives into his father and agrees to marry her, but then at the end changes his mind again, deciding to marry Amsatou, in part due to his admiration of her strength and spirit during the women's anti-excision rally.

The prevalence of the radios in the film evokes the importance of freedom of expression and access to the media. Throughout Sembène's narrative, radios play a fundamental role in the process of consciousness-raising among the villagers, including the spread of Collé's feminist ideology. From the beginning of the film, the constant murmuring of RFI and music serves as background noise for the story. When news of the women's rebellion against excision reaches the elders, they immediately decide to seize all the radios. Ciré angrily marches to his house, declaring that Amsatou will be purified and his wife Collé's radio confiscated. Amsatou strongly objects, stating that she received the radio from her namesake, the doctor who performed the caesarian that saved her (since Collé had lost her other babies as a result of having been cut as a girl). The radio is thus explicitly associated not only with the rebellion against excision but also with modern medicine; more broadly, it is an object protecting her from the harmful consequences of patriarchal traditions. When Ciré confronts Collé about disrespecting him, the elevator-like music emanating from the radio illustrates the contrast between the old, traditional ways and the new era of globalization.

The radios not only represent free-thinking and liberation; they also promote it. One woman, walking past the pile of burning radios, laments, "Our men want to lock up our minds," to which another responds, "But . . . how do you lock up something invisible?" Although the traditionalist men blame the radios for giving the women subversive ideas, the truth is that the women were against the practice of excision anyway, and the radios simply provided them with a discourse for expressing how they felt. During the revolt at the end of the film, Collé invokes an imam's sermon that she heard on the radio, and that partly inspired her rebellion: "Purification is not required by Islam. The Grand Imam said it on the radio. Each year millions of women go for pilgrimage to Mecca. All have not been cut." Thus the radios provide contact with the outside world in a way that encourages the women to assert themselves, form a collectivity, and ultimately revolt.

Many scenes in the film show the superposition of three images that represent the primary ideologies at play in the conflict. First, there is the mosque made of clay, which is in the background of many shots; this unique architectural structure is part of what drew Sembène to film in the village. At the top of the mosque there is an ostrich egg, representing the merger of Islam and ancestral traditions. Second, in front of the mosque lies an anthill that is in the middle ground of many shots. As we learn from an elder, this represents ancestral traditions and the spirit of the *moolaadé,* since it is a tomb for the first king who offered this form of protection. Third, in the foreground, we see the radios that the men gather together into a pile and burn, the smoke rising up as they continue to play French news programs and African music. In yet another layer of imagery suggesting the different forces of change, Mercenaire's shop is set up in front of the mosque, representing the arrival of capitalism and free market forces to the village. This triple superposition of images illustrates the changes that have come about in the village as the result of internal and external forces. In the end, it appears that excision is contrary to all of them: Collé states that the imam said it was not required by Islam; the *moolaadé* protects the girls from the practice; and the radios spread anti–female genital mutilation ideology.

The final scene of the film suggests the even greater changes that will come about in the future, this time as a result of television. During the women's anti-excision rally, Ibrahima declares: "Father, it is easy to hit a son, but the era of little tyrants is over . . . forever . . . ever. From now on I'll have TV. On." The last image is that of a television antenna sticking out from the ostrich egg at the top of the mosque. The implication is clear: the story we have just witnessed showed the great changes that came about as a result of radio. Now that television has arrived in the village, what will happen next? The end of the film thus suggests that even more changes will occur in this remote village, as it becomes increasingly connected to the outside world. David Murphy captures the significance of the final scene well:

> In the film's striking closing image, Sembène gestures towards an imagined future in a jarring cut to an image of a television aerial, before the screen fades to black. Sembene here seems to indicate that more change is on the way; those with a vested interest in the structures of power may seek to cast their position as predicated on a long and unbroken history but the film reveals that from animism to Islam to postcolonial modernity, the village has been a constant site of change and upheaval. Change is inevitable, although not necessarily positive (despite the positivist claims of the West): what matters is how one deals with it. ("Filming the Past, Present and Future" 169)

Indeed, Sembène himself affirmed the power of the media to enact social change soon after the film came out. In a 2004 interview, he states: "My view is that without the media, there's no future. It's not the media itself that are of importance—it's the content. I'm dealing with the issue of globalization" (Busch and Annas 207). He also describes radio and television, the primary focus of the film, as "very important tools" (207); "I don't think that Africa can afford to live in isolation nowadays, closed upon itself" (209).

The representation of radio and television in *Moolaadé* produces a metadiscourse that illustrates the role that the film itself can play in consciousness-raising in rural Africa. In a classic case of life imitating art, the process of making the film brought the inhabitants of the remote village of Burkina Faso in which it is set into contact with media. This village had no telephone, electricity, running water, or communications. According to Sembène, the villagers "didn't live as they did in the past but they didn't have the means of communication that we have today" (Interview, *Making*). Amy Borden writes: "As media, Sembène's production employed local craftsmen and was itself a tool of modernization that introduced a communication infrastructure to the village in Burkina Faso in which it was shot in 2002."

Beyond the confines of the village, Sembène considered *Moolaadé* to be an important "reference tool" for educating communities and promoting discussion about female genital mutilation in order to "fight to eradicate" it (Borden). This was reflected in its mode of distribution: dubbed into six African languages, *Moolaadé* was screened throughout the continent both by human rights organizations and Sembène himself. According to Borden, many different NGOs have employed the film as a tool for activism against female genital mutilation, including the United Kingdom–based Foundation for Women's Health and Research and Development, which used it to pursue an advocacy project in Ethiopia, Sudan, and Tanzania; and the Inter-African Committee, which incorporated it into a workshop for imams in Sudan as part of a broader initiative to use media to fight female genital mutilation.

Shortly after *Moolaadé*'s release in 2004, Sembène devoted most of his time to traveling from place to place, showing the film and leading discussions: "My main activity is to attend screenings in villages and conduct conversations with spectators in those villages" (Busch and Annas 208). In his work as a filmmaker, Sembène considers himself a modern-day griot or storyteller: "I think there are parallels between myself and these storytellers, because in that traditional society, the storyteller was his own writer, director, actor and musician. And I think his role was very important in cementing society. Now, with new technologies and the tools that we have acquired, I think we can take inspiration from them and do some work" (Interview, *Guardian*). He describes cinema as "a kind of evening school" (Busch and Annas 201) and believes that it can provide an educational forum that replaces traditional evening gatherings around a griot. In "Man Is Culture," Sembène argues that radio, television, press, and cinema should all be in national languages and that media (such as film) "should constitute night schools to replace traditional evening gatherings and to create an awareness" (9).

Sembène wanted to see *Moolaadé* become a communal work of art, belonging to all Africans (his intended audience): "The film does not belong to me anymore, but to all of African society" (Busch and Annas 207). He sought for spectators to identify with the characters and story lines: "With a communal approach, people can see themselves on screen" (Busch and Annas 208). In *The Making of Moolaadé,* Sembène explains: "As far as I am concerned, politically speaking, cinema allows me to show people their predicaments, so they take responsibility, they hold their destiny in their hands. Nobody other than ourselves can solve our problems." In a speech given in Ouagadougou at the premier for *Moolaadé* in Africa, Sembene declares: "Art is about bringing people together, about fostering understanding" (Interview, *Making of Moolaadé*). His practice of traveling around Africa screening *Moolaadé* recalls how Césaire collaborated with Serreau to stage multimedia spectacles of "theater of development." Although audience participation is not possible with film, in contrast to theater, Sembène led discussions after viewings as a means of inspiring the consciousness-raising necessary to adopt modern practices and beliefs, including the acceptance of technologies.

In his essay "Man Is Culture" (delivered as a lecture at Indiana University in 1973), Sembène critiques the discourse of the "civilizing mission": "For a while, certain races thought that they possessed the charismatic power over the destiny of other peoples which would lead them to progress and civilization" (2). He also openly questions how effective a traditionally minded African can be at resolving modern-day dilemmas: "Can the man of yesteryear—the Negro-African—with his values symbols, myths—can he solve the problems inherited by today's man? I wonder" (8–9).[12] While he believes that ancient culture should be valorized, he shuns a relationship to it that impedes progress from occurring: "If the demand for the ancient culture was a just cause, the servile imitation of it checks progress" (9); "The obligation to do today as the ancestors did is a sign of intellectual deficiency. What is worse, it reflects a lack of control over daily life" (9). Sembène continues: "It is not a matter of refusing modernity but rather of mastering it and directing it" (10).

In *God's Bits of Wood, Xala,* and *Moolaadé,* Sembène articulates how he believes modernity can be "controlled" and "given direction." He clearly demonstrates what he does *not* want the newly emerging Africa to be: dominated by Islam or Christianity, ruled by an idealization of African culture, or subjected to cultural imperialism in the form of "globalization." He feels that there are many forces at play, all working to dominate newly independent African nations. Sembène views globalization as cultural imperialism and believes it has not led to anything productive in Africa, as he states in a 2005 interview: "Globalization has brought nothing to Africa, and trumpeting that word is hypocrisy—

especially coming from the U.S., Britain and France" (Interview, *Socialist Worker*). While he speaks out repeatedly against this phenomenon, he does not seem to consider the appropriation of modern technologies to be part of it, since he views them as instruments that belong to the patrimony of all civilizations. Although he does not clearly state his vision of the ideal African nation, he is in favor of the strong presence of a number of different forces: Marxism and the "awakening" of the proletariat; a brand of humanism he associates with culture; and technology, progress, and modernization, which do not necessarily constitute part of "cultural imperialism" and "globalization" for him. In this independent Africa, French may be used to access scientific and technological knowledge, but Wolof is the national language of Senegal, African languages are used in the media, and everyone goes to the cinema and discusses the films afterward.

CHAPTER FIVE

Dams and Motorboats in Olympe Bhêly-Quénum and Aké Loba

In this chapter, as in the previous one on Sembène, I examine sub-Saharan African novels that focus on the transition between the colonial period and independence: Olympe Bhêly-Quénum's *Le chant du lac* (The song of the lake) and Aké Loba's *Les fils de Kouretcha* (The sons of Kouretcha). Much like the other works analyzed thus far, these novels view modernization and the transfer of Western technologies as an essential instigator of political, economic, and social progress.

The late 1950s and early 1960s marked the dawn of independence in sub-Saharan Africa, a region that had been dominated by Britain and France since the late nineteenth century. After Ghana achieved independence from Britain in 1957, the West African French colonies voted to become autonomous in a referendum held in 1958. This referendum was a prelude to independence, which was obtained in 1960, commonly known as "the year of Africa" due to the large number of former colonies that gained full independence at the same time: Cameroon, the Central African Republic, Chad, Congo-Brazzaville, Congo-Kinsasha, Dahomey (now known as Benin), Gabon, Côte d'Ivoire, Senegal, and Upper Volta (now known as Burkina Faso). As these nations entered into the new era, they faced crucial questions regarding development, and debates often focused on the role that Western technological innovations would play in economic progress. When the new African republics held elections, politicians spoke passionately about the need to develop economically, mainly by importing Western technologies and modernizing quickly. Modernization was equated with Westernization, and political leaders promised to raise the standard of living of the poor by producing rapid economic growth.[1] Marleen Renders notes that "development was the very raison d'être of the post-independence governments"; in Senegal, "the Parti Socialist, in power from 1960 until the 'élections d'alternance' in 2000, called itself 'PS-Parti du Développement' [Development Party]" (61). The prevailing sentiment was that colonialism had stagnated development in Africa, and now that the colonizers had been expelled, the continent would enter a period of unprecedented progress.

The tremendous political, cultural, and economic upheavals that occurred in the era of African independences are also reflected in the literature produced in the same period by West African authors. In the decade that followed the "year of Africa," which also saw the publication of Sembène's *God's Bits of Wood,* a number of other highly influential francophone authors from the sub-Saharan region confronted the question of Western technologies in African development, including Olympe Bhêly-Quénum, born in Dahomey (now know as Benin) in 1928, and Aké Loba, born in Côte d'Ivoire in 1927. Both of these authors quickly came to the attention of literary critics for moving away from the traditional theme of colonizer/colonized relations and addressing the place of newly independent African nations in modernity. In their second novels, *Le chant du lac* (1965) and *Les fils de Kouretcha* (1970), they directly confronted the question of how newly independent nations can incorporate modern Western technologies into the everyday lives of Africans. In this chapter, I analyze these two key novels, which exhibit remarkably similar ideologies regarding the role of technology in promoting economic development and social progress.

Bhêly-Quénum and Loba's works form part of a literary subgenre: 1950s–1970s African novels denouncing fetishism and advocating modern scientific, technological, and medical practices. Other such novels include David Ananou's *Le fils du fétiche* (The son of the fetish) and Jean Dodo Digbeu's *Sacrés dieux d'Afrique* (Sacred gods of Africa). In *Le fils du fétiche,* the Togolese author Ananou equates animism and traditional beliefs with backwardness, and Christianity with technological progress and modernity. This novel first appeared in 1955, a few years before the African independences, when the wave of decolonization was just beginning; it grapples with many of the issues faced by African societies as they attempt to enter into modernity while still maintaining their traditions and way of life.

Le fils du fétiche tells the story of Dansou, the son of Sodji, an inhabitant of a village in southern Togo. Throughout the narrative, the characters face many situations that could be resolved without recourse to fetishism, but they choose to pursue that route anyway. For instance, a couple struggling with infertility makes numerous sacrifices in honor of the gods, in the hope of having a child. When they are finally successful, the narrator implies that it is by means of modern medicine that their infertility was cured, even if they believe it was due to the rituals; this recalls Fanon's observation that Algerians consult both a doctor and a witch doctor, then attribute any improvement in their condition to the latter. Throughout *Le fils du fétiche,* Christianity is associated with scientific and technological progress, and animism with retrograde practices. In the introduction, the author praises the external influences that have brought enlightenment to the Dark Continent, including Togo, which still finds itself under the influence of fetishes and charlatans that the author views as nefarious.

In the epilogue, Ananou expresses his views on fetishism and modernity quite explicitly: "Since the last world war, an immense evolution was unleashed around the world" (215). He continues: "The very legitimate reform to which we aspire is a function of the reform of our customs"; "What can come of a liberation of people who are still fiercely loyal to their fetishistic practices? What kind of progress will have been truly accomplished in a country in chains from a thousand superstitions?" (216). "We do not categorically deny our customs," he says, "but would like to make our souls achieve the height of their times" and "obscurantism is not very favorable to progress" (216–17). Like some of the other novels from this subgenre, *Le fils du fétiche* focuses on denouncing fetishism and promoting modernity, and it makes virtually no reference to colonial domination. It has also been sharply attacked by some African critics for its condemnation of traditional values and praised by others for its embrace of modernity.

These texts as a group are a reaction against Negritude and the anticolonialist narratives of the 1950s pre-independence period, such as Camara Laye's *The Dark Child* (1954) and Ferdinand Oyono's *Houseboy* (1956),[2] which strongly criticized the colonial system and often focused on issues of tradition and race. In "African Literature and Modernity," Simon Gikandi states that in much of African literature from 1900 to 1960, the "unmodern—otherwise known as tradition" (5) was considered "the essence of African identity and its literature" (5) in a trend beginning with the Nigerian Chinua Achebe's *Things Fall Apart* (1958):

"The first generation of modern African writers posited their works, in clearly instrumental terms, as agents of recovering and inventing and celebrating the premodern" (11); and "this craving for the premodern was calibrated by the anxiety of modernity and modernization" (11).

Unlike the majority of francophone literature from the colonial period, Bhêly-Quénum and Loba do not have as their primary objective a vehement critique of colonialism, the valorization of a mythical African past, or a discussion of racial prejudices and injustices. Instead, their texts are a call to action: they are meant to provoke newly independent Africans to move forward and leave the past behind, reevaluate their own traditions, and above all, modernize. They portray modern Western technologies in an extremely positive manner, equating them with progress, and intentionally attempt to move away from the issue of race, toward a discussion of how to promote progress in the newly independent nations. While the anticolonialist novels focus on attacking the white colonizer, *Le chant du lac* and *Les fils de Kouretcha* often criticize this approach and satirize aspects of African society, especially religious beliefs (Islam, Christianity, and animism), which are considered contrary to progress. These works dissociate modern technological innovations from the white colonizers who initially brought them to Africa, and express the need to appropriate their instruments in the context of the society and environment of independent African nations. They assume a tone of hope and optimism, a strong belief in the changes that independence will bring and what modern technology can do for African society, and thus stand in stark contrast to the Afro-pessimism (disillusionment with postcolonial society) that characterizes much of francophone sub-Saharan African literature from the late 1960s to early 1970s, such as Amadou Kourouma's *The Suns of Independence* (1968) and Yambo Ouologuem's *Bound to Violence* (1968).

LE CHANT DU LAC (THE SONG OF THE LAKE)

Born in Dahomey (now Benin) in 1928, Olympe Bhêly-Quénum moved to France in 1948 to begin his studies, once his savings—which he earned as a warehouseman for a company—allowed him to do so. He studied classics in Normandy, and after receiving his diploma in 1955, he began teaching French, Latin, and Greek at the Lycée de Coutances in Normandy, before being transferred to other lycées in the Paris region. When Dahomey became independent in 1960, the first president, Hubert Maga, asked Bhêly-Quénum to place himself in the service of his country. From 1961 to 1963, Bhêly-Quénum trained as a diplomat before turning to journalism in 1964 and founding the magazine *L'Afrique actuelle* (Africa today). In 1968, he joined UNESCO headquarters in Paris and directed the publication of *UNESCO News.*[3]

Bhêly-Quénum emerged onto the literary scene in the early 1960s with the publication of *Un piège sans fin* (A never-ending trap) (1960). This novel caught the attention of critics, and, as Albert Gérard explains: "The book was hailed in some African circles as the first African novel that was not marred by obsessive preoccupation with such specifically African problems as the struggle against colonialism and the culture clash. The colonial background is presented as merely incidental, one aspect among others of the general malignity of fate" (533). Although this is no doubt a reductive characterization of the francophone novel during the colonial period, it reflects the innovative aspects of the work of Bhêly-Quénum, who from the time of his first novel was willing to move away from a focus on the evils of colonialism to a discussion of the role played by tradition and technology in the postindependence era. Gérard continues: "Bhêly-Quénum had perhaps deeper insight and originality than most African novelists of his generation" (535).

Bhêly-Quénum's success continued with his second novel, *Le chant du lac* (1965), which won the Grand Prix de littérature d'Afrique Noire in 1966. The story takes place in a small, fictive African village called Wésê, said to be located in Hadomé—a clear anagram for Dahomey. When a group of young students returning from abroad decides to wage a war against the local deities in order to pave the way for progress, the older inhabitants of Wésê must face the question of how the use of new technologies will affect their traditional beliefs. At the beginning of *Le chant du lac,* the young students who have gone to study abroad in Paris return to their native village and propose to use Western technologies to improve travel conditions on the lake: by adding lampposts along the side of the water for easier navigation at night and by motorizing the boats for protection against dangerous currents and improved fishing productivity. The older people of the village are against these improvements, since they believe that the lights and the motors will disrupt the gods of the lake and that such changes are sacrilegious because they interfere with their beliefs. At the end of the novel, the gods are chased out of the lake with guns and lanterns, thus making the way for the lampposts and motors that represent modernization and progress.

Le chant du lac represents the relationship between technology and colonialism according to a few basic principles. First, the story runs counter to the traditional discourse of the "civilizing mission" by suggesting that the colonial period did not lead to any development or modernization in West Africa. Second, the novel highlights a generational divide in the attitude of the inhabitants of Wêsé toward technology. Third, tradition (especially in the form of animism) is portrayed as tyrannical, while technology is depicted as a liberating, democratizing force. In fact, the final victory of the students over the deities at the end of the novel is a triumphant display of the possibilities for technological progress.

In *Le chant du lac,* there are no indications that the colonial period led to any technological or economic development in this region, since the African village of Wêsé appears to have remained virtually untouched by the forces of modernization. Contrary to the discourse of the "civilizing mission," colonization is portrayed as a political system that failed to bring any modern technologies to the village of Wêsé. This is markedly different from the representation of the railway in Sembène's *God's Bits of Wood,* as a technology that was built by the colonizers with the goal of providing for their own economic advancement. In Sembène's novel, the question of technology centers upon the way in which to relate to the machines that have already been transferred to the colonies by the French colonizers. *Le chant du lac,* however, has a fundamentally opposing view of how to bring innovations to the former colonies from the metropolis, since in this novel, the process of using Western technologies is initiated by the young students who have gone abroad to Paris to "learn the science of white men." Since their goal is to use these innovations for the benefit of the villagers, their plan contains no exploitative element and is thus very different from the colonial context of technology transfer.

The central conflict in *Le chant du lac* is not between French colonizers and African colonized but between the youth who favor technology transfer and the elders who fear the consequences of drastic changes in the landscape they inhabit. While colonization is mentioned sporadically throughout the story, it is by no means the focus of the narrative; this is the author's way of proposing a move away from the traditional dichotomy between colonizers and colonized to a new examination of the divisions within African society, and their effect on modernization following independence.

In *Le chant du lac,* as in Sembène's *God's Bits of Wood* and Loba's *Les fils de Kouretcha,* the young generation—including many who have studied abroad in France—constitutes the driving force behind technological progress, while the older generation is more resistant to change and associates technologies with the former colonizers. The ideology of the novel is expressed through the construction of two discourses about the lake and its deities, corresponding to the different viewpoints about the use of Western science and technological innovations held by the young students and the elders of the village. On the one hand, the elders associate Western technologies with their former colonizers and consider the beliefs in the gods as a sacred part of their cultural heritage. The young people of the village, on the other hand, do not possess the same attachment to the myths of the lake as the elders and definitely do not take the myths literally; they associate Western science and technology with the material they learned in France in order to bring it back and help the inhabitants of their native village. In the novel, modernization is an ideology adopted by the young students and initially rejected by the elders.

This division between the two generations is first made evident at the beginning of the story, when one of the students returning from abroad, Douk, recounts the death of Houngbé (who is also a character in Bhêly-Quénum's first novel, *Un piège sans fin* [*Snares without End*]), which occurred on the ship traveling back to Hadomé from France. Houngbé, once a member of the community, committed a heinous crime for which he was imprisoned and made an outcast in the village. During World War I, he became a *tirailleur sénégalais* (black African soldier) who fought side by side with the French against the Germans. On the ship, he contracts a mysterious fever and then, right before dying, gives a long speech, which is related by Douk.

Houngbé says that he will return to Wésê and liberate the people from the gods: "I will go to Wésê, village of my mother, I will destroy the gods, I will kill the gods of the lake" (21). The elders and the students interpret his character, speech, and death completely differently. When hearing Houngbé's last words, as related by Douk, the older people cry, "Héélu! Héélu!" meaning "A curse!," while the younger ones find inspiration in what he says. For the elders, Houngbé is a murderer, and his death is the revenge of the gods, who became angered by his desire to kill them. The mystery surrounding his fever, which is so high that it surprises even the doctor, confirms for them that it is the work of the gods. For the students, Houngbé is a hero and an inspiration: in his memory, they seek to carry out his final wish of eliminating the gods.

Although they understand the legend of the lake to be a beautiful piece of folklore, they do not think that a belief in the gods should be allowed to impede progress.

The narrator explicitly assumes an ideology in favor of technological progress and against the blind defense of archaic traditions; in other words, he openly takes the side of the students. When describing the position of the young people, he states: "The tyranny and lack of humanity of the gods of the lake, that is what these young men and women were protesting against" (96). He portrays the young people as attempting to move forward, while others seek to remain in the past: "Thus they wanted to put an end to certain ways of thinking and to force out of their native village its gangue of a distant past" (96). He calls those who oppose the students, "those who would settle for reliving the past instead of facing the future" (96).

Houngbé's speech on the boat associates animism, the gods, and tradition with tyranny; and technology and modernity with democracy and liberation. As someone who committed a murder and then fought in a war, all in the name of tradition, he states: "Take a look at this carnage we've been stuck in for the last four years. Blacks and Whites are exterminated left and right" (20). For him, the conflict in the war is not about racial distinctions, since soldiers are exterminated indiscriminately, but about oppression from the gods and tradition. In his speech, Houngbé establishes an enigmatic analogy between the liberation of France from German occupation, and the emancipation of the people of Wésê from the gods. He declares that the French would have been annihilated if they had not fought back in the name of maintaining the peace. He says that he will return to Wésê and liberate the people from the gods: "I will go to Wésê, village of my mother, I will destroy the gods, I will kill the gods of the lake. . . . I will cure the people of their fear and they will live free. Oh! Marvelously free" (21). For Houngbé, the question of liberation is not related to race but to the fear that results from belief in gods. In the story, the gods of the lake come to represent an irrational fear of change.

The association of traditional belief with tyranny, and of technological progress with liberation, is also evidenced in the second story line, which parallels the debate between the young students and the elders: the impending elections for the national assembly. In the elections, the candidates explicitly debate the potential merits and drawbacks of using technology on the lake.

Cocou Ounéhou is the candidate in favor of technological development and industrialization. He declares that "idiotic traditions should be wiped out. It is time for progress!" (61). He considers the potential ramifications of the use of motorboats on the lake: "Cocou Ounéhou had thought about it since then, thus he said with a princely ease that the lake would no longer be a simple body of water where fishermen would spend whole nights casting their nets, but on the contrary, one of the industrial sources of Wésê" (69). Reflecting upon the inefficiency of the current system of processing fish, he fantasizes about growing the industry: "The fish from the lake would be sold all over Hadomé, the salted fish industry would grow, the fish would be exported to other countries" (69). For Ounéhou, the essential instrument for increased production is the use of the latest European technologies: "For this magnificent body of water would be exploited according to the new methods of European technology" (69). The modernization of the village is the political mission of his party (69). Ounéhou calls the students who return from abroad, "young people full of goodwill, spurred on by the desire to give services of a technical and intellectual order back to the country" (70).

Ounéhou refutes the notion, repeated by the elders, that all aspects of European culture should be rejected, as exemplified in the phrase: "Beware of Europe, it is preparing the destruction of sub-Saharan Africa" (71). Speaking about the other politicians, Ounéhou says: "Us, we see in them only cowards, speaking at times of freedom and national independence, at other times of sacrifices to the spirits! . . . But what freedom is there when one fears the gods?" (71). According to Ounéhou, although the people of Wésê have freed themselves from the oppression of their colonizers, they will never be truly free until they liberate themselves from their beliefs in the deities, which impede technological progress. Both in the story of Houngbé and in Ounéhou's campaign, belief in the gods is considered a tyranny contrary to progress, much like that of the military occupation of a country by a foreign army. The liberation from the gods through the adoption of new technologies is meant to represent a second liberation of the nation.

The liberating power of new technologies is illustrated in *Le chant du lac* through the narration of an incident at the end of the novel. Several inhabitants of the village cross the lake to travel to the nearby town of Déhâ to buy and sell goods. When a fog falls over the lake, they are unable to return until it lifts. The narrator describes them waiting in their pirogues, with their lanterns lit, hungry and frightened. On the other side of the lake, the people of Wésê fear the worst, and one of the elderly women, grand-maman Tôtô, declares that "if her daughter-in-law came back, she would beg her to equip her boats with a motor" (115). Similarly, another elderly woman, "old aunt Ahouyonsi," states that it is time to let go of irrational beliefs: "We must finally dare to overcome certain unnecessary misgivings" (115). Yaga, yet another old woman, says that if it were up to her, her daughter would use only a motorboat to cross the lake.

This scene marks a turning point in the story, since the elderly who were so opposed to using the motorboats on the lake are willing to concede their use in the name of safety. Their beliefs in the gods symbolize the desire to preserve the landscape that surrounds them and in which their culture has been formed. The willingness to allow the motorboats represents an acceptance of some of the changes in this landscape that must occur in modernity. Overall, African societies are portrayed as highly malleable in the novel; although the elders were initially so adamantly opposed to any modifications in their dwelling place, they are capable of making some adjustments. In fact, the women of the novel are particularly open to these changes; as in Sembène's works, they do not fear change, since they believe that monumental societal transformations may lead to a greater amount of freedom for them and a more respected place in the family hierarchy.

At the end of the story, Noussi and her son chase the gods from the lake with motorboats and battery-powered lanterns, paving the way for progress. This final defeat of the gods at the hands of the people of Wésê represents their liberation from fear. Although the story focuses on a belief in animist gods, the narrator suggests that these deities represent all mythical forms of power that are contrary to progress, including (but not limited to) that of the colonizers, or the Germans occupying France. The initial mistake that the people of the village made, which caused the gods to reside at the bottom of the lake, according to the story, was to believe that they (the gods) were human, when in fact they were deities. Now, the narrator suggests that the people of Wésê are performing the opposite mistake: they believe that certain mortals (the leaders who promote animism) are gods.

Le chant du lac calls on the people of newly independent West African nations to demystify power and beliefs. At the beginning of the novel, a student states: "All folklore has its secrets which it is important to take apart, to make simple and understandable" (13). The narrator declares at the end of the story: "The African man would renounce the many gods for whom he exhausts himself and ruins himself, if he unveiled their secrets or the secrets with which their great priests surround them" (128).

In *Le chant du lac,* technology is portrayed as a democratizing force capable of eliminating the inequalities and conflicts existing within traditional African society, including the caste system. The narrative represents animist traditions impeding technology transfer as tyrannical and fully embraces the use of Western technologies in Africa, without mention of any negative ecological consequences.

LES FILS DE KOURETCHA (THE SONS OF KOURETCHA)

Aké Loba was the son of a traditional chief, who sent him to France to study and work as an agricultural laborer. Loba returned to Côte d'Ivoire in 1959 and emerged onto the francophone literary scene in 1960 with the publication of *Kocoumbo, l'étudiant noir* (Kocoumbo, the black student), the story of an African boy who goes abroad to France for his studies. This novel met with significant success and critical acclaim, winning the 1961 Grand prix littéraire d'Afrique noire. Loba spent most of the next ten years serving in various diplomatic and political positions at embassies in Bonn and Rome before returning to fiction writing in 1970 with the publication of *Les fils de Kouretcha.* In addition to *Kocoumbo* and *Les fils de Kouretcha,* Loba has published two novels, *Les dépossédés* (The depossessed) (1973) and *Le sas des parvenus* (The social climbers' ceiling) (1990).

Although issues associated with modernity had been addressed previously in Sembène's work, *Les fils de Kouretcha* stands out as one of the very first novels to deal directly with questions of modernization and industrialization by focusing on the debate surrounding the construction of a dam in a remote African village. Albert Gérard calls it "the first novel in French to deal in concrete imaginative terms with the social and psychological problems raised by the need for industrialization in a newly independent country" (531). While many of the francophone African novels that precede *Les fils de Kouretcha* dealt primarily with the conflict between the French colonizers and the West African colonized, associating modernity and technology with the former, and fetishism with the latter,[4] the primary focus of Loba's novel is on the role of European technology in the newly independent West African nations.

The story of *Les fils de Kouretcha* takes place in a former French colony of West Africa (although the narrator never specifies the precise location) during the period immediately following independence, that is, the early 1960s, when the question of the role of Western technologies in economic development was at the fore of all political debates. The main focus of *Les fils de Kouretcha* is on the debate about whether or not to build a dam, such that the narrative consists primarily of recounting the shifting positions of the characters, as well as their changing discourses, each of which reflects a particular attitude with regard to technological development in Africa. The novel reads like a carefully constructed argument in favor of technology transfer from the West, which takes the form of various literary techniques that are used to illustrate the superiority of progress and importance of constructing the dam. Throughout the novel, the narrator calls upon the reader to reexamine some of his or her own common assumptions about the politics discussed, through the use of surprise, irony, characterization, and point of view.

The preface to *Les fils de Kouretcha* sets the tone for the novel by expressing its predominant, protechnological ideology: "My concern is to present a current image of the rapidly changing Africa of today" (7). Since this preface was written in the late 1960s (the novel was published in 1970), Loba's statement refers to the dilemmas faced by African nations in the postindependence era, when they must strike a balance between rapid modernization and maintaining cultural traditions. He describes his objective as bringing to life a society caught between archaic beliefs and the necessity of being modern: "I set out to breathe new life into a society with medieval customs and beliefs, besieged by modern imperatives, forced to adopt the pace of the contemporary age and torn apart by its phenomenal delay/backwardness [*retard*]" (7). The language that Loba uses reflects his attitude toward the traditional beliefs and modernization: he calls them "medieval," describes modernizing as an "imperative," and speaks of the continent's "phenomenal delay/backwardness."

Although the conflict between tradition and modernity is one of the primary subjects of the novel, Loba emphasizes in the preface that he would also like to represent a struggle between individual ambitions and the interest of the community that the three main characters, Dam'no, Tougon, and the Old Man, must face. In the novel, the characters who oppose the construction of the dam—mainly Dam'no—represent the pursuit of selfish, individual interest, while those who argue in favor of it—especially Tougon and later le Vieux—are associated with a defense of collective interest. In fact, in *Les fils de Kouretcha,* egoism is associated with fetishism, and altruism with modernization and technological development.

The first few scenes of the novel establish the context for the debate about the dam by recounting the arrival of a number of characters to an African town shortly after independence: Dam'no, the French technicians, and Tougon. These characters represent the two opposing sides of the debate about the dam. Dam'no, a former official in the colonial administration, is against the construction, while Tougon, who is accompanied by the technicians, is a representative of the new independent government, having been assigned the task of obtaining the consent of the "sons of Kouretcha" without any bloodshed.

The opening scene strikingly confronts two key associations found in much of francophone African literature, especially the novels of the 1950s: that of the colonizer with the white man, and of colonialism with modernity. *Les fils de Kouretcha* undermines these associations by portraying a black African character, Pierre Dam'no, as a reactionary who would like nothing more than to restore the old colonial regime, thus equating colonialism with the obsolete and associating Tougon with independence and modernity.

At the very beginning of the novel, Dam'no returns to the home of the sons of Kouretcha, his native tribe, named after Kouretcha, the god of the river that borders their village. He returns in order to see if, in the period of independence, he can regain some of the power he held as the right-hand man of the Commandant de Note, the "head of the canton" in the French colonial administration.[5] The power of the opening sequence lies in an ingenious trick that the narrator plays on the reader. First, he describes Dam'no as the ultimate colonizer, without explicitly stating his race. All aspects of his character appear to signal that he is a white colonizer: his name is "Pierre," and when he arrives in the town, people notice him as someone who is different; he wears the traditional colonial garb, including the hat worn by administrators of the colonial regime; the narrator states that he used forced labor (10). Given the literary context of this novel, the reader most likely either assumes that Dam'no is a white Frenchmen or feels a sense of confusion about his race and nationality. When the narrator finally states that Dam'no is a son of Kouretcha, the reader is confronted with a shocking truth: Dam'no is a black African who was instrumental in the abuse and exploitation of his former tribesmen under the colonial regime and who mourns the disappearance of the French administration.

More generally, *Les fils de Kouretcha* dissociates colonialism from modernity and associates technology with independence. In the initial scene and throughout the entire novel, colonialism is equated with obsolete, archaic practices. When Dam'no, the former colonial administrator, marches into the town, "the young people for whom colonialism already seemed like an obsolete, even historical, phenomenon" (10) perceive him as the symbol of a bygone era. The narrator uses the pluperfect tense in these passages to further emphasize Dam'no's temporal distance from the others. The occasion for his arrival is the celebration of the anniversary of the French Revolution, which Loba presents as the epitome of all that is obsolete; Dam'no wears colonial garb evoking a past that was never experienced firsthand by the young sons of Kouretcha.

The opposition between animism and technology, which is central to the debate over the dam at the core of the novel, corresponds to the battle between two main characters: Dam'no and Tougon. The debate about the dam initially divides the sons of Kouretcha into two now familiar camps: the young people who seek the wages and electricity that the dam will bring; and the elders, who still associate the project of building a dam with exploitation by their former colonizers. Dam'no and Tougon fight to win the favor of the villagers: Dam'no does so by opposing the dam's construction and claiming to defend the animist beliefs of the sons of Kouretcha; Tougon emphasizes the material gains that the dam will bring, including wages for labor and electricity for the town.

Dam'no, the former officer nostalgic for the colonial era, takes the side of animism against modern technology. In an attempt to increase his power, Dam'no forms an alliance with the local *fêticheur,* or witch doctor, Moussa Dombyia. Although Dam'no claims to defend the indigenous beliefs of the village, the novel presents him as a ruthless egotist who appropriates the discourse of animism as a mode of persuasion; his primary objective is his election as a representative of the town in the newly formed independent government. Through the character of Dam'no, Loba seeks to show how some African leaders attempt to use animism to assert their power.

Tougon, a young son of Kouretcha who misses the Parisian Latin Quarter where he lived as a student, takes the side of modern technology. Unlike Dam'no, who represents the old order, Tougon is a representative of the new independent government, the prefect of the region, and has been sent by the authorities to oversee the construction of the dam. When he arrives with the French technicians, they face the opposition of most of the villagers. Before embarking on this endeavor, they must obtain permission from the locals, especially their unquestioned leader, called "the Old Man." The villagers, known as the "sons of Kouretcha," believe that the river Kouretcha is a god and fear that building the dam will disrupt this deity. Moreover, they were once told that if the river is destroyed, the sons of Kouretcha will all die. In the end, Tougon convinces the Old Man to allow the dam to be built, such that progress triumphs over fear and the tactics of the power-hungry Dam'no.

The debate about the dam has its origins in the colonial period, when the French government decided to build a dam on the river. When the colonial government sent technicians and engineers to begin work, the villagers opposed the construction at this earlier time (just as they did later on), also because of their belief in Kouretcha. But the opposition of the sons of Kouretcha was considered irrelevant, since the French administration felt no need to consult them. The older people of the village were deeply opposed to the project, which they interpreted as a declaration of war. They understood that the construction and use of the dam constituted a means of exploiting the people of the sons of Kouretcha and their natural habitat. The dam was to be built using forced labor, much of it from men in the region, and the colonial government was to be the exclusive beneficiary, using electricity for its own needs.

As an official of the colonial administration, Dam'no—who was once a son of Kouretcha—favored the building of the dam and did not fear the revenge of the god of the river. Dam'no is clearly demarcated as a "colonizer" and had no qualms about using his fellow tribesmen for forced labor, as the narrator clearly indicates at the beginning of the narrative. Thus, the two sides of the colonial debate over the dam did not split down neatly along racial lines, since Dam'no is portrayed as a "black colonizer" who was as much a part of the colonial administration as the white French commandants.

The French government's plan ultimately fails, and the dam is never built. The sons of Kouretcha interpret this as a victory of their people and their mighty god over the powerful French, but the narrator states that the colonial government abandoned the project due to technical and engineering difficulties. Dam'no also changes his mind about the wisdom of pursuing the project when the Old Man casts a spell on him that makes him extremely ill. He then opposes the construction and uses the story of the spell to persuade the villagers to take his side in order to increase his power. In this case, as in others, the narrator presents an event that took place and provides two interpretations of it: the viewpoint of the sons of Kouretcha, which generally involves animism and the god Kouretcha; and another, rational explanation. The narrator takes an ideological stance by stating that the rational explanation is the correct one; he does not believe that fear of the gods should impede construction of the dam. This defense of rationalism is consistent with the prevailing ideology of the novel, which promotes the use of science and technology.

The debate about the dam in the colonial period prefigures the position of different groups in the novel with regard to technological development in the postcolonial era. The village of the sons of Kouretcha functions as a microcosm for the entire nation, in which the dam represents the transfer of technologies from the metropolis. Since the dam was equated with the exploitation of the colonized by the colonizers, the metaphor of the dam in *Les fils de Kouretcha* suggests that during the colonial period, Western technologies brought to the colonies were primarily used as instruments for exploiting African workers and disrupting their environment. The economy was built for the exportation of goods abroad and not for the benefit of the local populations.

The novel seeks to highlight the differences between the debate about the dam in the colonial era and the current period of independence, in order to dissociate technological development from the painful period of colonization. After the French abandon the project, a decade goes by without another attempt. Then, when the new independent government comes into power, they decide to begin construction on the dam. This represents a remarkable turn of events: while in the past the two sides of the debate corresponded to the colonizers and the colonized, now it is the authorities of the independent government, referred to in the novel as "our young republic," who send the French technicians.

In the context of independence, the construction of the dam is portrayed much more positively, as a stimulus for technological progress and economic development, since a number of key changes have occurred. First, the leader of the French technicians, and representative of the authorities, is Tougon, a young man who studied in Paris (he is also a character in Loba's *Koucombo*). Tougon is portrayed as an intelligent young man who seeks to reconcile sides and make progress; this is in contrast to Dam'no, who takes the side of animism and forms an alliance with Moussa with the sole objective of regaining his lost power. Second, while the French administration did not consult the sons of Kouretcha, the new independent government insists that the approval of the tribe be obtained. Although the French technicians wonder why this approval is even necessary, Tougon is given the task of assuring the construction of the dam will begin without any bloodshed; the authorities declare that any bloodshed will be interpreted by the rest of the world as proof that the Africans of his country cannot govern themselves.

Ultimately, the novel favorably portrays characters who are receptive to change and critiques those who resist it. Both Western and African cultures and characters are portrayed as highly malleable and capable of evolving, if they are willing to adapt themselves. Moreover, the people of the African village and nation are capable of doing something that the French failed to do: build the dam. They promote technological progress when the French did not; and yet, the presence of the French technicians suggests that it is not possible to appropriate modern innovations without foreign assistance. Loba suggests that the young people of the newly independent African nations, who have a fainter memory of colonialism and are therefore less likely to reject all Western products, should address this dependence by going abroad to educate themselves and transferring technologies back to their homelands.

Les fils de Kouretcha enthusiastically promotes the transfer of Western technologies to Africa, indicating at times the dangers of modernizing too quickly. Although it explores both sides of the debate about the dam and, by implication, the role of Western technologies in economic development in Africa, progress triumphantly prevails at the end of the story. Loba's primary innovation in the novel is to establish an opposition between what is old, outdated, and archaic (represented by fetishism and the colonial order) and what is modern and progressive (corresponding to technology and the dam), which exists independently of racial and cultural divisions. For Loba, both Western and African societies possess elements that are obsolete and contrary to progress, and there are aspects of both these cultures that are capable of evolving and inducing positive change. The novel suggests that any element that originally pertained to one society can be appropriated by another; this is the case not only with regard to the Western technology of the dam but also the animist beliefs, which the French engineers come to adopt after encountering difficulties while performing construction on the river. Loba seeks to counter the notion that Western technologies should automatically be rejected as the inventions of the colonizers, and fetishism fully embraced as the authentic religious beliefs of African peoples.

The authors of *Le chant du lac* and *Les fils de Kouretcha* disrupt the conventional discourses surrounding the relationship between colonialism and technology in the colonial and postcolonial periods, particularly that of the "civilizing mission," which equates colonialism with modernization and technological progress. First, they portray European colonization as a force contrary to progress, which leads to backwardness and underdevelopment. Second, they emphasize the differences between the exploitative use of technology in the colonial era—in which the colonizers reaped the benefits of African labor—and its potential benefits in the era of independence. Third, they portray modern technologies as universal entities that can be appropriated by any culture. In the end, both authors suggest a need to move past the memory of colonization and to adapt beliefs to a modern world in order to progress as a nation.

There are a number of significant differences between the portrayal of modern technological innovations in the postindependence novels of Bhêly-Quénum and Loba and in *God's Bits of Wood.* Sembène's novel (which takes place in 1947 and 1948, was written in 1957, and published in 1960) focuses primarily on the colonial period, all the while gesturing toward a future of independence, which is still unknown. Although Sembène frequently describes the internal divisions between the African peoples and highlights the benevolent actions of some of the white characters, the central plot is the battle between the colonizers and the African peoples, who ultimately come together to defeat their oppressors. The technology discussed, the railway line, was built by the colonizers, and although the workers begin to appropriate the machines through their labor, at the end of the novel they are still very much the property of the French.

In contrast, the postindependence authors Bhêly-Quénum and Loba document the conflict between the young African intellectuals and political leaders, all of whom advocate all-out modernization, and an older generation, which resists rapid change; colonialism is rarely mentioned, except as an era that must be forgotten. In their novels, the debate between the characters is over the consequences of bringing Western technologies to their villages in the period following independence, and the focus is on the impact that machines will have on the natural and cultural landscape of African peoples. Bhêly-Quénum and Loba address the conflicts that arise when the introduction of new technologies threatens to transform this landscape, according to which the societies have built entire belief systems.

In *Le chant du lac* and *Les fils de Kouretcha,* the primary issue is less the association of technology with its colonial inventors than the fear that Western innovations will perturb the gods and destroy traditional

African religion. Whereas in *God's Bits of Wood*, Islam and Christianity are the main religious beliefs represented and there is little discussion of animism, the postindependence novels of Loba and Bhêly-Quénum focus on the animist beliefs of the inhabitants of the African villages and show how they conflict with modernization. Although Sembène centers his critique on different religions than do Bhêly-Quénum and Loba, all three of these authors portray religions as systems of beliefs and practices that must evolve and adapt themselves to modernity and that can often be contrary to progress.

There are a number of key similarities between these three novels that reflect the changes in the representation of technology in francophone literature during the era of independence. First, for all three authors, the moment of independence marks a shift in the notion of ownership of modern technologies: while in the colonial era, according to these authors, technological innovations were necessarily associated with the Europeans who brought them to the colonies, in the postindependence period, they should be embraced as a liberating force. They call upon the newly independent African nations to modernize; technological innovations are presented as part of a universal patrimony that does not belong to any one group of people but is the property of all of humanity.

Second, in all three novels, it is the elders who continue to associate technologies with colonial exploitation, and the young African intellectuals who propose to move away from these associations and to embrace modern innovations: Bakayoko in *God's Bits of Wood*, the young students in *Le chant du lac*, and Tougon in *Les fils de Kouretcha*. This generation includes students who have gone abroad for their studies and acquired ideas there that they bring back to their native countries. They are young enough not to have experienced many of the hardships of colonialism, including the use of machinery for the exploitation of African workers. Sembène, Bhêly-Quénum, and Loba—who all lived in France and were greatly influenced by intellectual life there—most likely identified quite closely with these young characters, who often assume the role of spokesperson for the author in the novels. These characters are extremely optimistic in their views on modern technologies, which they believe can provide the means for liberation.

Third, Sembène, Bhêly-Quénum, and Loba all assign women a vital role in the struggle for decolonization. In their novels and films, the female characters are consistently the most active in seeking change: in *God's Bits of Wood*, it is the march of the women that ultimately leads to the victory of the strike; in *Moolaadé*, the women, empowered by their radio-listening, revolt against female genital mutilation; in *Les fils de Kouretcha,* they favor the building of the dam; and in *Le chant du lac,* it is a woman who finally kills the gods of the lake. Women in these novels are portrayed as a powerful, progressive force; they have no interest in upholding the existing order, which oppresses them, and are thus inclined to embrace the change represented by the advent of modern technologies. The ideology of the novels echoes Sembène's declaration in a 2005 interview that "the liberation of Africa will never happen without the liberation of women" (Interview, *Socialist Worker*).

Ultimately, these novels call upon readers to dissociate the instruments and materials of the colonizers—whether the French language, writing, or modern technologies—from colonialism. For the most part, the authors do not point out the dangers of rapid modernization (including ecological consequences) but view cultural factors surrounding the use of technologies as obstacles that must be overcome for the sake of African development. Their writings do not manifest a fear that technology transfer from Europe to the former colonies will lead to neocolonialism or economic dependence; far from rejecting this transfer, they fully embrace it as the primary (and perhaps the only) road to progress. This marks a contrast between these African authors and their Caribbean counterparts writing about contemporary postcolonial society, such as Édouard Glissant and Patrick Chamoiseau, whom I discuss in the following chapters. While many Caribbean authors also advocate technology transfer as a means of instigating progress, they highlight the difference between a negative form of transfer that reinforces oppressive hierarchies and also destroys the natural environment; and a more beneficial form, controlled by the local inhabitants of the islands, that promotes an ecologically responsible mode of development and modernization.

CHAPTER SIX

Globalization and the Internet in Édouard Glissant

The authors examined thus far—Césaire, Senghor, Fanon, Sembène, Loba, and Bhêly-Quénum—focused primarily on the reception in their cultures of the numerous inventions that were developed in the earlier parts of the twentieth century and whose dissemination characterizes the notion of "modernization." Writing in the era directly prior to and immediately following political independence, these authors emphasized the need to dissociate modern technologies from the (former) colonizers and argued for their important role in the nation-building process.

The following chapters consider two contemporary Caribbean authors, Édouard Glissant and Patrick Chamoiseau, who also approach questions of technology in their works, albeit from a slightly different perspective. As authors from Martinique (an island that remains a department of France) writing in the late twentieth and early twenty-first centuries, Glissant and Chamoiseau address questions of technology by focusing on the relationship between modern communications technologies (such as radio, television, and the Internet) and global culture. Although they have advocated for independence from France, the discussion of technology in their works does not generally emphasize their role in the process of nation building but rather the potential function of communications technologies as defenders of diversity in an increasingly globalized community.

The works of Glissant have generally been divided into two primary stages. The first stage begins with his early novels from the late 1950s and early 1960s, *La Lézarde* (1958) and *Le quatrième siècle* (The fourth century) (1964); continues with his poetry collections and ars poetica, *L'intention poétique* (The poetic intention) (1969); and ends with the *Caribbean Discourse*, published in 1981. During this initial period, which is characterized by the production of a great deal of narrative fiction, poetry, and essays on literature, Glissant focuses primarily on the contemporary political and social issues faced by Martinique and the Antilles, confronting especially the trauma of slavery and the need to develop a distinct form of cultural identity.

Caribbean Discourse marks a transition to the second stage in Glissant's thinking by proposing his now famous notion of *Antillanité*, defined as a specifically West Indian identity. This concept seeks to counter the movement of Negritude through the creation of a cultural identity based on a fluid multiplicity of elements. From the early 1980s onward, Glissant shifts his focus from the relatively localized politics of Martinique and the French Caribbean and approaches globalization from a theoretical standpoint.[1] In *Poetics of Relation* (1990), *Introduction à une poétique du divers* (Introduction to a poetics of the diverse) (1995), *La Cohée du Lamentin: Poétique V* (The Lamentin hill: Poetics V) (1996), *Traité du tout-monde* (Treaty of the everything-world) (1997) and *Une nouvelle région du monde* (A new region of the world) (2006), Glissant develops his now famous concepts of Relation and rhizome-identity, and articulates his notion of a new, global culture created by the interaction of new technologies, which he denotes variously as the "*tout-monde*," "*totalité-monde*," "*mondialité*," "*chaos-monde*," and "*nouvelle région du monde*."

Many critics, most notably Peter Hallward and Chris Bongie, have argued that the shift from the first stage to the second represents an abandonment of politics for Glissant. Hallward believes that the famous concepts Glissant develops for addressing questions of globalization, the *tout-monde*, *totalité-monde*, and *chaos-monde*, have the effect of flattening all differences by referring to all localities with a language of sameness.[2] In Hallward's frequently cited essay in *Absolutely Postcolonial*, he describes these two stages in the development of Glissant's thinking, tracing a movement from a "specific," grounded engagement with national independence to a vision of the world as an immanent totality, outside the control of conscious political intervention. According to Hallward, the theoretical concepts that Glissant develops for examining globalization are so abstract that they cause any concrete referent to be lost in the flux of global movement and chaos that they describe. For Hallward, the apolitical dimension of Glissant's later writings exemplifies some of the problems with postcolonial theory in general, namely the tendency to embrace hybridity and ambivalence over political engagements that involve polarized oppositions.

I will argue, in contrast, that Glissant does seriously consider how his notion of the *tout-monde* (the "everything-" or "all-world" that he equates with globalization) relates to the precise political and social reality of Martinique, and the French Caribbean more generally. For Glissant, the constant flux and chaos of the *tout-monde* finds its embodiment in the flow of images, language, and ideas produced by new media, and in particular the Internet, which he considers the ultimate embodiment of the "global village." In fact, Glissant's turn to contemporary issues from 2000 until his death in 2008 suggests a third stage in his thinking, in which he attempts to politicize the abstract concepts that he developed in the 1990s. Glissant anchors his theories about the *tout-monde* into the real world through the Internet, which provides a concrete embodiment of his theories of globalization—contrary to Hallward's assertions, which, of course, were directed at earlier writings. This third stage is also marked by an increasing concern for ecology and the development of a theory about the role of technology in what he calls "*mondialisation*" (globalization as hegemonic) and "*mondialité*" (globalization as the promotion of diversity).

In my reading of Glissant, I argue that the shift from the local to the global in the 1990s, as well as the politicization of theory after 2000, reflects a coherent attitude in his works about the role of modern technologies and ecologies in Caribbean globalizations. In particular, I explore how each of the major concepts about globalization developed by Glissant—including the Relation, rhizome-identity, and the *tout-monde*—relate to his views about modern technologies, including television, radio, and the Internet; and to ecology as both a form of mysticism and a political practice. Moreover, I will show how the Internet, for Glissant, constitutes the key instrument for furthering political projects, with their new focus on ecology.

POETICS OF RELATION

In *Poetics of Relation* (1990), Glissant begins to articulate his theories about globalization, introducing some of his most famous concepts, especially the fundamental notions of the "Relation" and "rhizome-identity." In this text, Glissant defines the "Relation" (written with a capital "R" analogous to the one used for the "Other") as the irreducible difference of the Other, a nonhierarchical form of exchange. Notably, the concept of Relation applies not only to individuals but also to other cultures and societies. Indeed, as Celia Britton notes: "The elements which interact in Relation are preponderantly *cultures,* rather than human beings. . . . Glissant, in other words, is primarily interested in the multiple forms of relation between the cultures of the world" (*Sense of Community* 38). Glissant further describes Relation as a system rather than as a series of separate, distinct relations. "Relation" is in the first place a relation of equality with, and respect for, the Other as different from oneself; it represents dynamic, flexible, and constantly changing modes of interaction rather than fixed relationships. Britton writes that "Relation is fundamentally dynamic, 'turbulent' in a way that being-in-common is not" (*Sense of Community* 39). For Glissant, Relation constitutes an ideal form of interaction, albeit one that is not frequently achieved.

For Glissant, the interaction involved in Relation does not—and should not—necessarily lead to a profound understanding of the Other, since he adamantly proclaims the fundamental "right to opacity" (*droit à l'opacité*). This entails the right *not* to be understood, to interact with peoples and become aware of their presence in the world, without seeking a complete (and potentially reductive) understanding of them. In other words, Relation involves an exposure, an interaction with others that makes one aware of one's own position, relativizing it, but does not claim to produce a total mutual understanding.[3]

Indeed, Glissant notes that the word "Relation" evokes both the adjective *relatif* (relative), marking its ability to conquer the existence of an absolute; and the verb *relater,* meaning to narrate or tell a story: "We have already said that Relation informs not simply what is relayed but also the relative and the related" (*Poetics of Relation* 27). In this sense, the Relation constitutes an alternative narrative, one that does not present an absolute story or truth but takes into account all the relative perspectives: "Because what it relates, in reality, proceeds from no absolute, it proves to be the totality of relatives, put in touch and told" (28). These alternative narratives force people to abandon the idea that their own culture is singular or absolute, by causing them to become aware of the relative nature of their own way of perceiving the world. Thus the "coming into relation" (*mise en relation*) entails not only a form of contact between cultures and peoples but a relativizing of their points of view.

According to Glissant, cultures are transformed by the ongoing process of coming into "Relation" with one another; through this process, the West becomes relativized and its dominance is undermined.

In *Poetics of Relation,* Glissant asserts that modern technologies of transportation and communication, especially the Internet, produce a "coming into relation" of peoples and cultures.[4] In particular, he predicts a "coming into relation" of Martinique with surrounding societies, including the "Other America" (other Caribbean countries and the United States, especially Louisiana) and the rest of the world, which he believes to be so fundamental to its progress. Glissant's argument rests on two observations. First, and most basically, modern technologies end the isolation of local communities by creating links to other cultures. Here he appeals to the personal experience of his childhood in Martinique, as in this somewhat nostalgic description of youthful isolation from a 1998 interview with Claude Couffon: "My childhood was—I might be mistaken, I might embellish things—at once marvelous and legendary, and at the same time very poor. When I was barely ten years old, at the height of the World War, from 1939 to 1943, Martinique was completely isolated from the rest of the world" (Couffon 43). In retrospect, Glissant sees the extent to which his society was far removed from the outside world: "Don't forget that at that time there was no television, no radio, no newspapers, but we were imagining the world in a fantastic way" (44–45). In this same interview, he declares that he believes that modern technologies are putting an end to this isolation.[5] Second, Glissant believes that new communications technologies provide a voice for small, solitary communities by projecting them onto a global stage. Specifically, in the era of globalization, as a result of the dissemination of technologies, injustices can be rapidly publicized by new media, in a way that creates global pressure to end them.[6]

Glissant does not deny that a "coming into relation" of peoples and cultures existed before the advent of modern technology; the difference is the rapidly accelerating frequency at which cultural contact, especially, is occurring: "The cultures of the world have always maintained relations among themselves that were close or active to varying degrees, but it is only in modern times that some of the right conditions came together to speed up the nature of these connections" (*Poetics of Relation* 26). Whereas before many regions remained unexplored or unfamiliar, now the distance between these areas appears to have contracted; Glissant writes of the "shrinking of unexplored regions on the map of the world" (*Poetics of Relation* 26). Moreover, there is no longer an enormous time lag involved in cultural contact, which now occurs rapidly: "Contacts among cultures—one of the givens of modernity—will no longer come across the huge spans of time that have historically allowed meetings and interchanges to be active but almost imperceptibly so. Whatever happens elsewhere has repercussions here" (*Poetics of Relation* 26). For Glissant, the resulting changes are truly significant: the individual, independently of his/her community, can be directly influenced by other cultures, whereas before, according to Glissant, influences occurred primarily through a sort of collective exchange between groups of people (*Poetics of Relation* 26–27).

Glissant values the ability of communications technologies to build communities, especially across the borders of nations. He writes that they can lead to "an unexpected call to other modes of relation between communities of people" (Glissant and Lepin, *Les entretiens de Baton Rouge* 120). As Glissant frequently emphasizes throughout his work, any contemporary author writes in the presence of other languages, whether or not he or she knows them.[7] As we will see, this multilinguistic background for writers is embodied by the Internet for Glissant, since, for the first time in history, not only are people from diverse cultures in simultaneous contact with one another, but they are fully aware of the exchanges as a result of new media.

In addition to enacting a "coming into relation" between Caribbean societies and the rest of the world, Glissant believes that modern technologies provide the basis for two more of his later theoretical constructs, namely the "relation-identities" and "rhizome-identities." In *Poetics of Relation*, Glissant famously establishes an opposition between the fixed root-identity and the more diverse rhizome-identity. About the root-identity, Glissant writes, "*Root identity* is founded in the distant past in a vision, a myth of the creation of the world" (143). Additionally, the root-identity is "arborescent"; it is anchored in one place, and there is no interaction between the roots and surroundings. Like the root of a tree, all growth is structured from a single central point. Glissant argues that Negritude, with its emphasis on African roots, and Créolité, with its somewhat fixed notion of Creole identity, constitute forms of root-identity, as do monolingualism and even bilingualism, to an extent (143). He also associates the root-identity with certain collectivities that seek to band together and establish common roots. The root-identity is "absolute" or "totalitarian"; it is associated with the total absence of Relation, since the roots fail to interact (come into relation) with the surroundings (others). In sum, Glissant's root-identity represents fixed notions of identity that emphasize singular origins, even essentialism. The rhizome-identity, by contrast, is based on Relation rather than essence: it is anchored in different places (nodes), from which it simultaneous proliferates, with roots that interact with the surroundings.

In developing the concept of the rhizome-identity, Glissant appropriates the notion of the "rhizome" from Gilles Deleuze and Félix Guattari's *A Thousand Plateaux: Capitalism and Schizophrenia* (1980). The rhizome, unlike the root, is *both* root and stem: it simultaneously proliferates from different nodes. As individuals experience a constant mix of languages and cultural elements, identities are viewed as anchored in a number of places. At the same time, Glissant develops the concept of the relation-identity, which is basically identical to the rhizome-identity. The relation-identity is more attuned to lived reality: "Relation identity is linked not to a creation of the world but to the conscious and contradictory experience of contacts among cultures" (*Poetics of Relation* 144) and is therefore more suited to the ebb and flow of globalization. Although some have interpreted the rhizome to be completely fluid and displaced, as well as transient in nature, Glissant emphasizes that the rhizome is a "demultiplied root," meaning that it is still a root, but one anchored in a plurality of places. This notion of the rhizome provides for Glissant the basis for a new form of poetics, one that finds its inspiration in a wide variety of places.

According to Glissant, the proliferation of modern technologies in the global era fosters the creation of rhizome-identities. This is because communication technologies accelerate the process of establishing the individual and collective rhizome-identities that he associates with creolization, by creating new spaces of identity-formation, ones that are not necessarily anchored in a particular place. The Internet has no doubt played a significant role in this process for Glissant, since it harbors the *mise en relation* between peoples, the creation of rhizome-identities, and the "creolization" that leads to the creation of composite cultures, as well as the disintegration of atavistic ones. As Glissant writes in his 1997 *Traité du tout-monde,* the Internet is emblematic of a space that supports the creation and assumption of rhizome-identities; in cyberspace, each participant can be anchored in a number of different locations at once, thus assuming a multiple rhizome-identity. Moreover, the Internet produces a space of "creolization" (a term coined by Glissant in the *Caribbean Discourse* for hybrid identities), where languages constantly mix together, changing and evolving through contact with other languages. This acceleration of the "process" of creolization and the creation of rhizome-identities is associated with the emergence of a new poetics for Glissant, what he calls the "poetics of relation."

As a result of processes of globalization—including the proliferation of the Internet—Glissant believes that root-identities are progressively giving way to rhizome-identities, which are now beginning to dominate, mainly due to their more open and flexible nature. In a 1998 interview with Andrea Schwieger Hiepko, "Europe and the Antilles," Glissant states that in the era of globalization, "we have moved from the single root to the rhizome. . . . We have shifted from believing in identity as a single root to hoping for identity as a rhizome" (Hiepko 259). In addition to its open (as opposed to hierarchical) and global nature, as Helmtrud Rumpf notes, "rhizomatic identity claims the right to opacity, which is opposed to the transparency of root-identity" (266–67).

For Glissant, the idea that a technology is the sole possession of the society that created it is linked to the idea of root-identity that he finds to be so detrimental, while the notion of technologies as elements in a universal patrimony and thus existing in multiple locales is associated with the rhizome-identity, which he views much more positively. As is the case for the other thinkers analyzed in this study, Glissant suggests that the appropriation of a modern technology by a formerly colonized culture destroys the associations between this particular technology and its Western origins.

In the *Traité du tout-monde*, Glissant revisits the opposition between the root-identity and rhizome-identity first introduced in the *Poetics of Relation* in light of his theories about globalization. As Britton observes: "Glissant's increasing emphasis on the political dangers of the 'root-identity,' as opposed to the plural, relational 'rhizomatic' identity, continues throughout the *Traité*" (*Glissant and Postcolonial Theory* 180). Glissant finds the notion of the root-identity to be a profoundly oppressive one: "The idea of identity as coming from a single root explains why these communities were subjugated by others, and why a number of them took on their struggles for liberation" (21). He argues that the single root kills everything around it, while the rhizome—which is rooted nonetheless, just in multiple places—does not usurp the surrounding territory (21). Glissant would like to change the way that identity is imagined, such that it is more of a rhizome-identity (anchored in various places), as well as a relation-identity, that is, an identity constructed on the basis of mutual exchange and interaction with others (22).

Glissant's distinction between rhizomatic and root identities is strongly correlated to the crucial one that he establishes between "atavistic" and "composite" cultures, which in turn is fundamental to his ideas about technology. He defines an atavistic society as one that is predominantly focused on its own origins and strongly emphasizes that its status as a "native" people gives it a legitimate claim to the land it inhabits. In "A Visit to Édouard Glissant," he declares: "Atavistic cultures are those that, over an extended span of time, were able to create, to dream up, to imagine a myth of the creation of the world, of a genesis, which they are connected to by an uninterrupted line of descent, by legitimacy" (Couffon 54). In the Hiepko interview "Europe and the Antilles," he describes an atavistic society as "a culture that has felt the need to create a myth related to the creation of the world, a genesis" (Hiepko 256). In other words, atavistic societies are obsessed with presenting myths about their own origins, and they are firmly anchored in their beliefs and territory; this makes them the collective equivalent of the root-identity (*Traité* 35). Composite cultures, by contrast, are more malleable and consist of the creolization of various peoples; they constitute the collective equivalent of the rhizome-identity or relation-identity.

For Glissant, the cultures of the Caribbean and the Americas are necessarily composite, due to their history (*Traité* 36). Contact between atavistic cultures led to the creation of composite societies, with each kind of society battling the other for the rightful possession of the land; and now, in the era of globalization, "composite" societies have fully replaced the "atavistic" ones that once dominated (*Traité* 36). Glissant sees a tendency, in the *tout-monde,* toward the abandonment of atavistic cultures and establishment of composite cultures, as atavistic cultures fall apart and lose their sacred quality, much as root-identities make way for rhizome-identities.

Later in the decade (1990s), after the gradual emergence of the World Wide Web, Glissant explicitly associates the Internet with his famous concept of the "poetics of relation." Following his notion of "Relation," Glissant defines this as a mode of writing that represents difference as relations with others and invents new forms of expression to denote these relations. Glissant's own novels, such as *Tout-Monde* (1993), are an example of this genre, since they seek both to represent cultural differences and to initiate contact between cultures.

In "Europe and the Antilles," Glissant explores the relationship between the Internet and a "poetics of relation." He believes that the Internet's sense of relation and accumulation, as well as its unpredictability and lack of measure, causes it to resemble a poetics of relation: "That is why I think that a poetics of relation is akin to electronic technologies. All the concepts of the poetics of relation are present in information technology" (Hiepko 260). According to Glissant, the Internet, like the poetics of relation, has no moral, no primary theme; therefore all notions of the poetics of relation are represented within it. Glissant believes that both the poetics of relation and the Internet have the ability to change our imagination and our relationship to the unforeseeable, which is necessary for finding a new identity that is ultimately a rhizomatic one (260).

Glissant asserts that the Internet is capable of forging the poetics of relation by providing new forms of inspiration for poetry and literature more broadly. In "Concerning the Poem's Information," an essay from *Poetics of Relation,* Glissant addresses himself to all those who declare that in the information age, poetry has become irrelevant, since it is generally associated with the distant past, with what is traditional and outdated, and thus seems out of place in the modern computer age (81). He writes that the question is always the same one: "What's the use of poetry?" (81). Glissant refutes these ideas by pointing out the extent to which poets have found inspiration in new technologies: "Poets today, fascinated by the adventure of computers [*l'informatique*], sense that here lies . . . at least a chance to reconnect the two orders of knowledge, the poetic and the scientific" (81). Much as Césaire once wrote that poetry and science are two different perspectives on reality, capable of coming together,[8] Glissant suggests that by providing new forms of inspiration, information technology offers opportunities for bridging the gap between science and poetry. Whereas science once felt very distant for poets, the computer has now made the "scientific intention" more approachable to them (81). Glissant believes that this increased approachability forces the poet to rethink the message conveyed in his/her work, which often passes through the channels of the "*machine informatique.*"

Glissant believes that the advent of computer technology transformed poetry by changing the perception of speed for both the reader and writer; it has made speed banal: "The advent of computers has, nonetheless, thrown poetics into reverse. By making speed commonplace" (82). When describing this "banalization of speed," Glissant intentionally breaks the sentence into two, stopping/slowing the reading process by placing an unorthodox period after "*poétique*" (poetics) and before "*Par*" (By). This serves to illustrate his point that information/digital technologies make readers accustomed to reading very quickly, skimming text and skipping over words, sentences, and paragraphs. The speed-reading mode of the Internet eventually changes our perception of everything in life, such that we always find ourselves in its constant flux: "We are in the incessant Internet of life" (*Traité* 173). Glissant proposes the need for pauses and breaks within this movement of acceleration, and occasionally to slow down and stop: "In our ever-accelerating familiarity with the diversity of the world, we need breaks, moments of meditation" (*Traité* 172). For Glissant, it is precisely the book that provides these moments of meditation, by forcing the reader to slow down. He feels that there must be a balance between these two kinds of reading and perceiving, the speed-consumption of words and images, and the more thoughtful pondering of a text.

Glissant writes that as a result, two kinds of poetics have been created. The first finds inspiration in the dramatic speed of the information age and tries to use it for literary effect. This is the poetic of the instant: "The sudden flash, this poetics of the moment, has become established and in some ways obliterated by the unimaginable instantaneousness of the computer" (82). The second is the poetics of "duration" (*une poétique de la durée*) (82), which seeks to slow down the reading process; he gives as an example Mallarmé's *Un coup de dès,* a highly visual poem presenting the phrase "*Un coup de dès jamais n'abolira le hasard*" (a roll of the dice will never abolish chance) spread across numerous pages in a variety of font sizes.

Glissant concedes that the book, as a physical object, is in danger of disappearing, but he appears nonchalant about this development, which he believes will forge new, as of yet unimaginable possibilities in terms of genres and forms of expression. Fundamental differences exist between the Internet and the book, with regard not only to their form but also their essence. According to Glissant, the Internet presents the world in its crudest form, whereas the book illuminates it, showing its invariables (*Traité* 161). Glissant mocks those who declare the death of the book: "Everyone agrees in thinking that the book is threatened by advancements in audiovisual technology" (*Traité* 170); "The audiovisual has allegedly put an end to reading, rendering it useless, and has apparently signaled the death of the book" (*Traité* 171). He believes that books and computers will ultimately complement each other, with each one forging a sense of purpose for the other (*Traité* 171).

The constant movement of the Internet affects not only how we read, according to Glissant, but how we write: "Today we write the way we read and vice versa"; "In an incredibly active and rapid way, adapted to all of this momentum that the world has and to the surge of the technologies of modernity, which carry us along in their unstoppable flow" (*Traité* 175). He ponders the poetic possibilities of the Internet and whether it is realistic to believe that anything can be firmly created in its constant flux: "But will we be able to compose poems, to illustrate a Creole language [*langue*], to weave a language [*langage*], in this suspended space?" (*Traité* 167). Evidently, he believes that the answer is "yes"; with changing expectations of form and content, ultimately new artistic possibilities will emerge. Glissant believes that the Internet has led to the opening up of a wide variety of new genres, as a result of the constant exposure to diversity: "Diversity makes it so that little by little the writer renounces the former division between literary genres" (*Traité* 174); its elimination of genres and creation of a feeling of simultaneity make it ideal for inspiring new literary forms.

Glissant also critiques those who herald the death of writing in the new information age (*Poetics of Relation* 97); on the contrary, he believes that this age will lead to new forms of interaction between writing and orality: "But the drama does not simply boil down to a possible deathblow for writing. Now the crisis of writing as a form of expression meets the sudden burgeoning of oral languages" (*Poetics of Relation* 83). Although the differences between writing and orality have long been contemplated by scholars and writers alike and often form the crux of issues explored in postcolonial literature, Glissant believes that this question has reached a critical point today, as modern technologies change our relationship to the oral and the written. In the past, according to Glissant, the oral and the written existed in opposition to each other, with the written associated with the transcendent and absolute: "Yesterday we distinguished between the oral and the written, with the latter being transcendent" (*Poetics of Relation* 84). Glissant believes that the computer will merge them together, producing new forms of expression consisting of orality transcribed onto the page or screen, two entities that he refers to interchangeably, since he appears to believe that they will become one and the same: "Maybe tomorrow we shall be living through a synthesis that could be summed up as the written resolution, or transcription onto the page (which is our screen), of an economy of orality" (*Poetics of Relation* 84).

Indeed, Glissant associates the Internet with orality—that which is organic and malleable, a life form—and *not* with the written word. This is paradoxical, to say the least, given that such a large amount of what is posted online consists of written texts that are then silently read by the

Web user. But for Glissant, the transient, fluid nature of the Internet—in which language is constantly in flux—causes it to resemble orality. In "Europe and the Antilles," he states that although "electronic technologies are first and foremost techniques of written communication . . . the fact is that orality, which is also a technique, is quite comparable to what we see on the Internet" (Hiepko 260). This is because "both show wild forms of accumulation, the excessiveness of an unexpected and unstoppable flow" (260). For Glissant, these are precisely the signs of an oral culture: "this sense of relation, of the unexpected, the excessive, and the cumulative" (Hiepko 260).

Glissant associates the Internet—and the many communications technologies that it envelops, such as television and radio—with orality and the organic, due to the speed of transmission and modification; and writing with the inorganic. Whereas in the past orality, due to its fluid nature—including its constant repetition and contact with other words—accelerated the mixing of cultures that Glissant describes as "creolization," it is now primarily the Internet that produces a similar process, speeding up the mixing and merging of cultures by instigating clashes of languages and cultures in cyberspace that provoke a *mise en relation* of individuals and societies.

In *Introduction à une poétique du divers,* Glissant once again contemplates the role of information technologies in the "poetics of relation," this time by exploring the relationship between oral and written language, and what he calls "transcendence." According to Glissant, distantly echoing Plato's *Phaedrus* and Jacques Derrida, writing has always been associated with "transcendence," the word of God (*dictée du dieu*), and "the immobility of the body" (38), since it is fixed, rigid, and generally expresses a linear mode of thinking. Orality, on the other hand, is related to movement, including repetition, redundance, and rhythm (38), and is much more distant from thoughts of transcendence. Since Glissant considers orality to be more distant from transcendence than writing and the book, and he associates the Internet with orality, this suggests that he also considers the Internet to be more distant from notions of transcendence.

Glissant distinguishes between two kinds of orality with profoundly different objectives, and that are closely related to his globalization/globality opposition.[9] The first kind of orality, which he associates with the homogenizing forces of globalization, is associated with the media; it involves standardization, "banalization," and is very much the linguistic equivalent of "cementization" (*bétonisation*), the term that

Chamoiseau uses to describe negative changes in the Martinican landscape.[10] For Glissant, the predominance of French TV and radio stations in Martinique represents precisely this kind of orality: the use of technology to impose an oral discourse at the expense of more local ones. Glissant views this homogenizing orality as a by-product of the "globalization" and departmentalization that he views so negatively. Although this form of orality might originate in written form, since it often follows a script commissioned by governments and corporations, it has nothing to do with transcendence; likewise, it does not produce a *mise en relation* or interaction between cultures, since the discourse is merely imposed from above with no opportunity for dialogue or feedback.

The second kind of orality is the one that Glissant associates with "globality," the form of globalization that he celebrates enthusiastically. This modern form of orality is also the product of new media technologies, but unlike the first, it is open, interactive, inclusive, and thus highly democratic; it emerges naturally from cultures that have longstanding traditions of embracing orality. Glissant describes this kind of orality as "shivering and creative" and writes that it has become the mode of expression of choice for cultures newly thrust onto the global stage (*Poétique du divers* 39). According to Glissant, the transition from oral traditions (in the forms of songs, stories, dialects, and other means of communication) to media culture (radio, television) is a natural one for many societies that are already in the habit of communicating via oral forms. Much like Fanon's analysis of the radio in Algeria, Glissant believes that the central place of orality in traditional Caribbean cultures actually makes them *more* inclined, rather than less so, to embrace new technologies of communication.[11]

In "Technology-Based Orality: A Force for Social Change in the Caribbean," Helmtrud Rumpf describes the notion of a "technology-" or "media-based" orality in Glissant, which is roughly the equivalent of this second form of orality (which Glissant associates with globality): "The new 'technology-based orality,' for example, the Internet, presents not a subordinate relationship (*mise-sous-relation*) as do radio, television etc. It is no longer a matter of a hierarchical relationship in which one person informs another, but of reciprocal communication—an equal relationship (*mise-en-relation*)" (262). "It is first of all necessary," Rumpf continues, "to distinguish between the orality arising from communication technology and the orality of non-print cultures. Glissant stresses the fact that people of oral cultures such as those of the Caribbean should rediscover their orality, which serves to transmit history. Only after the recovery of orally transmitted history—in the form of a creation myth—can orality lead to writing, and then to media-based orality" (267).

Unlike traditional orality, however, the "media-based" orality that Rumpf describes surpasses national borders, connecting peoples and cultures in the imaginary domain of cyberspace:[12] "Whereas the orality of societies with an oral culture requires proximity, as the storyteller and his listeners are in direct contact and share the same space and cultural values, writing puts distance between the author and his readers, who may live in very different cultural spaces. The evolution of new communications technology, however, restores proximity, which is then no longer physical but virtual. . . . Media-based orality re-establishes this proximity and thus the omnipresence of the whole-world" (270).

In this cultural turn, from the privileging of the written over the oral, to a synthesis of the two on the page/screen, traditional oral poetry will provide a major source of inspiration. Glissant therefore heralds a new relationship between the oral and the written, in which the transience, fluidity, and diversity of orality and oral cultures infuse the written form.

Paradoxically, in the constant flux of information and globalization, the computer, for Glissant, suggests not only instability but also stability, since it provides a potential means of recording endangered languages and speech (*Poetics of Relation* 84); and it represents not only the hypermodern but also the traditional. He believes that modern technologies will promote new means of expression for predominantly oral cultures, since the medium of the Web allows them to be thrust onto the world stage; their songs and oral literatures, in the various indigenous languages and dialects, can be recorded and preserved in the fluid form of blogs, forums, articles, MP3s, and Youtube videos, accessible to all. All one needs is an Internet connection to produce a *mise en relation* between societies, a process that was extremely difficult, even impossible, for Glissant as a child in Martinique, growing up in a village relatively isolated from the rest of the world.

Although Glissant celebrates the revolutionary potential of information technologies to inspire new forms of poetics, he nonetheless warns against the dangers of their use by hegemonic powers. The relationship between the oral and the written he describes is rendered even more complex by the practices of political and economic oppressions he delineates in the next section of *Poetics of Relation* (104–5). One of these oppressions is what he calls the "relationship of domination," which takes place primarily through technological expansion and leads to a neutral uniformity (104). Within this context, the "dominated languages" are reduced to folklore or "technical irresponsibility" (104–5), meaning that they are viewed as useless since they do not assist in the oppressive process of technological expansion by the dominant power. As a result, these languages are subjugated to a "universal" that is not generalizing, meaning that it consists of one language imposed on all the others, without representing them in some way, as Esperanto presumably could do. Glissant does not specifically name the domineering language, although one could imagine that it is English, and moreover an English that is highly standardized and does not take into account linguistic differences between groups of speakers.

Similarly, French, which likewise is considered the primary means of gaining technological knowledge in the former colonies, can become domineering if it is imposed as a standardized language that does not consider variations in speech. About this phenomenon, Britton writes: "An important aspect of the 'Tout-monde' is thus communication, and therefore language. Globalization has, paradoxically, created the conditions both for much greater contact between different language communities as a result of migration and hybridization, and at the same time for the increasing dominance of the major world languages at the expense of those spoken by smaller and economically weaker communities" ("Transnational Languages" 63).

Nevertheless, although globalization can lead to the dominance of one language, Glissant nonetheless highlights the potentially positive—albeit at times unintended—consequences of the spread of new technologies. In the *Poetics of Relation,* Glissant writes that even when information technology is used for less than noble objectives—such as opening up markets—it can nevertheless lead to a valuable preservation of languages. He gives the example of a project executed by the Société en informatique du Japon (Informatics Society of Japan), which invested large sums of money into the study of African languages. Although the goal of the study was to conquer a potential market, the project nonetheless led to a necessary recognition of these languages: "Still, it should be noted how the most self-interested technology was thereby sanctioning not the (actual) liberation of the languages of orality, of course, but already their right to be recognized" (109). So paradoxically, even projects of dissemination that originally have a sinister intent can lead to the preservation of important cultural heritage.

FLASH AGENTS

A fundamental yet highly neglected element of Glissant's theories of globalization—especially as they relate to technological innovations—is his notion of the "flash agents" (*agents-d'éclat*). Glissant calls modern communications technologies—such as television, film, and the radio—"agents," a term that emphasizes the extent to which the use of media implies a sense of agency or intentionality, even though these media often present themselves as objective recorders of reality. In *Poetics of Relation,* he makes a key distinction between the relay agents (*agents de relais*), which he views positively and associates with Relation, and the nefarious flash agents, which form part of the destructive forces of globalization for him. The relay agents are the technologies that relay information back and forth between different subjects, fostering productive exchange and interaction between cultures and peoples. Glissant describes these "intermediaries" as fundamental instruments in the *mise en relation* of individuals and societies; they are the building blocks of the Relation: "they are *échos-monde* working with the matter of Relation" (178).

Unlike the relay agents, which foster dialogue and the mutual exchange of ideas, the flash agents create flashes before spectators or listeners in order to shock, shake, and startle them. They lose their effect through overuse, as they numb the spectator's perception of reality, especially in cases of Internet addiction. These flash agents consist of media that produce brutal and immediate contact, such as television, newspapers, film, radio, and, of course, the communications technology that contains all others within it: the Internet.[13] In the essay, "That That" from *Poetics of Relation,* Glissant provides a somewhat enigmatic definition of the flash agents: "Today flash agents are the relay agents who are in tune with the implicit violence of contacts between cultures and the lightning speed of techniques [technologies] of relation" (166). In other words, these flash agents are the vectors through which contact between cultures occurs, and at the lightning speed of communications technologies Glissants calls the "technologies of relation" (*techniques de relation*). They are the original relay agents (which participated in Relation) sped up indefinitely and rendered violent. Glissant writes that the flash agents neutralize the "relay agents by causing them to lose their ability to signify.[14] For Glissant, the primary difference between the positive, productive relay agents and the destructive flash agents is the speed at which contacts occur. With the relay agents, the contact occurs more slowly and deliberately, such that there may be a mutual exchange of ideas; but with the flash agents, the contact is too quick; the agent emits signals without receiving a response. The flash agents impress with their immediacy: "The flash agents impress us especially through the immediacy (pure pressure) of their communication techniques [technologies]" (*Poetics of Relation* 166). Glissant reiterates Marshall McLuhan's famous statement that the "medium is the message":[15] "Their action is sufficient unto itself here; there is no stated ideology of communication" (*Poetics of Relation* 166).

Glissant's use of the term "flash agents" to denote media technologies echoes the French philosopher Felix Guattari's 1993 essay "On Machines" in which Guattari refers to technologies as "assemblages" that play a role in various "ideological instruments" (8). According to Guattari, each technology is a machine that forms part of a broader machine: the city, and also the ideological apparatus. While technologies themselves are neutral, in their actual function within the social order they carry an intentionality or agency, since as part of the ideological apparatus, they can be used to subjugate and to reinforce hierarchies. Glissant, like Guattari, is interested in how technology is inserted into social practices. He views modern communications technologies, such as the Internet, as a way of inserting oneself into the network of the "world-as-totality" (*totalité-monde*) and fully experiencing it. He frequently presents these technologies as inextricably linked to the networks of which they are a part, including the endless circulation between viewers/spectators and producers.

Glissant's notion of the flash agents has broad ramifications for cultural relations. When all contact between cultures occurs through flash agents rather than relay agents, it becomes superficial and meaningless, consisting of one people blindly perceiving the flashes produced by another. Glissant states in an interview with Lise Gauvin, *L'imaginaire des langues* (The imaginary of languages) that these flash agents produce the illusion of knowing the world and cultures that we do not truly understand: "the total 'literality' transmitted by televisions, radios, and newspapers, that is to say the illusion that one knows the world because it is brought to the same level, because one knows what has happened on the other side of the world, through the media" (56).

Glissant believes that the actual knowledge of the *totalité-monde,* what he calls a "real imaginary," is the only way to counter these media illusions: "It is this real imaginary of the *totalité-monde* which acts as a counterweight to the media illusion of real knowledge of the world" (56). This "real imaginary" is a way of imagining the world, how the world as a whole is perceived and envisioned by people on a daily basis. This is the essence of what he calls the "poetics of relation," the awareness of the existence of other peoples, cultures, and languages, even if these safeguard their "right to opacity" and are not understood. He writes that multilingualism has become a "mode of the imaginary" (*Traité* 26), such that this new way of imagining the world necessarily includes an awareness of distinct cultures and languages.

For Glissant, the role of the flash agents in globalization reflects some of the wider problems he sees with modern technologies: their ability to essentialize objects and cultures by reducing them to spurts of information and then dividing them by creating an insuperable gap between the producers and consumers of these flashing images and sound bites. As a result of their mass production and their desire to shock and dazzle, flash agents have ceased to produce a communicative effect, because all they spread is radiance rather than real information; the receptors (people) have grown accustomed to and bored by them, their radiance dulled. Glissant emphasizes the brevity of communication through technological agents. These agents produce effects that obscure reality, by reducing it to a short sound bite or flash of light (*Poetics of Relation* 176; see also xiii). Talking and writing become one and the same, since all speech is reduced to short segments that form part of an endless chatter.

In this constant flux created by the flash agents, there is a massive dissemination of commonplaces (*lieux-communs*): the clichés, sound bites, and phrases that are often heard over and over again, ad infinitum, eventually losing all meaning. "Indeed," Glissant writes, "what we have is a sequence of moments of inebriation whose sense no fashion could fathom. Commonplaces are rambling, ephemeral particles within communication, this cold nodule; all the ideas are in the air, but it is the public manifestation of these (pushed, whenever possible, to the limit or simplified) that counts" (*Poetics of Relation* 176). Seanna Sumalee Oakley has argued: "Glissant speculates that traditionally, *lieux communs*, 'commonplaces,' arose from the migration of peoples, trade, or imperial expansion. The hyphen in *lieux-communs*, 'common-places,' indicates the 'spectacular' and near-instantaneity of their transport through info-technological channels in the now commercial forms of trends, fashions, and other consumer-oriented ephemera" (20). Although it presents an interesting interpretation of Glissant's notion of commonplaces, Oakley's analysis ultimately falls short because of her assumption that

Glissant views technology, and thus the commonplaces it produces, in an entirely negative light. On the contrary, Glissant believes that this process has both positive and negative repercussions. On the one hand, it leads to what he calls the "the presumed barbaric nation of fashion"; it forms part of the standardization, lack of uniqueness and individuality that he views as so detrimental (and equates with globalization). Yet, on the other hand, it bears the profound impact of the back-and-forth movement of the Relation (*Poetics of Relation* 175).

The so-called First World nations ("roughly, the industrialized countries") own most of the flash agents, which makes them the "generators" of commonplaces who impose them on the Third World nations ("roughly, the countries existing in absolute poverty"), who are the passive "receptors" (*Poetics of Relation* 176). Alternately, Glissant calls these two groups "cultures of intervention" and "surfacing cultures," respectively: "cultures of intervention" are the powerful First World nations that are capable of directing the course of global events, while "surfacing cultures" are the Third World societies that are currently trying to enter into the global community. Glissant likewise describes this gap as one between the "producing" and "recipient" countries. In other words, since Third World societies are not actively producing flash agents, they remain completely silent, passively receiving the flashes and sounds, unable to participate in their creation; they are consumers rather than creators, to use the terminology of Paulo Freire, appropriated by Césaire in his essay "L'homme de culture et ses responsabilités."[16] Glissant believes that the creation of a profound gap between the First World "generators" and Third World "receptors" is necessary for the very existence of these agents, which continually strive to maintain their state of dominance.

Glissant argues that the flash agents work actively to maintain the stark divide between cultures, the separation between the colonizer and the formerly colonized (*Poetics of Relation* 179). Since in many instances, such as that of France and Martinique, the receptors are the former colonies of the generators, the massive dissemination of commonplaces via the flash agents reinforces previous colonial power structures. In a process of "historical precipitousness," the wealthier, producing nations have become more and more focused on increasing the speed and production of these flash agents, causing them to become exhausted and no longer able to create anything, while the poorer "recipient nations" feel excluded and fantasize about taking ownership of these agents (175). This in turn widens the gap between rich and poor countries: "The latter are kept in a state of sluggish, passive receptivity in which fantasies of spectacular development and overwhelming consumption remain fantasies" (175).

Although Glissant is highly critical of the flash agents and finds their effects destructive, he warns against idealizing the recipient or Third World cultures that do not possess these agents. He emphasizes that these cultures, such as Martinique, are still active in the Relation as "active relays" (*relais actifs*)—meaning that they create contact with others and work as intermediaries—even if they believe themselves to be separate (*dans un écart*) from the constant flux (176–77). According to Glissant, all peoples and cultures have become part of this global circulation of ideas and commonplaces established by the flash agents and relay agents, whether or not they are aware of it and/or accept it. The very existence of a culture causes it to become present to another in the contemporary flow and movement of the *tout-monde*. Moreover, Glissant finds it would be naïve to suggest that the Third World cultures that do not control the flash agents are somehow advantaged by having more deeply ingrained values (173); Glissant believes that these cultures are more or less powerless in the encounter with the flash agents. He writes that although many respond by creating an "ethnotechnology" (science of technology as part of a "primitive" culture) that glorifies local traditions, this does nothing more than produce neutral, powerless agents that will be worn out in the "dazzling diffraction of the flash agents" (179).

TECHNOLOGY AND LITERATURE

In light of the theories about the role of technologies in globalization that we have examined thus far, what is the relationship between these technologies and the production of literature for Glissant—his notion of a modern, partly technological "poetics of relation"? In "Révéler les invariants de la Relation mondiale" (Revealing the invariables of the global relation), a 2008 interview with Alexandre Lepin, Glissant explores the relationship between literary production and modern technologies. He writes that whereas in the past, Western literature might have focused on a literary approach to the world, now the investigation of the world and reality often takes a technological form, and focuses on the search for profit (Glissant and Lepin, *Les entretiens* 100). Glissant addresses the ubiquitous, highly relevant question circulating today: What is the utility of literature in an increasingly technological world?

In this sense, his analysis very much echoes that of Heidegger in "The Question Concerning Technology," who declares that the greatest danger facing humanity with regard to the proliferation of modern technologies is the mode of "Enframing" that accompanies it, and that he characterizes as a perspective according to which everything (all of reality and the world itself) is viewed in terms of potential use value, and as "standing-reserve."[17] Like Heidegger—of whom he was an avid reader[18]—Glissant views literature, even that which is disseminated by technological means, as a powerful means of responding to this nefarious worldview provoked by modern technologies.

For Glissant, it is precisely literature's ability to provoke contact between cultures—the *mise en relation* that he so favorably describes—that allows it not only to maintain its revolutionary potential but possibly to magnify it. In fact, Glissant views literature itself as a *mise en relation* and believes that the Internet's transformation of different modes of cultural contact is greatly expanding literature's revolutionary potential. As a result of this increased contact between cultures, literature has taken on a more global dimension, becoming the very means of expressing "the global Relation" rather than the customs and beliefs of a particular language, culture, or nation ("Révéler les invariants" 100). This is, of course, closely related to the notion of a *littérature-monde,* as articulated in the 2007 manifesto in *Le Monde,* cowritten by many illustrious francophone writers such as Maryse Condé, Césaire, and Dany Laferrière, since this "world-literature in French" (*littérature-monde en français*) constitutes a prime means of expressing the "global Relation" for Glissant.

THE INTERNET AND THE *TOUT-MONDE*

In *Traité du tout-monde* (1997), Glissant approaches issues of globalization, including the role of modern technologies in the "global village." Echoing his assertions in the *Poetics of Relation,* Glissant insists that new technologies, as well as the changes they bring about, are not to be feared (168). For Glissant, these changes take place not only on a global level but within each individual, whose perspective is transformed by an increased awareness of the existence of an entire world of diverse peoples and cultures. In particular, he reflects upon the role of new communications technologies in his notion of the *tout-monde.*

Glissant defines the *tout-monde* as the world considered and experienced as a totality rather than in pieces; he uses the term along with the notions of *totalité-monde, mondialité,* and *chaos-monde,* to denote the semi-chaotic state of globalization for him. The *tout-monde, totalité-monde,* and *chaos-monde,* as words stuck together without articles, are meant to emphasize the awkwardness of what they describe, objects thrown together and constantly in flux; they are best characterized as an awareness of the entirety of the world, including its tremendous breadth and diversity. As Eric Prieto effectively writes: "What is the Tout-monde? It is emphatically not the world itself, in the geospatial or geopolitical sense of the term. It is, in fact, more a mode of cognition than a geographical construct" (115). "But," he continues, "if phenomenologists such as Husserl and Merleau-Ponty tend to think in terms of the relationship between a consciousness and its immediately perceptible environment, Tout-monde emphasizes a more properly global awareness, an intuition of the extent to which distant places and events impinge on my understanding of the immediate environment" (115).

For Glissant, the *tout-monde, totalité-monde,* and the *chaos-monde* find their concrete embodiment[19] in the Internet, which allows us to experience—willingly or unwillingly—the presence of the whole world, by placing people into contact with one another and often collapsing hierarchies by creating a vast, expansive flow of words and images. Glissant presents the Internet as that which plunges us into the *totalité-monde:* "The Internet, which we choose as a symbol and model for the moment, plunges us right into the surge of our *totalité-monde*" (160). He describes it as a constant flux of words and images, like a river that flows and is never the same in one place, or from one moment to the next; a perpetual current, in which we constantly try to anchor ourselves, reaching for some kind of stability. To those who claim the Internet is more of an accumulation, an archive, Glissant counters that it is a wave (160).

Glissant ponders whether it is realistic to believe that anything can be firmly created in its constant flux: "But will we be able to compose poems, to illustrate a Creole language [*langue*], to weave a language [*langage*], in this suspended space?" (167). Evidently he believes that the answer is yes, maintaining his optimistic approach to the Web. It is just a matter of changing expectations in terms of form and content, and ultimately new artistic possibilities will emerge: "The explosion of this diversity, the acceleration of audiovisual and computer technologies have opened up the field to an infinite variety of possible genres" (174).

In the *Traité du tout-monde,* Glissant writes that new communications technologies, especially the Internet, lead to the *mise en relation* and production of rhizomic identities and are thus the embodiment of the *tout-monde.* He believes that, largely as a result of new technologies of communication and transportation, "For the first time, human cultures in their semi-totality are entirely and simultaneously put into contact and into an effervescence of reaction with one another" (23). Not only are peoples "entirely" and "simultaneously" placed into contact, according to Glissant, but they are more *aware* of this contact and exchange: "Also for the first time, people are totally aware of the exchange. Television of all things provokes this kind of relationship" (23). As Prieto notes, "Glissant emphasizes the decisive role of globalization, which has irrevocably marked even the most remote communities, often in damaging, even catastrophic, ways but which has also enabled unprecedented levels of mutually beneficial contact between cultures" (113).

In the *Traité du tout-monde,* Glissant suggests that knowledge in general is in need of these new modes of dissemination in order to thrive. He sees nothing wrong with libraries being replaced by mediathèques, a process that is now happening across the university system: "If visual and computer technologies, as well as technologies of orality, change the material of books, if they even replace books with strange objects which we cannot imagine, if they transform libraries into something other than médiathèques," that's fine with him (159). "The Internet appears to be the instrument of the supremacy of technological societies over all others," Glissant declares; "In this way, it has purely and simply replaced the book" (167). He points to the endless artistic possibilities inspired by the advent of new technologies and creation of the *tout-monde:* "The explosion of this diversity and the acceleration of audiovisual and computer technologies have opened up the field to an infinite variety of possible genres, which we can't even imagine" (122). In fact, rather than a diminishment or downgrading of literature, Glissant views the representation of the *totalité-monde* as the ultimate literary ideal: "an opening of speech to the world-dimension and that the highest object of literature is precisely this world-totality" (182). This idea is, of course, strongly linked to his notion of the *littérature-monde,* a transnational corpus of literature written in French, which includes works by authors not only from France's former colonies but also French-speaking European nations.[20]

Building upon the idea, presented in the *Traité du tout-monde,* that communications technologies can build communities, in his *Nouvelle région du monde* (2005) Glissant proposes that technology will lead to the creation of a "new region of the world," which is not anchored in a particular place and is characterized by a constant *mise en relation* of peoples and cultures. In this "new region of the world," akin to the *tout-monde* and the *chaos-monde,* the use of the Internet and communications technologies establishes a system of *mise en relations* between individuals, cultures, peoples, and their environment. Glissant believes that the existence of this "new region of the world"—which appears to resemble cyberspace—has fundamentally transformed literature. Previously, according to Glissant, literary texts were primarily concerned with expressing an absolute truth and mode of being; literature sought to present its own subjectivity, to project a closed whole. Now, as he states in a 1993 interview with Lise Gauvin, literary works are more focused on producing a *mise en relation* between peoples and cultures, communicating a relative point of view to outsiders unfamiliar with it. That is, they strive to bridge gaps between cultures, and to come into contact with other peoples, such that a singular subjectivity is replaced by an intersubjectivity (*L'imaginaire des langues* 44).

GLOBALIZATION / GLOBALITY

In *La Cohée du Lamentin* (The Lamentin hill) (2005), a series of essays that constitute Glissant's most extended reflection on globalization, he explicitly articulates the opposition between globalization (*mondialisation*) and globality (*mondialité*) to which he alludes in earlier essays and interviews, and that forms the crux of his theories about modern technologies. Pointing to the political dimensions of the use of technologies, he states that they can either be the instruments of the globalization that he views as so destructive, or establish the equal exchanges between people that he extols in his notion of globality.

For Glissant, "globalization" refers to everything that is negative about globalization; it represents a hierarchical relationship between cultures, where the West dominates due to its current technological superiority. Glissant considers the greatest danger of technology to lie in its capacity to standardize everything, therefore establishing singular ideas, languages, and universals: "A number of technical inventions are thus motivated or secretly moved by this need to rally the Unique, even if the scientific need is not yet there" (*Traité* 99). He describes globalization as "standardization from the bottom up, the reign of multinational companies, wild ultraliberalism on the world markets" (*Cohée* 15); it is the dominance of the "flash agents" disseminating "commonplaces": "it is the procession of commonplaces repeated by everyone" (*Cohée* 15). Glissant equates globalization with the imposition of certain noninteractive media and technologies, such as French radio and television stations broadcast in Martinique, which force ideologies upon viewers and listeners without receiving any feedback. He also associates it with departmentalization, lack of technological and industrial development, and ecological destruction through the tourist industry.[21]

"Globality," on the other hand, with its form that mimics "diversity" (*diversité*) is characterized by the celebration of differences and preservation of each culture's "right to opacity." It entails the chaotic *mise en relation* of peoples and cultures, where the hierarchies present in globalization are eliminated in the vast, transnational circulation of goods and peoples, and the landscape is respected. While globalization is strictly hierarchical, globality involves exchange on an equal footing. Globality is the global equivalent of "rhizomatic identities" and respects the existence of these, whereas globalization is associated with the "root-identities" Glissant considers so oppressive. Chris Bongie summarizes Glissant's notion of globality as "a process of aesthetic enlightenment in which we learn how to sense what is already right there in front of us: Mondialité, the positive flipside of globalization" (335); he calls it a "poetics of 'solidarity-in-diversity'" (335). Bongie writes that *mondialité* for Glissant is "a way of seeing and living the Tout-Monde" and that to embrace it means "to gain this sense of planetary consciousness, to live what we have newly learned to sense is the pre-condition for social change" (335). Britton, for her part, sees an equivalence between this positive notion of globality and the *tout-monde:* "The 'Tout-monde' thus comes to stand as a kind of shorthand for a 'good' version of globalization: contact which not only preserves diversity but creates new forms of it. Globalization in the negative sense of 'the reign of the multinationals, standardization, the unchecked ultra-liberalism of world markets' cannot be resisted from a purely local standpoint" ("Transnational Languages" 63).

Glissant believes that all technologies, while themselves neutral, can play a role either in the globalization he considers so nefarious or the globality he views as liberating. He warns that the Internet, like most communications technologies, is currently in the hands of the West and can be the instrument of globalization by establishing hierarchies and imposing one language (generally, English). Glissant does indeed worry about groups that have been excluded from global communications networks: "The most hidden privilege of communication technologies is to deny a portion of people today the possibility of communicating" (*Cohée* 168). For him, the widespread use of communications technologies leads necessarily to the creation of a vast territory of "incommunication" (169) (apparently a metaphor for a kind of anti-Web). He writes that it is all too easy to block the sharing of such technologies, between a "North" that has and a "South" that has not (171). Nevertheless, Glissant states the control of these instruments is not destined to be forever in the hands of the "overdeveloped" economies of the Tout-Empire (169).

On the other hand, Glissant believes that the Internet can be used to promote diversity and the positive *mise en relation* of peoples. He states that the means of countering globalization in favor of globality is to support diversity, which can be done through the use of communications technologies. For Glissant, globality is a way of life; he describes it as "this unprecedented adventure which we all have the chance to experience, in a space-time that for the first time, genuinely and rapidly, is conceived of all at once as unique and multiple, and inextricable" (23). He believes that living globality becomes a means of combating globalization; in a call to arms of sorts to his compatriots and readers, he writes: "If you are living *mondialité,* then you are on the brink of truly combatting *mondialisation*" (139).

For Glissant, there are two primary means of resisting the nefarious order of globalization. The first, as he states in his *Traité du tout-monde,* is to avoid falling under the spell of the flash agents: "Moreover, we must not give in to the effects of the audiovisual media and written press" (110). He suggests that each individual, by becoming aware of the oppressive presence and effects of these agents, has the power to ignore them and thus combat them. The second (related) means is to create a shared and diverse cultural imaginary, which actively opposes the standardizing pressures of globalization. As Bongie writes, "The struggle against the terrifying indistinction of a globalized, universal order (the Tout-Empire) is best promoted, Glissant insists, not through principled, armed resistance . . . but in 'an ever more active opposition to the very idea of empire,' and it is in support of this form of opposition that 'the cultural imaginary comes into play'" (336).

A diversity of languages forms a fundamental part of this imaginary for Glissant; he takes an almost ecological perspective toward languages, stating that losing one is like losing a piece of the landscape, such as the savannah (*Traité du tout-monde* 85). Glissant believes that poets will play the primary role in creating this diverse, cultural imaginary, because they are the ones most attuned to the "trembling" of the *tout-monde* and capable of grasping its diversity. The celebration of diversity through literary texts provides the primary means for Glissant of countering the homogenizing forces of globalization and the Tout-Empire.

ECOLOGY

When discussing the effects of the proliferation of modern technologies, Glissant is keen to address questions of ecology, in a conscious parody of the distinction between nature and technology. Environmentalism, like the Internet, represents yet another way that he tries to anchor his ideas about the *tout-monde,* rhizome-identity, and Relation in the concrete political and social reality of contemporary Martinique. Glissant does not believe that technological development and the preservation of the environment are mutually exclusive. On the contrary, he believes that new technologies can play an important role in the creation of ecologically responsible modernization, especially in the case of tourism. According to Glissant, technological transfer under the rubric of globalization generally entails ecological destruction; while technological development in the name of globality can actually lead to the preservation of the landscape.

In *Poetics of Relation,* Glissant approaches the question of ecology, already eminently present in his work from the early days of *La Lézarde* (his 1958 novel that addresses issues of water conservation) from a theoretical standpoint. He begins by establishing an opposition between two contemporary forms of ecology that he views very differently: ecology as "mysticism," and ecology as "politics" (146). The first form, ecology as mysticism, is the notion that the environment is sacred and belongs to its initial inhabitants, a group of "natives" who originally settled the land and thus possess a sacred right to the territory (again, much like Negritude). Since this mysticism privileges indigeneity and purity, it is associated for Glissant with atavistic cultures (which do not mix or "creolize," as composite cultures do), as well as the notion of root-identity, which he views so negatively.

Glissant equates the mode of relating to the environment of ecology as mysticism with "deep ecology," which he describes as the mystification of relations to the land. As Timothy Clark writes: "Glissant sees such romantic notions of community as implicated in discredited forms of nationalism, the notion of a proper, exclusive territory, of *this* land for *this* people"; "He criticises those environmental thinkers who would sacralise the indigenous or the local as a basis of ideas of rootedness" (133). Glissant believes that in the Caribbean, given the extent of migration and flux of peoples and cultures throughout its history, such a notion of ecology is simply untenable.[22] Moreover, Glissant believes that ecology as mysticism impedes progress by preventing the development of a more constructive form of ecological awareness.

The second form, ecology as politics, formulates a critique of ecology as mysticism, especially its notions of sacred territoriality, by emphasizing the inter-relationality and interdependence of all lands and peoples, regardless of origins. As Clark writes, "Glissant endorses another 'ecology,' which would be a politics of relation, questioning ethnic and cultural purism and stressing interdependence and interrelation across the earth" (133). This contemporary form of ecology emphasizes a politics that prioritizes the landscape and is thus a more positive, constructive ideology for Glissant. It also seeks to protect the diversity of peoples and cultures, although not necessarily by claiming their unique right to the land. Unlike mystical ecology, which can lead to an intolerance of foreigners (those not originally from the region), political ecology emphasizes solidarity among lands: "For, far from consenting to sacred intolerance, it is a driving force for the relational interdependence of all lands, of the whole Earth" (*Poetics of Relation* 146).

For Glissant, communications technologies such as the Internet foster the notion of ecology as politics, by emphasizing the connections between not only different peoples but also distant lands. In an essay from the *Poetics of Relation,* Glissant argues for an "aesthetics of the earth" and puts forth an ecological interpretation of his notion of Relation. Relation, for Glissant, is not only a relationship between individuals and cultures but also between peoples and landscapes. He argues in favor of a new politics of ecology, which establishes new connections with the land and allows individuals to enact a *mise en relation* with their environment.

Glissant strongly believes that the globality he favors fosters these forms of contact, while the globalization he denigrates does not. According to Glissant, globalization imposes one form of construction and technology without considering differences in landscape. It results in what Patrick Chamoiseau has termed in *Écrire en pays dominé* (Writing in a dominated land) (1997) the "cementization" (*la bétonisation*) or "cementing over the landscape" of a country, in this case, Martinique. In particular, Glissant attacks the international standardization of consumer products, which destroys local economies, cultures, and ecologies. He believes that the relationship to the land has changed dramatically as a result of new technologies such as agricultural machinery, which lead to the mass production of standardized, artificial goods for an elite few (*Poetics of Relation* 149–50), no doubt a dark side of globalization for Glissant. In the case of globality, however, differences in landscape are considered and valued, leading to a *mise en relation* between peoples and the land; Glissant believes that tourism, especially the new trend of ecological tourism, is still very much possible according to the concept of globality.

Glissant describes how some societies have developed an "ethnotechnics" that valorizes and celebrates traditional techniques and instruments, as a defense mechanism against the massive influx of foreign imports, believing that this will protect them from the excesses (*Poetics of Relation* 152–53). He warns, however, that this ethnotechnics will eventually lead to the return to a pretechnological, artisanal culture, leaving to others the procurement of industrial goods (*Poetics of Relation* 153), thus doing nothing more than establishing a strong dependence on other, more industrial cultures. In order to combat this notion, Glissant believes that the people of the Antilles must find a way to produce objects for exchange that are the result of creative endeavors, not just the cultivation of the land (*Poetics of Relation* 153).

Glissant considers the Internet to be a key tool for developing alternatives to ethnotechnics, as well as fostering the "ecology as politics" that he favors so strongly. An example of this form of ecology can be found in a recent manifesto, the *Manifeste pour les "produits" de haute nécessité* (Manifest for "products" of high necessity) (2009) cowritten with Chamoiseau and proliferated on the Internet.[23] In this essay, Glissant and Chamoiseau propose the creation of an "organic zone" in the French Caribbean, which would produce high-quality organic goods for export. These goods would be sold at a high price with the goal of transforming the Caribbean into a region known for the quality of its organic goods. In another highly publicized manifesto, "Quand les murs tombent: l'identité nationale hors-la-loi?" (When the walls fall down: National identity outside the law?),[24] also cowritten with Chamoiseau, Glissant argues in favor of eliminating the "walls" that impede "relation" and establishing new forms of collective identity existing outside the traditional structure of the nation and fostered through Internet forums. In fact, Glissant has long been very active in his use of the Internet to further his political projects, including founding the website

L'Institut du tout-monde (Institute of the everything-world), which was responsible for the online publication of this manifesto.

Glissant's theoretical writings from the 1990s onward have increasingly addressed questions of technologies, especially the Internet, and their roles in the processes of globalization. Glissant emphasizes the potential role of new communications technologies in providing new forms of poetic inspiration (the "poetics of relation"), increasing the amount of interaction between Caribbean societies and the rest of the world (the *mise en relation*), creating transnational forms of communities and collective imaginaries and defending local causes (such as the protection of Creole language and culture) by projecting them onto a global stage. He celebrates the role of technologies in the creation of a second, more democratic form of orality, which he describes as open and interactive, and that emerges from cultures that naturally embrace oral modes of expression. Nevertheless, he warns of the potentially destructive effects of the communications technologies he calls flash agents. For Glissant, the greatest danger of technology lies in its ability to standardize and create uniformity where there should be diversity. At the same time, he points to the endless possibilities of using technologies to preserve diversity, including recording endangered languages and protecting minor cultures by providing a global platform for their defense.

Ultimately, like Césaire and Fanon before him, Glissant considers modern technologies to be part of a universal patrimony that all peoples should acquire; and he believes that negatively associating these inventions with their European origins constitutes a form of the "nativism" and "atavism" (including the notion of root-identity) that he so vehemently opposes. Although Glissant's notions of the *tout-monde, totalité-monde,* and *chaos-monde* have been critiqued by scholars, most notably Peter Hallward in *Absolutely Postcolonial,* as being essentially apolitical, this perspective needs to be reassessed. The relationship between Glissant's various concepts for globalization and the coherent theory about technology transfer and ecology as politics that he articulates in his later texts demonstrates a high level of engagement with contemporary social, cultural, and economic issues, including the desire to halt "cementization" and safeguard a sustainable natural environment.

CHAPTER SEVEN

Urban Space and Cyberspace in Patrick Chamoiseau

Aimé Césaire, while a representative in the French National Assembly, drafted in 1946 the legislation that would turn Martinique, Guadeloupe, and French Guyana into departments of France. He supported departmentalization because he viewed it as a means of promoting development and technological progress in Martinique, while offering protection from U.S. hegemony, the dangers of which were evidenced by the numerous occupations of Haiti. Césaire believed that departmentalization would be temporary, one step in the process toward independence, although it eventually proved to be much more permanent than he had ever imagined (as he acknowledged at the end of his life). This chapter examines technological progress and development in Martinique post-departmentalization from the perspective of Patrick Chamoiseau.

Throughout his entire literary career, from the 1980s to the present, Chamoiseau has considered questions of modernization and technology transfer in the Caribbean in his writings. Although many of his novels highlight the negative elements that accompany development—such as the cementing over of the landscape—he is also optimistic about the potential of communications technologies to preserve oral cultures and establish new, democratic forms of community. As stated in his novels and interviews, he is not against these forces per se but rather the way in which they have been imposed in a top-down manner through departmentalization. His most recent works have also emphasized the ecological concerns associated with globalization and the rise of the tourist industry in the Caribbean.

Chamoiseau's novels and essays focusing on questions of technology can be divided chronologically into two stages. The first extends from the mid-1980s to early 1990s and includes some of his earliest novels, *Chronicle of the Seven Sorrows* (1986), *Solibo Magnificent* (1988), and *Texaco* (1992), which explore issues of modernization and development. These novels present a scathing critique of departmentalization, which is portrayed as a destructive force that flattens the landscape and eliminates local traditions. The second stage begins in the late 1990s with *Écrire en pays dominé* (Writing in a dominated country) (1997) and continues with *Biblique des derniers gestes* (Bible of the last acts) (2002); it is characterized by a focus on questions surrounding globalization and communications technologies, especially the Internet, as well as the emergence of an ecological sensibility.

FIRST STAGE

Chamoiseau's early novels *Chronicle of the Seven Sorrows* (1986), *Solibo Magnificent* (1988), and *Texaco* (1992) present a critique of neocolonial influences in Martinique by focusing on how departmentalization has changed the urban environment of Fort-de-France, transforming neighborhoods flourishing with Creole culture into vast cement wastelands. Following the law of 1946, the country began to change rapidly, with substantial construction and the mass importation of French goods. Chamoiseau calls this process the "cementization" (*bétonisation*) of Martinique, a neologism he invents from the French word for cement (*béton*).

Chronicle of the Seven Sorrows traces Martinique's transition "from an economy based on the local Creole market in the early twentieth century to its brutal entry into the world of modernity, consumerism and global capital in the aftermath of World War II" (McCusker 21). The novel concentrates on a marketplace in Fort-de-France, telling the story of the "djobbers" (a term derived from the English term "odd job"), especially Pipi Sun (Pipi Soleil) known as the "king of the wheelbarrow." These laborers scramble to make a living day to day by meeting the changing needs of the vendors.

The *Chronicle* is divided into two parts, marking the before and after of departmentalization. The title of the first part, "Inspiration," suggests the breath of life, while that of the second, "Expiration," implies a slow exhalation leading to death. The changes brought about following the 1946 law are described at the beginning of part 2: "Ladies and Gentlemen here present, as time passed, more boats and planes kept coming from France. They brought crates of inexpensive merchandise, exotic apples and grapes that capsized our hearts, unfamiliar produce in cans, in vacuum pouches, or wrapped in cellophane. . . . Soon they were covering the country with self-service grocery stores, supermarkets, and mega-markets that made ours look pretty sad" (97). In one scene, a group of local politicians, including Fort-de-France mayor Césaire, visit Pipi's garden and offer financing to "industrialize" his "gardening techniques" (144). This consists mainly of applying a toxic pesticide that is environmentally noxious. The visit represents the French administration's desire to regulate and control the island's natural horticulture. In the *Chronicle,* the chaotic disorder of the marketplace and Pipi's vegetable garden is presented in stark contrast to the rationality and regimentation of the French administration.

Similarly, departmentalization replaces a dynamic, diverse part of Creole culture—the marketplace and its "djobbers"—with supermarkets and departments stores in which there is no dialogue, bartering, or exchange. These stores, as emphasized in their names (Prisunic and Monoprix), present just one price, take it or leave it, and sell goods shipped from abroad (rather than the surrounding Caribbean) at low prices meant to drive local vendors out of business and establish a monopoly. This represents a move from diversity to uniformity, as the abundant variety of the marketplace and Creole culture is replaced by standardized stores. By the end of the novel, the colorful characters of the first part have all but disappeared, which is ironic because the appendix includes an article stating that millions of euros will be spent to reconstruct the marketplace as it was before, primarily to turn it into a tourist attraction. A note below this newspaper clipping suggests that such a reconstruction is not even possible because the vibrant characters and life have already disappeared. Overall, the *Chronicle* suggests that the economic and political forces of departmentalization (equated with modernization) have produced a form of neocolonialism that stifles local Creole culture.

Like the *Chronicle, Solibo Magnificent* takes place in the urban setting of Fort-de-France, this time not in the marketplace but rather in the "Savane" plaza, where the storyteller Solibo has just died. This work takes the form of a detective novel and is characterized by an innovative oral style in which the Creole language infuses the French writing.

Whereas the *Chronicle* stages the conflict between the predepartmentalization marketplace and postdepartmentalization supermarket, *Solibo Magnificent* (like Chamoiseau's subsequent novel, *Texaco*) presents the confrontation of two discourses: the oral traditions of Creole culture and the technological, scientific approach of the French investigators. Solibo, a legendary storyteller, utters the words "Patat'sa" and suddenly dies in the middle of a performance, right in front of countless witnesses. By all indications, he choked on his own words. The autopsy confirms death via asphyxiation, although the discourse of modern Western medicine is unable to provide an adequate explanation. Just as the scientific perspective cannot explain Solibo's death, many of the witnesses—including the "djobbers" and the author himself, called "bird of Cham" (*oiseau de Cham*)—are described in the police report as being unemployed, emphasizing the extent to which their valuable labor is invisible to the rational, scientific eye. This novel laments the decline of Creole culture as a result of the rise of a technological worldview akin to the one described by Heidegger.

The third work from this first stage is perhaps his most celebrated: *Texaco* (1992), winner of the prestigious Goncourt Prize. This novel recounts the story of a shantytown on the outskirts of Fort-de-France called "Texaco" by its residents due to the large oil tanks nearby. In this text, the "bird of Cham" authorial figure (who appears in much of Chamoiseau's work) relates the oral narrative of Marie-Sophie Laborieux, founder and first inhabitant of the shantytown. As the "Word Scratcher" states in the first sentence of the novel, a highway aptly named "Penetrating West" has already reached the edge of the neighborhood, connecting it to the city center; this makes the residents nervous, since they worry that their houses will be bulldozed in order to extend it. The novel opens with the arrival of an employee of the urban services bureau who has been sent to "rationalize" and "sanitize" the town. This character represents the forces of departmentalization, which are attempting to eliminate Creole culture in favor of progress and development. Someone throws a stone at him, and the residents ironically call him "the Christ," since he is presumably the savior sent by the "City" and the metropole to "save" them; he is like a missionary spreading the ideology of modernization.

Speaking in the first-person singular, Marie-Sophie tells the urban planner the story of three generations of her family, especially her father, Esternome, as a means of conveying the rich cultural history of the neighborhood, which represents the experience of black Antilleans during the last two centuries. The planner's shifting reactions to Marie-Sophie's narrative—which are conveyed through the "Urban Planner's Notes to the Word Scratcher" interspersed throughout the text—show that although he was intent on bulldozing the homes to extend the highway, he ultimately decides to preserve the neighborhood, which he comes to see as a sort of "urban mangrove" of Creole culture.

Richard Watts argues that the characters of Marie-Sophie's narrative "and their dwellings constitute living counterpoints to the deadening impulses of industrial modernity and reclaim a connection to the natural environment that urbanization had severed" ("Chamoiseau's Birds" 183). Celia Britton writes about the city of Fort-de-France in *Texaco:* "By the 1980s, the town is characterized by its soulless, inflexible, geometrical order and its dedication to a process of modernization, inspired by Europe and North America, that threatens to destroy the countryside around it" (*Sense of Community* 96). Similarly, Michael Dash declares that in Chamoiseau's portrayal of the City (*en-ville*), "the binary pattern is clear: the destructive spirit of modernization at the center is confronted by the organic, rooted (however precariously) community at the outskirts" (237–38). Watts writes that in each of these early novels, "the 'urban' is suffused with the 'rural,' and unruly Creole—or simply African—identified 'nature' disrupts the workings of the paved, rectilinear 'culture' of the city that is linked to the legacies of French colonialism" ("Chamoiseau's Birds" 182). This is clearly the case in the *Chronicle,* in which the administration of the DOM (*départements d'outre-mer*) seeks to tame and regulate both Pipi's garden and the marketplace; in *Solibo Magnificent,* in which the Creole oraliture is at odds with the scientific and medical discourses of the detectives; and in *Texaco,* in which the urban planner seeks to "sanitize" and "regularize" the shantytown by paving over it with concrete.

These early novels exhibit a negative view of departmentalization-led modernization, which is referred to as "cementization." In the *Chronicle,* Chamoiseau addresses the technologies of agricultural production and transportation that flood supermarkets with fruits and vegetables grown in France instead of fresher, more local varieties. In *Solibo Magnificent,* he illustrates how the technologies of construction, agricultural production, and communications that have come to the island after the implementation of the 1946 law have been accompanied by a scientific worldview that fails to represent Creole culture. And *Texaco* satirizes the notion of a "civilizing mission" bringing progress to the shantytown, since the construction projects will do nothing but destroy it. In these early novels, the relationship between the center (metropolitan France, Paris) and the periphery (the *départements d'outre-mer*, or DOM) is one of hierarchical imposition, characteristic of what Glissant calls globalization in opposition to the more relational globality. Overall, they exhibit a highly critical stance toward technology transfer, one that Chamoiseau will temper in his later writings.

This view of technology and modernization in turn corresponds to Chamoiseau's early perspective on writing and the role of the author in the preservation of local cultures. In each of these novels, writing provides a means of preserving what the forces of progress destroy: the culture of the "djobbers" and the marketplace; the rich *oraliture* of storytellers such as Solibo; the history of the Texaco neighborhood and the experience of the black diaspora. The emblematic figure of this first stage is the "Word Scratcher," who takes down onto the page the oral traditions of Creole culture. The author identifies himself as such a figure: someone who preserves the oral narratives of storytellers such as Solibo and Marie-Sophie. This figure is virtually nonexistent to the technological, scientific worldview of the detectives in Solibo, since the author is described as being unemployed (*sans profession*); nevertheless, he represents the key to liberating the imaginary. The second stage of Chamoiseau's writings, to be examined in the next section, demonstrates how new technologies can assist the Word Scratcher in his efforts to record oral languages and traditions.

SECOND STAGE

From the late 1990s to the present, the focus of Chamoiseau's work shifts from an emphasis on local Creole cultures to an analysis of the processes of globalization, including the rise of communications technologies, the emergence of vast networks, and ecological destruction through the tourist industry. This second stage in Chamoiseau's treatment of technology begins with the semi-autobiographical *Écrire en pays dominé* (Writing in a dominated land) (1997) and continues with the lengthy novel *Biblique des derniers gestes* (2002) (Bible of the last acts). The emblematic figure of this stage is the "Warrior of the Imaginary" (*guerrier de l'imaginaire*)—also called the "Old Warrior" (*vieux guerrier*)—who first emerges in *Écrire en pays dominé* and is then more fully developed as the protagonist/narrator of *Biblique des derniers gestes*.

The semi-autobiographical *Écrire en pays dominé* intersperses Chamoiseau's nostalgic ruminations about his library (which he calls a *senti-*

menthèque due to the books' ability to stir up memories and feelings), his tirades against departmentalization, reflections on Césaire (who appears in one form or another in almost all his works), and analysis of the Internet and globalization. The text includes long passages printed in a smaller font spoken by the Warrior of the Imaginary, whose relationship to the author is somewhat unclear: at times, he appears to be Chamoiseau's spokesperson; at others, an extreme rebellious figure intended to provoke more than analyze.[1]

Écrire en pays dominé opens by pondering the question of how to write when the imaginary has been overtaken. The first part, "Anagogie" (a nostalgic and sentimental reflection on books) delineates a theory about the different forms of domination: brutal, silent, and furtive. According to Chamoiseau, the "brutal domination" of the colonial period has ended, but new forms have emerged: these are the "silent" and "furtive" dominations, which involve brainwashing and thought control rather than physical violence. For Chamoiseau, these forms are in many ways more difficult to fight because they are invisible and often permeate thinking without leaving any trace of their presence. *Écrire en pays dominé* stages the author's attempts to liberate himself from the "silent" and "furtive" forms of domination by narrating his stream of consciousness as he struggles to find a mode of writing that is free from mind control, often through dialogue with the Warrior of the Imaginary.

Chamoiseau believes that departmentalization, assimilation, and the media all play crucial roles in sustaining this system of domination, namely the colonization of the imaginary of Martinicans (18). In the era of postdepartmentalization, a soundscape of television and radio now blankets the island, speaking of things that have little relevance to the people of Martinique. For Chamoiseau, the prime example of this is weather forecasts, which refer to four seasons when in the Caribbean there are only two; a Parisian meteorologist talks about how much it's snowing in the French Alps, while in Fort-de-France it's hot and humid.[2] The absurdity of Martinique being a department of France is manifested by this disconnect from the reality of life on the island; television and other European media impose a strictly hierarchical discourse in which there is no interaction or exchange with Martinicans.

Chamoiseau believes that all communications technologies can be used either to impose a discourse or produce dialogue and exchange. Wendy Knepper notes that "Chamoiseau expresses an ambivalent view of technology: for at the same time that technology enables the sharing of local knowledge, it also functions as a diffuse system of domination" (180). This is especially true of the Internet, as the medium that encompasses all others within it. On the one hand, it appears to encourage a more interactive form of communication; on the other, as Watts observes, "for the Old Warrior, one can still be subject to domination within the ostensibly decentered space that is the Internet" ("Wounds of Locality" 119). In this sense, Chamoiseau echoes Glissant's distinction between globalization and globality, since the Internet can promote either one of these phenomena.

In interviews, Chamoiseau has expressed a markedly ambivalent view of globalization/globality:

> I see globalization as the emergence of a *totalité-monde* that will penetrate all the world's languages, cultures, and conditions. Of course capitalists can profit from globalization. But globalization affords us opportunities, too. It gives us more freedom, both individually and culturally. It's easier to be Antillean or Breton or black in a world that is linked up than it was in the old shackles of the nation-states. There is no reason to abandon this vast electronic network which now hangs over the world to the dominating powers. If we do so, then we'll all be subject to homogenization. (Lucien Taylor, "Créolité Bites" 137, qtd. in Gyssels)

In other words, capitalism may take advantage of globalization for profitable ventures, but that does not preclude minority cultures from using electronic networks (for instance, social media) to establish contact with others. In fact, Chamoiseau appears to believe that those who ignore the existence of such networks make themselves particularly susceptible to homogenization.

Chamoiseau further asserts that the nefarious forces of globalization can be countered through reading and writing, which he describes as a "cry" that "opposes those radios, those televisions, those publicity campaigns, that so-called 'news,' that monologue of fascinating Western images" (18–19). In particular, reading and writing—whether in books or online—constitute practices that transform the imaginary and thus combat the silent and furtive dominations. And cyberspace provides a potential place of resistance, due to its association not only with reading and writing but also with orality and the organic. More precisely, Chamoiseau recognizes the Internet's potential for recording and therefore saving oral traditions, which are so valued by him in his earlier works. In *Écrire en pays dominé*, Chamoiseau writes: "The oral, oraliture are there, in the world and within me, and their spirit finds unexpected awakenings in new media" (179). Helmtrud Rumpf argues that Chamoiseau's "media-based orality" reestablishes the proximity of the storyteller with his or her audience: "Whereas the orality of societies with an oral culture requires proximity, as the storyteller and his listeners are in direct contact and share the same space and cultural values, writing puts distance between the author and his readers, who may live in very different cultural spaces. The evolution of new communications technology, however, restores proximity, which is then no longer physical but virtual" (270). Interestingly, it appears that for Chamoiseau, a visual connection is not necessary for significant virtual communication.

Chamoiseau explores the relationship between the Internet and traditional oral cultures primarily through the figure of the Old Warrior, a rebel who has fought in countless revolutions and whose purpose now is to fight against standardization in the hyper/cyberspace, thus allowing it to become the privileged space of orality. As the narrator of *Biblique,* the Old Warrior is the "Word Scratcher" set free, presenting an endless series of stories over more than eight hundred pages; like a cyberhacker, the Old Warrior, "to be sure of saying everything, begins by saying nothing" (*Écrire* 23). Chamoiseau's mysterious figure declares: "Oral traditions can find a surprising support in cyberspace. Imagine the griots [African storytellers] or creole storytellers, those forgotten, dominated, crushed languages, those imaginaries from the margins that can now circulate there, that could make their sounds heard on the other side of the world" (*Écrire* 281). Much as Sembène believed that film could create new narrative genres for the griot, Chamoiseau envisions cyberspace as a refuge for endangered stories, languages, and imaginaries.

Chamoiseau envisions the malleable and interactive nature of cyberspace as productive of orality. Both *Écrire en pays dominé* and *Biblique* are presented in a written format and narrative mode that seek to reproduce for the reader the experience of browsing the Web. *Écrire en pays dominé* offers a blog-like style of writing, and at times the page almost appears to be a computer screen with running lines of text. *Biblique* presents a wide variety of fonts that give the impression of a compilation of different texts and genres, thereby opening up the space in which the Old Warrior must lead his struggle for revolution. This is the domain of the "imaginary," the cyberspace that Chamoiseau feels must be possessed by orality in order to escape the dangers of a furtive domination by hegemonic powers in Europe and the United States.

In one key passage of *Écrire en pays dominé,* Chamoiseau highlights the new mode of reading in the digital era: "Read and reread," "read-without-reading," "read-by-skipping-over-pages" (33). He describes this innovative reading—which is likewise a new form of writing—as a kind of wandering of words and phrases and encourages the reader to imitate the movement by wandering him or herself around the book, much as one might do on the Web: "begin to wander yourself, gather your phrases" (23). Chamoiseau describes the written page, in a paperback book, as a Web page being downloaded before the reader (23). Furthermore, the structure of the narrative is marked by constant digressions, with each one appearing almost as a highlighted link that the reader has clicked on, leading the story in another direction. The wide variety of speakers also evokes the online "wiki" format, where authorship is shared, fluid, or undetermined. Reading and writing have thus become less solitary endeavors, given the awareness of a broader audience simultaneously consuming the text: "Writing today represents an end to solitude, and—if it agrees to it, if it is open to it—an erosion of its pride" (179).

Whereas Glissant often portrays cyberspace as a free-flowing territory of *mise en relation,* for Chamoiseau it is a battleground, one in which the Warrior of the Imaginary must fight against the forms of furtive and silent domination. This is reflected in the layout of the book, in which the Old Warrior's words are printed in a smaller font in rectangular passages interspersed throughout, like boxes of text flashing onto the screen as he hacks into the space of the narrative, inserting his thoughts into the narration. His discourse is one of excess, as if he is trying to overwhelm cyberspace and thus take over the imaginary. His extensive lists create a snowball effect, an uncontrolled accumulation of technologies piling up against each other to create a new "Electro-world": "The screens, the cables, the satellites, the telephones, the modems, the interactive faxes, the Minitels, the information highways, the fiber optics, totalitarian multimedia . . . : this old world which I had never really imagined as a whole materialized in the net of an Electro-world" (*Écrire* 216). For Chamoiseau, Glissant's *mise en relation* between peoples is not a given but must be attained by fighting for it in the domain of the imaginary.

Despite the physicality of media in the "Electro-world," Chamoiseau believes that the Internet leads to the "dematerialization" of knowledge, which enters into flux and comes to exist only in the imaginary domain of cyberspace. By linking oral traditions to cyberspace, the people of

Martinique will all become "warriors of the imaginary," just like the Old Warrior. In an image striking for its colonial implications, Chamoiseau sees cyberspace as a territory that must be occupied by the inhabitants of the developing regions of the world, to empower them through control over the global imaginary. This will be accomplished by using the information age to revive the dormant texts of many cultures, that is, to preserve and bring to light forgotten arts and knowledge (*Écrire* 30). In *Écrire en pays dominé* he describes experiencing the pleasure of a great book that awakens (29).[3]

CRITIQUE OF GLISSANT

Throughout *Écrire en pays dominé,* Chamoiseau presents a subtle critique of Glissant's theories of globalization. According to Watts, Chamoiseau differs from Glissant in that he "refuses to see globalization as an unproblematic means for escaping the oppressive center/periphery relationship, for it too can be a vehicle for domination" ("Wounds of Locality" 120). Through a tongue-in-check parody of his concepts and writing style, Chamoiseau asserts that Glissant's notions of Relation and rhizome are much less egalitarian and more hierarchical than he suggests.

In the first part of *Écrire en pays dominé,* Chamoiseau calls the system of social welfare established through departmentalization a "putting under welfares and subsidies" (*une mise sous assistances et subventions*) (18), a phrase whose structure parallels that of Glissant's concept of the *mise en relation.* Through this turn of phrase, Chamoiseau illustrates how this silent domination functions: Martinicans are subjugated through the generous French welfare system that keeps them in their place and prevents them for rebelling (or at least voting for independence in referendums), a process that is masked by calling it a *mise en relation.*

Chamoiseau's critique of Glissant often consists of reconceptualizing his terms and theories through the addition of localized components.[4] This is best illustrated through the notion of the "Stone-World" (*Pierre-monde*), which is Chamoiseau's equivalent of the *tout-monde* or *chaos-monde.* Rather than evoking free-floating movement and large, undefined space, the "stone" of the title denotes a concrete object, as a way of anchoring the noun in a particular place. It also suggests the processes of creolization, which Chamoiseau likens to the alchemic transformation of base metals into a composite through the Philosopher's Stone. For Chamoiseau, this is precisely the process involved in globality: local elements are brought into contact with each other and transformed to produce new ideas and identities. This image also emphasizes the potential role of the marvelous—depicted in many of Chamoiseau's novels—as a means of countering the forces of globalization.

In the second part of *Écrire en pays dominé,* "Anabase," Chamoiseau parodies Glissant's style of writing with hyphenated nouns. Whereas Glissant's *tout-monde* and *chaos-monde* imply abstract concepts, Chamoiseau's *Moi-colons, Moi-Amérindiens, Moi-Africains,* and so on convey the particular components of Antillean identities. This is meant to assert what Watts (following Chamoiseau) has called "the wounds of locality," that is, the necessity of grounding cultural identities in a particular place and the difficulties faced by those who do so ("Wounds of Locality" 112–13).

In the third part of *Écrire en pays dominé,* "Anabiose," which constitutes his most explicit statement on technology, Chamoiseau describes the "blaze" (*flambée*) of communications, recalling Glissant's notion of flash agents: "In the blaze of communications, the 'putting-under-relations' [*mises-sous-relations*] have attained a globality, a systematicity and a flash-speed" (216). Just as Glissant describes the accelerated speed and shock value of flash agents, Chamoiseau writes of the "flash-speed" of the "spark" of communications. But the reference to Glissant in this passage alters his terminology slightly to perform a subtle critique of his notion of Relation: whereas Glissant talks about the "putting *into* relation" (*mise en relation*) of cultures through technologies (as discussed in chapter 6), Chamoiseau speaks of the "putting-*under*-relation" (*mises*-sous-*relations*) (my emphasis). Chamoiseau's use of the preposition "under" underscores how the forces of globalization can exert an oppressive control over a society like Martinique, stomping it "under" its boot, so to speak. For Chamoiseau, "the putting-under-relations [*mises-sous-relations*] is vertical" (285) in contrast to the more horizontal "putting-into-relation" (*mise en relation*). While Glissant's concept denotes a nonhierarchical form of exchange, Chamoiseau's equivalent emphasizes the imposition of communications technologies in a top-down manner, such that the receivers (as in the case of Glissant's receptors of flash agents) become the blind consumers of hegemonic transmissions.

In order to enact a true *mise en relation,* the silent and furtive forms of domination must be brought into the open, where they are no longer invisible. Once this has occurred, subjects become aware of their functioning, thus allowing for resistance in the domain of the imaginary: "Open resistance is not imaginable except in full conscience of the clockwork of the silent or furtive domination. Exposing them, like seeds in the sun, is the founding act of the *mise-en-relations*" (*Écrire* 285). Chamoiseau believes that global networks can provide the opportunity to produce *mise en relations* by raising consciousness about the processes involved in the "silent" and "furtive" dominations: "By becoming aware of these processes, by mastering these machines, we can make out from this flow the principles of a true relation, rich with differences and unlimited exchanges, and far from dominations" (*Écrire* 292–93). This cannot be done by acquiring financial power but by mastering the imaginary, and through writing and artistic creation more generally (*Écrire* 293).

Like the Relation, "for Chamoiseau, the rhizome is a neutral concept, capable of being experienced in both negative and positive ways," and "at the local level as a mode of domination" (Knepper 180). The Old Warrior reconceptualizes Glissant's notion of the rhizome as a gigantic network of meganetworks that takes over the world: "The circuits of communications joined together into networks, the networks into mega-networks, the mega-networks into a technotronic rhizome that covered the entire earth, and plunged me, at every instant of my life (by a credit card, a cellular phone, a Minitel command, an exploration of the Internet, a parabolic antenna . . .), and from year to year a little more, in the omnipotent fog of a cyberspace" (216). This imperialistic vision is tempered by Chamoiseau's assertion that the rhizome can provide local cultures with "hooks" or points of entry into global society: "The rhizome offers hooks (electronic maps, parabolic antennas, emitters, satellites, cables, Minitels, faxes, visio-faxes, modems, multimedia . . .)" (292). These "hooks" have tremendous subversive potential by allowing individuals to insert themselves into the broader networks of the "Electro-world"—much like the Old Warrior who acts as a cyberhacker—and thus to defend local cultures and counter oppression. Ultimately, Chamoiseau seeks to emphasize that the equal exchange and diversity that characterize the Relation and rhizome for Glissant are not a given, but must be fought for, according to the example of the Warrior of the Imaginary.

ECOLOGY

More than any other author in this study, Chamoiseau expresses grave concerns about the ecological consequences of massive technology transfer, modernization, and development. Chamoiseau is an influential "green" activist on an island in which ecological issues are closely tied to independence movements, and his environmentalism correlates closely with his politics.[5] Several scholars, notably Renée Gosson,[6] Heidi Bojsen,[7] and Watts[8] have explored the representation of the tropical landscape and natural world in his fiction, including his use of the orchid instead of the rhizome as a metaphor for cultural identity.[9] Although the question of environmentalism in francophone Caribbean literature is a vast topic outside the scope of this book, I will offer a brief analysis of how technology relates to ecology in Chamoiseau's corpus.

The relationship between technology and ecology for Chamoiseau is inextricably linked to his distinction between territory and place. Territory is composed of a center and peripheries; it implies an act of colonization—the marking of territory—and implies a power dynamic of dominance. To conceive of the DOMs (*départements d'outre-mer*) as "territories" is to consider them modern-day colonies of France. Place (*Lieu*), on the other hand, lives in a network; it is not fixed in a relationship of domination but remains mobile while attached to a locality. If territory is the domain of the *mise sous relation* for Chamoiseau, place is that of the *mise en relation*. When nations utilize technology to mark and maintain "territories," the result is environmental devastation; when technology is used to establish "places," it becomes an instrument for preservation and liberation.

In Chamoiseau's work, the representation of innovations is often a means of illustrating these very different functions of technology in the creation of territories and places, respectively. The arrival of planes and ships at the beginning of the second section of the *Chronicle* reflects the new post-1946 economy: trade laws promote the import of fruits and vegetables (among other things) from France by making inter-Caribbean commerce prohibitively expensive, thereby causing an unnecessary transportation of goods across oceans that burns massive quantities of fossil fuel. This arrival is presented as nothing less than an invasion, a second act of colonization that marks the island as a territory and will ultimately lead to the destruction of its landscape. The arrival of tourists from France is likewise portrayed as a sort of occupation, as inexpensive flights and vacation deals encourage metropolitans to travel to Martinique, and entrepreneurs build resorts and take over communal beaches. Important elements of Creole culture—such as the marketplace depicted in the *Chronicle*—become picturesque images for tourist consumption, a temporary stop on a guided tour of Fort-de-France.

In addition, Chamoiseau is highly critical of the way in which departmentalization leads to the imposition of urban planning models that are more appropriate for a European city and do not take into account the specific qualities of the Caribbean landscape (such as its tropical climate, Creole culture, native vegetation, etc.). This is the case, for instance, when the administration of Fort-de-France proposes to build a highway through the Texaco neighborhood, failing to see it as an "urban mangrove" full of life. Chamoiseau's use of this term is highly significant, since it illustrates his conception of the landscape that should be preserved: not necessarily the native vegetation and geography of the island but the rich bastions of Creole culture that combine urban and rural, traditional and modern elements.

Technology can also play a role in the creation of *places* for Chamoiseau. Places exist within networks and can be linked via cyberspace; they are the "hooks" that he describes in relation to the rhizome. They also exist within the geography of the Caribbean, including not only the natural habitats of fauna and flora but also the Creole neighborhoods of Fort-de-France. Chamoiseau's Internet manifesto, "Manifest for 'Products' of High Necessity" (coauthored with Glissant, among others), proposes a means of organizing Martinicans by advocating the creation of an organic zone in the French Caribbean known for the export of high-quality goods. The island will thus be preserved as a natural, eco-friendly environment, free from contamination, which will allow the crops grown there to be of the finest quality and command the maximum price in the global market. Chamoiseau believes that cyberspace, with its organic orality, provides a means of bringing Martinicans together to achieve lofty goals, including the protection of the landscape and production of such high-quality goods.

For Chamoiseau, as evidenced in his work from the early 1980s to the present, the way to fight the negative impact of modernization and globalization—which lead to uniformity and standardization—is to assert diversity through the preservation of local, oral cultures, as well as taking control of the imaginary through writing (not only in books, but cyberspace). Paradoxically, technologies—whether in the form of the agricultural techniques imposed on Pipi's garden in the *Chronicle,* the autopsy of Solibo by the medical examiners in *Solibo Magnificent,* or the construction of the highway in *Texaco*—not only constitute the means of imposing ideas through furtive and silent domination but also provide the instruments for liberating the imaginary. The Internet, in its all-encompassing "Electro-World," enables both possibilities at their most extreme.

Chamoiseau asserts that modern communications technologies can be used to combat the negative effects of globalization by preserving oral languages and oraliture, creating more democratic spaces of writing (such as online blogs and manifestos) and establishing new forms of community in cyberspace. Together, these perform a key role in reappropriating the imaginary from the silent and furtive dominations by making it the domain of orality. Chamoiseau, like Glissant, associates cyberspace with orality and the organic and believes in its potential to inspire a new poetics. Both thinkers have become extremely interested in practices of reading in the era of the Internet, especially the effects of Web browsing on the reception of literature. They believe that digital technologies not only have the potential to inspire new poetic forms and genres but can also play an important role in the preservation of the orality and authentic Caribbean cultures that Chamoiseau valorizes so highly in his early novels. For Chamoiseau and Glissant, the Internet, unlike previous technologies, presents an interactive, highly malleable form of communication. Whereas radio and television often take the form of a subordinate relationship—as in the case of French stations broadcasting in Martinique—Web-based dialogue can create reciprocal forms of engagement for these authors, a true *mise en relation* (putting into relation). As a result, they are cautiously optimistic about the potential of communications technologies to facilitate a transition to a more egalitarian relationship between countries and regions.

Nevertheless, Chamoiseau (like Glissant) signals the dangers of abusing technologies, especially given their potential use as instruments of hegemony perpetuating the dominance of Western powers. In particular, he expresses serious concerns about the current hegemonic nature of the World Wide Web, which both he and Glissant consider to be dominated by a nonpoetic and decidedly corporate form of the English language. Both authors consider technology's greatest danger to lie in its ability to standardize—establishing singular ideas, languages, and universals—and they speak openly about the need to make cyberspace the domain of orality, thus asserting the presence of lesser-known cultures within the global imaginary. For Chamoiseau, technology can either allow an opening up to the "totality-world" in the form of Relation, or perpetuate the dominance of technologically superior Western powers, a distinction that is inextricably bound to Glissant's opposition between globalization and globality. Both thinkers emphasize the importance of liberating the "imaginary" in the minds of the Antillean people, that is, how they think and conceive of their place in the world; this imaginary is the site of a power struggle, and it is already under the sway of new technologies.

In the works of Glissant and Chamoiseau, the question of technology begins to merge with that of ecology. The earlier authors in my study (Senghor, Fanon, Sembène) focus on the postindependence moment of nation building, considering technologies such as railways and the radio. Their texts served as a means of trying to persuade the reader, spectator, and more generally the public to view the utility of these technologies independently of their origins in a colonized culture, as a means of promoting modernization. As a result, they often exhibit a complete disregard for ecological concerns. Glissant and Chamoiseau, on the other hand, recognize the utility of modern communications technologies while emphasizing the environmental consequences of departmentalization and the tourist industry in the Caribbean; they believe that modernization can occur in a responsible manner, but this requires preserving the natural habitats of fauna, flora, and Creole culture, as well as pursuing modes of commerce and urban planning that take into account the tropical landscape of Martinique.

Epilogue

Francophone African and Caribbean literature exhibits a momentous shift in attitudes toward technology transfer, from an association with capitalism, exploitation, hegemony, and hierarchy in the colonial period (before the 1960s), to a much more positive—though complex—perspective in the years following decolonization (1960s to present). The authors of this study view modern technology as a liberating, democratizing force, capable of freeing the proletariat and promoting equality by instigating economic and social development and creating an endless circulation of commodities and peoples—a nomadism—which is equated with dismantling the hierarchical relationships that separate the periphery from the center. While many West African and Caribbean writers advocate an all-out drive toward modernization, others are more cautiously optimistic, considering the political and ecological consequences of excessively rapid development.

During the period considered in my study—from the beginnings of Negritude in the 1930s, to the independence-era African novels of the 1960s and 1970s, to Glissant and Chamoiseau's latest writings on the Internet—the question of technology in the work of francophone authors has shifted fundamentally. Before the 1970s, many francophone authors (Césaire, Senghor, Sembène, Loba, Bhêly-Quénum) focused on the industrial innovations necessary for modernization—such as railways, dams, and motorboats—which were still strongly associated with the colonizer. The discussion of these technologies generally focused on their physicality and instrumentality, how to transfer and appropriate them. In this earlier francophone literature, the arrival of a modern invention to a remote village was a significant event that sparked passionate debates and the formation of alliances. Later on, authors grapple with how to integrate technologies into daily life, including the appropriate relationship to them. These authors (Fanon, Sembène, Glissant, and Chamoiseau) focus more on technologies of communication—including radio, television, film, and the Internet—which are at once localized in a particular place and disseminated on a global scale. Although these modern innovations are portrayed as universal instruments, they still retain vestiges of their associations with the former colonizer's culture: in contemporary Caribbean literature, the question is less about the utility of technologies, which is generally accepted, than it is about who controls them and how to prevent others from using them in a hegemonic way.

The role of technology in colonization and its aftermath continues to be debated in the public sphere. Depictions of Africa as backward and uncivilized were invoked by a French president as recently as July 26, 2007, when Nicolas Sarkozy gave a speech at Cheikh Anta Diop University in Dakar shortly after his election. Speaking in broad, sweeping terms about the African continent from a viewpoint that Dominic Thomas rightly characterizes as "strikingly paternalistic and reductive" (*Africa and France* 97), Sarkozy echoes the colonial discourse of the civilizing mission: "The colonizer took, but I want to say with respect, that he also gave. He built bridges, roads, hospitals, dispensaries and schools. He turned virgin soil fertile" (*Africa and France* 98). These sentiments recall those of the colonizers and elders in *God's Bits of Wood,* who praise the "white men" for bringing the railway to Senegal and claim that if they ever left, the brush would takeover.

Sarkozy even goes so far as to openly defend principles of the "civilizing mission": rewriting colonial history as a humanitarian mission, he portrays the colonizers of Africa as hardworking people who "meant well": "He [the colonizer] gave all of his effort, his work, his know-how. I want to say it here, not all the colonialists were thieves and exploiters. There were among them evil men but there were also men of goodwill. People who believed they were fulfilling a civilizing mission, people who believed they were doing good. They were wrong, but some were sincere" (*Africa and France* 98). Sarkozy's speech suggests that Africa possesses a lack of development *despite* these attempts to civilize Africans rather than *because* of them, as many of the authors in my study (Césaire, Fanon, Bhêly-Quénum, and Loba) assert.

For Sarkozy, the way of progress has been blocked by the "natural spirit" of Africa, a continent that he describes as an ahistoric, underdeveloped world, entirely prisoner of its natural spirit (Mbembe, "Sarkozy's Africa"). Indeed, Sarkozy equates "modern man" with the European, and "traditional, natural man" with the African. He claims the values of African civilization will provide the perfect "antidote to the materialism and individualism that enslaves modern man" and that modern man "has much to learn from the African that has lived in a symbiotic relationship with nature for thousands of years" (Sarkozy).

For Sarkozy, African culture is an agglomeration of peasant societies, existing outside of history and stuck in the past: "The tragedy of Africa is that the African has not fully entered into history. The African peasant, who for thousands of years has lived according to the seasons, whose life ideal was to be in harmony with nature, only knew the eternal renewal of time, rhythmed by the endless repetition of the same gestures and the same words. In this imaginary world where everything starts over and over again there is no place for human adventure or for the idea of progress" (Sarkozy). For Sarkozy, not only have Africans failed to instigate progress, but he also suggests that they are incapable and unwilling to do so: "This man (the traditional African) never launched himself towards the future. The idea never came to him to get out of this repetition and to invent his own destiny" (Sarkozy). According to Sarkozy, given these circumstances, "Africa's challenge . . . is to appropriate for itself modern science and technology as the product of all human intelligence" (Sarkozy). Overall, he implies that Africans possess an inherent resistance to technological progress that must be overcome.

In an ironic twist, African intellectuals took to the Internet to respond to the speech, making use of the latest modern technologies to express their outrage at being called backward and pretechnological. In a scathing critique published on the Africultures website, linked to Alain Mabanckou's blog, Achille Mbembe highlights the offensive nature of Sarkozy's speech and the extent to which it echoes the discourse of the civilizing mission: "Nicolas Sarkozy openly revealed what, until now, went unspoken: that is that, both in terms of form and content, the intellectual framework underlying France's policy to Africa literally dates back to the end of the 19th century" ("Sarkozy's Africa"). Particularly troubled by Sarkozy's opposition between the modern,

European man and the traditional, African one, Mbembe continues: "Indeed, our ethno-philosopher president's 'African man' is above all characterized either by *what he hasn't got, what he isn't or by what he has never managed to achieve* (the dialectic of lack and incompletion), or by his opposition to 'modern man' (read 'white man'), an opposition which apparently results from his irrational attachment to the kingdom of childhood, the world of night, to simple pleasures and a golden age that never existed" ("Sarkozy's Africa"). Mbembe also takes issue with Sarkozy's depiction of Africa as a vast, primitive peasant society: "The new French ruling elite's Africa is essentially a rural, magical, phantom Africa, partly bucolic, partly nightmarish, inhabited by peasant folk" ("Sarkozy's Africa"). According to Mbembe, Sarkozy and other French intellectuals are making a concerted atttempt to rewrite the history of France and its empire "as a history of 'pacification,' of 'the valorization of empty, leaderless territories,' of 'the spreading of education,' of 'the founding of modern medicine and of the creation of road and rail infrastructures'" ("Sarkozy's Africa").

In another essay published on Africultures, Cheikh Thiam openly wonders, "Should African intellectuals waste any more time responding to Mr. Sarkozy?," answering his own question with an emphatic "no." In addition to the numerous declarations published online, many essays by notable intellectuals—such as Souleymane Bachir Diagne, Boubacar Boris Diop, and Jean-Luc Raharimanana—were collected into a lengthy volume, *L'Afrique répond à Sarkozy: Contre le discours de Dakar* (Africa responds to Sarkozy: Against the Dakar speech), edited by Makhily Gassama.

As evidenced by Sarkozy's speech and the responses of African intellectuals, the authors of my study are not simply addressing a historical discourse—that of the civilizing mission—that no longer exists but rather one that has persisted even after independence and that continues to be propagated to this day. As Thomas emphasizes, the statements made by Sarkozy are much more than just social blunders, since such constructs and perceptions continue to play a significant role "in policy making and in shaping perceptions of Africa (as continent), Africans (as people), and ethnic minorities and diasporic populations (in France and in the E.U.)" (99). Debates about the process of modernization in formerly colonized nations continue to rage on, albeit now on Internet forums and widely disseminated media rather than in the newspapers, journals, and printed books of Senghor's and Fanon's day.

The Internet appears to be ill-suited for Daniel Headrick's analysis of technological transfer, described in the introduction to this work, and especially his assumed separation between instruments or tools and the knowledge required to use them. In the case of the Internet, the instrument itself seems to provide the knowledge necessary for its use, and the relevant scientific and technological knowledge is much more readily available, even if access is still severely limited in many formerly colonized nations. In today's digital age, the question of technology becomes less about physical objects, and Headrick's distinction between the relocation of technological instruments and the cultural diffusion of knowledge appears to unravel. While in the case of the radio a transmitter is necessary, the Internet can provide not only knowledge about how to appropriate technologies but sometimes also access to them via downloads or online ordering.

Most of the authors examined in my study are open to using new technologies to reach a wider audience and are willing to change their preferred medium of expression in order to do so. For Césaire, it was the decision to shift from poetry to theater, which he viewed as a multimedia spectacle. Senghor's numerous essays and speeches reflect an attempt to communicate his message to a public broader than the readers of his poetry. Fanon's journalistic writings demonstrate his determination to reach Algerians and his sensitivity to technology's revolutionary potential. Sembène's turn to film was a consequence of his desire to use technology to speak to a wider audience and instigate social progress, just as the radios do in *Moolaadé*. Loba and Bhêly-Quénum's novels illustrate for African readers how new technologies can provoke change. And Glissant and Chamoiseau value the Internet's ability to enact *mise en relations* between cultures, preserve orality, and provide a domain for the imaginary.

In recent years, francophone authors have increasingly gone online in order to express themselves. Although these authors are of course anchored in concrete geographical locations, the Web provides them with a space existing outside the boundaries of nation-states in which they can communicate with a global audience, including members of African and Caribbean diasporas living throughout the world. In this sense, cyberspace becomes a sort of transnational phenomenon. The Web also transforms the relationship between writers and readers; as Robert Burnett and David Marshall note in *Web Theory: An Introduction*, "The internet plays with the boundaries that have traditionally delineated three modes of communication: interpersonal (one-to-one), mass (one-to-many) and computing (many-to-one)"; it "allows for all three types of communication, as well as a fourth, many-to-many, mode of communication" (48).

African and Caribbean writers have taken advantage of these new modes of communication through the creation of websites and blogs and by posting to social media. Sites such as Femmes écrivains et littérature africaine (Women writers and African literature) and Africultures: Le site des cultures africaines (Africultures: The website of African cultures) now enjoy substantial popularity. Odile Cazenave and Patricia Célérier believe that the rise of Internet forums has counterbalanced the use of African literatures in an educational setting by promoting a democratic means of distribution to a larger audience (171–72). As they point out, many francophone authors—including Ilboudo Ebodé, Raharimana, Ken Bugul, Marie-Célie Agnant, Tadjo, and Boni—now publish some works exclusively online, especially short pieces such as essays, short stories, or poems (172). A number of them—Mabanckou, Kangni Alem, Waberi, Boni, Devi, and Léonore Miano—have developed their own websites and blogs, which have become important sites for the promotion of African literatures (172).[1] Nevertheless, Cazenave and Célérier acknowledge the digital divides that exist not only between Africa and the rest of the world but between individual African countries:

> The benefits of the Internet are not evenly distributed in Europe, Asia, the Americas, and the African continent. . . . While the African telecommunications market has dramatically expanded during the past ten years, there remains a digital divide with the rest of the world, a digital divide that also plays out between individual African countries—with South Africa, Morocco, Egypt, Mauritius, and the Seychelles ahead of the game—and between urban centers and rural areas. Not everyone in Africa can spend money and time in cybercafés. Furthermore, the number of cybercafés varies from country to country. (174)

Despite this divide, Cazenave and Célérier believe that the Internet ultimately contributes to the democratization of African literatures by making them part of global economies of cultural production, and thus more visible on an international scale (175).

Some Creole authors believe that the rise of the Internet creates the illusion of proximity when in reality there is none. While browsing the Web, the Martinican might feel as if he or she is not thousands of miles away from France. For instance, Raphaël Confiant states in a 1998 interview: "In fact we are trapped by electronics. Before it was absurd that Martinique depended on France, but as electronics minimize distances . . . [p]eople who are pro-France use this as an argument: it's not a problem that there are seven thousand kilometers between France and Martinique because of fax and e-mail" (Julia Watts, "An Interview with Raphaël Confiant" 49, qtd. in Gyssels). Consequently, the failure of referendums for independence has at times been attributed to the rise of the Internet and media culture.

This assessment of the promise and pitfalls of the Internet for francophone culture is confirmed by the later authors in this study. As discussed in chapters 6 and 7, Glissant and Chamoiseau published several manifestos online: "Quand les murs tombent: L'identité nationale hors la loi?" (When the walls fall: National identity outside of the law?); "L'Intraitable beauté du monde: Adresse à Barack Obama" (The uncomprimising beauty of this world: Address to Barack Obama); and the "Manifest for 'Products' of High Quality." These appeared on the website Institute of the Tout-Monde, founded by Glissant in 2006 (www.tout-monde.com), and also in print as pamphlets, a continuation of the trend begun with "Manifeste pour une littérature-monde." Chamoiseau also maintains a Facebook page to which he posts regularly, often with announcements of events of interest for readers of Martinican literature, such as a theatrical adaptation in Brussels of his most recent novel, *Les neufs consciences du Malfini* (The nine consciences of the Malfini birds).

The Cameroonian Calixthe Beyala also has a particularly strong Internet presence. Famous not only as a novelist but also as a public intellectual, she is known for her incendiary Facebook posts, which seek to provoke discussion. A post from April 22, 2015, sparked a lively conversation: "What is admirable in today's world is that the Westerner is at home in Africa, in fact everyone is at home in Africa, and it is only the African who is not at home in the West, in the end, the African is not at home anywhere." Ironically, Beyala's post on the African's lack of belonging is done from cyberspace—which exists at once everywhere and nowhere—and allows Africans situated all over the world to react and comment on her words.

In a series of posts, Beyala develops a personal theory about Facebook, which she views as a fantasyland of friends and supporters. She has the maximum number of Facebook friends allowed by the site, such that it is no longer possible for anyone to add her as a friend. On September 26, 2010, she announced that her account was full and shared a link to a new account that replicates the old one exactly but allows her to have twice the number of friends and followers. In a post from April 18, 2015, she claims to "de-friend" three hundred people a day, between those who insult her, contradict her without an argument, and commit other offenses. In this post, she states her Facebook philosophy: "It's simple, my friends: Facebook is a friends page and not the opposite; if I don't like someone, I don't visit his/her page." She goes on to say that it is not about democracy. In the world of Facebook, everyone establishes their own rules, and there is liberty in that; unlike the real world, if you don't like something on Facebook, you can just ignore it, and she finds freedom in the right to ignore others (although some may call this censorship).

In Beyala's Facebook world, there are "real friends" (*vrais amis*) and virtual ones (*amis virtuels*): real friends are those who support her and have met her; virtual friends exist only online. For Beyala, every virtual friend has the potential to become a real one by making actual contact, often as a result of events announced on her page. For instance, in an announcement for a talk at the Catholic University of Yaoundé, she encourages her Facebook friends and followers to attend, declaring, "The Internet is great, but reality is even better!" Afterward she displayed a message expressing her joy at finally meeting her Facebook friends.

In a post from April 21, 2015, Beyala provides a makeshift theory about Facebook, which she then relates to her ideas about the French language and technology more generally. She begins by responding to those who say that she uses the "white people's platform" to criticize them. According to Beyala, everyone who uses Facebook has paid for the service by viewing advertising, and this conveys ownership of the site to the users, providing them with freedom to do as they choose. When someone comments that it is the same with the French language and inventions (that they don't belong only to French people, but to Africans as well), Beyala wholeheartedly agrees, sending her kisses and perhaps even promoting her from a "virtual friend" to a real one.

Alain Mabanckou is also known for his Internet persona, which is markedly different and more subdued than Beyala's. In "New Technologies and the Popular: Alain Mabanckou's Blog," Dominic Thomas performs a fascinating interview with the Congolese writer about the very popular blog that he maintains as part of the website Congopage. Thomas writes that the blog form provides a "new forum for conversations, debate, and exchange between people located in different parts of the world" (58). While understanding the limitations of the Internet, Mabanckou appears optimistic about its potential to democratize. He wants the energy from his blog to come from "anywhere or anyone" (67) and declares that he is very happy when people from disadvantaged areas such as the Congo intervene (70). Mabanckou believes that "blogs in general will play an increasingly important role in society" (70) and that Africans will need "to adapt to these news technologies as they gradually replace traditional forms of print culture" (70).

When asked by Thomas about "the democratization of access," Mabanckou responds: "One of the main advantages of a blog is the feeling of presence. When people in Brazzaville connect to the internet they have the impression of having the writer right there in front of them on the screen, and of being in a conversation of dialogue with the writer himself. As far as they are concerned, I am speaking to them directly, except for the fact that there is a third eye watching, namely, the other visitors" (62). When Thomas asks if he views his blog as a *radio-trottoir* (pavement radio)—that is, a grassroots network used in urban African settings to relay information—Mabanckou responds that he sees it more as a *case à palabres,* that is, "a locality in which people gather to discuss the affairs of the village" (65). And much as in an African village, "all the protagonists are to be found on the blog, from the intellectual pedant to the more down to earth person who says things as they are and in street French! This creates an ambiance and each visitor becomes a kind of actor on the blog" (65). In other words, Mabanckou considers himself a modern-day griot who narrates and leads discussions in cyberspace rather than around a fire.

The notion of the Web as a gathering place for discussion akin to the square in an African village echoes the place of technology in the works of the francophone authors in this study. Césaire views his multimedia theatrical productions as a means of sparking dialogue and debate; Senghor emphasizes technology's role in the collective project of nation building; Fanon notes the radio's potential to organize; Sembène describes film as an "evening school" that replaces gatherings around a storyteller; Glissant views communications as forms of *mise en relation;* and Chamoiseau reconceptualizes the griot as a cyberhacker in the domain of the imaginary. As African and Caribbean nations move forward with development, transferring and appropriating the latest technologies—from cell phones to satellite TV to the Internet and beyond—francophone authors will continue to invent new literary techniques for their represention, and find in them new modes of poetic inspiration and expression.

NOTES

INTRODUCTION

1. I will discuss in greater detail my definition of "modern technology" in the next section of this introduction.

2. Elizabeth Ezra defines "colonialism" as "the images of its colonial enterprise that France presented to itself and to the world" (2).

3. In James Arnold's classic study *Modernism and Negritude: The Poetry and Poetics of Aimé Césaire,* he recounts Césaire's appropriation of various European movements and authors, including surrealism and André Breton. Another pivotal study, Lilyan Kesteloot's *Black Writers in French: A Literary History of Negritude* (Philadelphia: Temple UP, 1974) approaches Césaire and Senghor from a historical standpoint, by focusing on the development and evolution of Negritude in the context of postindependence West African and Caribbean politics and culture. More recently, Carrie Noland, *Voices of Negritude in Modernist Print: Aesthetic Subjectivity, Diaspora, and the Lyric Regime* (New York: Columbia UP, 2015), approaches Negritude "as an experimental, text-based poetic movement developed by diasporic authors of African descent during the interwar period in France through the means of modernist print culture" (1).

4. In *Freedom Time: Negritude, Decolonization and the Future of the World,* Wilder likewise argues that Negritude thought has all too often been dismissed as irrelevant to questions of modernity: "Scholarship long promoted one-sided understandings of Césaire and Senghor as either essentialist nativists or naive humanists. Tied to the territorialism that dominated histories of decolonization, Negritude, whether embraced or criticized, was treated as an affirmative

theory of Africanity rather than a critical theory of modernity" (8). While my study also explores Negritude as a "critical theory of modernity," it differs from Wilder's in that I focus on representations of technology in literary works, while he produces an intellectual history of Césaire and Senghor through readings of their political writings.

5. Mildred Mortimer's *Journeys through the French African Novel* considers the motif of the journey in francophone African bildungsromans, focusing on the formation of personal cultural identity under colonialism. Christopher L. Miller's *Theories of Africans: Francophone Literature and Anthropology in Africa* argues for the importance of anthropology in approaching francophone texts from sub-Saharan Africa and performs readings of them from this perspective. Michael Syrotinski's *Singular Performances: Reinscribing the Subject in Francophone African Writing* takes V. Y. Mudimbe's reconceptualization of the subject in the African context as a point of departure for examining subjectivity in the francophone African novel.

6. Although there are numerous studies that focus on literature from the Caribbean region, often from a comparative perspective, none has focused on the question of technology or examined its relation to the predominant issues facing Caribbean communities today: tourism, globalization, modernization, and ecology. Recently, Maria Christina Fumagalli's *Caribbean Perspectives on Modernity: Returning Medusa's Gaze* examines the way that modernity has been represented in discourses by Caribbean authors, or European writers describing the Caribbean, from the Renaissance to the present.

7. In addition, the discovery of quinine as a malarial prophilaxis greatly facilitated the conquest of territories (see Curtin, *The Image of Africa: British Ideas and Action, 1780–1850*).

8. I intentionally refer to these authors as "avid readers of Marx's work" rather than "Marxists" since they make clear allusions to his writings but did not identify themselves as Marxists and at times even resisted this label.

9. See Karl Marx, "Critique of the Gotha Programme" (1875), *Marx and Engels: Selected Works* 3 (Moscow: Progress, 1970), 13–30.

10. Marx's views on this subject show the influence of Hegel's thinking about Africa in *Philosophy of Right.* In this text, Hegel describes Africa as outside of history, and, according to his logic, colonialism benefited Africa by providing it with the reason, ethics, and culture that historicized it (Hegel, *Philosophy of Right*).

11. See, for instance, Bimber, "Marx and the Three Faces of Technological Determinism."

12. For an overview of perspectives on Marx's treatment of technology, see Amy Wendling, *Karl Marx on Technology and Alienation* (New York: Palgrave Macmillan, 2011).

13. Although Senghor was an avid reader of Marx and developed his theories of African socialism by appropriating many Marxist concepts, it should

be noted that he was not a member of the Communist Party, as were Césaire, for a time, and Sembène.

14. See Louis Althusser, "Ideology and Ideological State Apparatuses," *Lenin and Philosophy and Other Essays,* trans. Ben Brewster (New York: Monthly Review Press, 1971), 127–86.

15. See Bhabha, *The Location of Culture.*

16. See, for instance, Corcoran, *The Cambridge Introduction to Francophone Literature;* and Moura, *Littératures francophones et théorie postcoloniale.*

17. Félix Guattari uses this term to refer to technologies in his essay "On Machines." For Guattari, the machine constitutes interaction itself.

18. In "Sociéte et littérature des Antilles" (Society and literature in the Antilles).

19. Fitzpatrick, "The Humanities, Done Digitally."

1. SCIENCE, MODERNIZATION, AND THE "THEATER OF DEVELOPMENT" IN AIMÉ CÉSAIRE

1. The notion of Negritude as antimodern and antitechnological has its origins in the essay that put it on the map: Jean-Paul Sartre's "Black Orpheus," in which he characterizes it as a spiritual and emotional poetic movement capable of countering the alienation produced by Western capitalism and modern technology. Sartre views Negritude poetry as fundamentally antithetical to technological progress, since he openly ponders whether technological development in Africa and the Caribbean will cause the poets' sources of inspiration to run dry.

2. Although Freire's *Pedagogy of the Oppressed,* which lays out some of the basic precepts of his theories on literacy and education, was not published until 1970, the ideas articulated in this text were already exerting a tremendous influence on the production of plays in Africa, Latin America, and the Caribbean in the early 1960s.

3. Unless otherwise noted, all translations of French texts are my own.

4. Serreau is perhaps best remembered as the director who sparked the New Theater movement, which included Adamov, Ionesco, Becket, and Genet, by directing some of their plays and allowing others to stage them at his Théâtre de Babylone in Paris.

5. Boal writes: "I believe that all truly revolutionary theatrical groups should transfer to the people the means of production in the theatre so that the people themselves may utilize them. The theatre is a weapon, and it is the people who should wield it" (122).

6. This description appears in the original version (in French) but not in the translation.

7. He does this in his political speeches, which I will discuss later in this chapter.

8. In *Freedom Time,* Wilder asserts that French African and Antillean legislators and intellectuals, including Césaire and Senghor, made unrealized attempts "to invent forms of decolonization that would secure self-determination without the need for state sovereignty" (1). According to Wilder, "Rather than allow France and its former colonies to be reified as independent entities in an external relationship to each other, the task was to institutionalize a longstanding internal relationship that would persist even after a legal separation" (2). This analysis is consistent with mine, since I argue that both Césaire and Senghor advocated maintaining ties to the metropole even after departmentalization and independence as a means of ensuring sufficient technological and economic development.

2. TECHNICS AND POETICS IN LÉOPOLD SÉDAR SENGHOR

1. See Stanislas Adotevi, *Négritude et Négrologues* (Paris: Union Générale d'Éditions, 1972).

2. See Towa, *Léopold Sédar Senghor, Négritude ou servitude?;* and Jones, *The Racial Discourses of Life Philosophy.*

3. Abiola Irele writes in "What Is Negritude?": "The recourse to traditionalism, to the values of the past as a global reference, gives Négritude the character of conservatism which is felt to be at variance with the exigencies of the moment. And the spiritualist terms in which even the theory of African socialism is cast in Senghor's writings give his ideas an air of unreality that seem to bear no relation to practical issues of socio-economic and technological development" (85).

4. He also briefly alludes to technology in the "Épître à la Princesse V" (Epistle to Princess V), in which the narrator calls the arrival of the Europeans "the year of Discovery" and "the year of Reason," before declaring, "It will be the year of Technology" (82) and "All will be sterile" (83).

5. This essay was the preface to the groundbreaking *Anthologie de la poésie nègre et malgache,* ed. Léopold Sédar Senghor (Paris: Presses Universitaires de France, 1948), which put Senghor on the map, so to speak.

6. I will discuss this idea in more detail during my analysis of Senghor's reading of Heidegger.

7. Senghor's singling out of the Japanese here as a technologically advanced society that is not European echoes Césaire claim (discussed in chapter 1) that the Japanese are one of the few examples of a society that has acquired the "self-confidence" necessary for assimilating borrowed elements, such as technologies, all the while maintaining cultural traditions.

8. For an overview of various critiques of Senghor's racial essentialism, see Barbara Ischinger, "Negritude: Some Dissident Voices," *Issue: A Journal of Opinion* 4 (1974): 23–25.

9. Although some critics have pointed to the influence of Spengler's *The*

Decline of the West on Senghor's thought, the impact of *Man and Technics* has not been evaluated.

10. As we will see in chapter 6, this is surprisingly close to what Glissant writes about the book in the age of the Internet.

3. RADIOS AND REVOLUTION IN FRANTZ FANON

1. See Nigel Gibson, introduction to *Fanon: The Postcolonial Imagination,* 2–14.

2. According to Gibson, this is largely the result of Homi Bhabha's famous preface to the English translation of the *The Wretched of the Earth,* as well as an increased interest in Fanon's earlier essays in *Black Skin, White Masks.* See, for instance, Diana Fuss's classic essay "Interior Colonies: Frantz Fanon and the Politics of Identification."

3. The most notable instances of this trend are Hannah Arendt's critique of Fanon's theory of violence in *On Violence,* in which she traces outbreaks of violence on college campuses during the 1960s to Fanon's influence on black culture, including the Black Panthers (65). Some more recent examples of this trend can be found in Gordon, Sharpley-Whiting, and White, eds., *Fanon: A Critical Reader*; for instance, "Fanon, Oppression, and Resentment: The Black Experience in the United States," by Floyd W. Hayes III, and "Perspectives of Du Bois and Fanon on the Psychology of Oppression," by Stanley O. Gaines Jr.

4. Sekyi-Otu is one of very few scholars to have questioned the version of Fanon as a strong critic of Western modernity: "Fanon worried that the allegiances to 'tradition,' from which the spontaneous action of the country people and ethnic communities often derived its inspiration, contained the seeds of centrifugal 'federalism,' to say nothing of separatist and genocidal forms of tribalism" (169). In other words, as Sekyi-Otu suggests, Fanon was far more concerned with the dangers of obsessively safeguarding tradition than those of embracing a novel modernity. In Sekyi-Otu's view, Fanon had a vision of "the rebirth of the colonized as an autonomous modern subject" (181). Far from condemning modernity, he sought its liberation "from colonial and postcolonial underdevelopment, and the democratic salvaging of the radical intelligentsia's 'technical and intellectual capital' from alienating usages" (181). In this chapter, I build on Sekyi-Otu's brief analysis by focusing on the representation of technology and, by implication, modernity in Fanon's work.

5. Sekyi-Otu writes that McCulloch conflates "the concept of *national culture,* which Fanon saw as a revolutionary postcolonial achievement, with the 'familiar idea of a specific black sensibility' and 'precolonial culture'" (261).

6. Sekyi-Otu points this out: "Those who discern in his texts that deep-seated romance with the African personality promoted by Negritude and its decorous revolt against modernity in the name of primordial racial virtues" (261).

7. My use of the masculine "he" to denote the impersonal pronoun here is

intentional since it corresponds to Fanon's own gendered analysis. For intriguing accounts of Fanon and gender, see Françoise Vergès, "'I Am Not the Slave of Slavery': The Politics of Reparation in (French) Postslavery Communities" (258–75); and T. Denean Sharpley-Whiting, "Fanon and Capécia" (57–74) in *Frantz Fanon: Critical Perspectives,* ed. Anthony Alessandri (London and New York: Routledge, 1999).

8. Senghor makes this highly controversial statement in "Ce que l'homme noir apporte" ("What the black man has to offer"). Fanon, like the majority of readers of Senghor, considered him to be an opponent of modern technologies, an interpretation that I refute in the second chapter of this book.

9. A few articles of note have analyzed this essay, though without considering the question of technology in Fanon's broader corpus. In a chapter of Gordon, Sharpley-Whiting, and White, eds., *Fanon: A Critical Reader,* titled "Jammin' the Airwaves and Tuning into the Revolution: The Dialectics of the Radio in *L'an V de la révolution algérienne,*" Nigel Gibson examines "This Is the Voice of Algeria," focusing on the "dialectics" of Fanon's thinking. Gibson writes, "The distinction between the time *before* the rebellion and the time *of* the rebellion constitutes an important division in Fanon's thought" (274).

10. "Primed by their discovery of the political and military importance of information, Algerians, beginning in 1956, start to demand more radios"; "As a result, and Fanon is keen to emphasize this, the radio is deprived of its status as a modern . . . object" (92).

11. In *Bourdieu in Algeria: Colonial Politics, Ethnographic Practices, Theoretical Developments,* Jane E. Goodman writes about some of the ongoing conflicts between Fanon and other major intellectual figures of his era, even ones advocating similar positions with regard to the Algerian question: "Bourdieu sharply demarcated himself from other leading intellectual proponents of 'Algerian Algeria'—most notably, Jean-Paul Sartre and Frantz Fanon" (10). In particular, Fanon and Bourdieu sharply disagreed about the role of the peasants in the Revolution, and the extent to which they were aware of their own position and expressed a collective will for change. Whereas Fanon attributed to them a rising consciousness and credited them with a revolutionary fighting spirit, Bourdieu was much more skeptical about their conscious involvement in the struggle; the latter states, "Algerians' support for the war did not necessarily make them—sociologically speaking 'revolutionaries'" (Bourdieu 1961, 1962; qtd. in Goodman 11). In general, the relationship between Fanon and Bourdieu is a highly neglected topic.

12. Germaine Tillon could be another example.

13. As Goodman writes, "In Bourdieu's implicit equilibrium model of traditional Algerian society, to alter such a significant element was to produce a domino effect in which the entire social and cultural edifice would come crumbling down" (Goodman 16). She further notes that "both *Travail et tra-*

vailleurs en Algérie and *Déracinement* are predicated on a 'clash of civilizations' (*choc de civilizations*) model that Bourdieu had initially outlined in an article of that title" (14–15).

14. On the level of the individual, Bourdieu argued that "the antinomies of modernity and tradition lead to what he will later call hysteresis, in which learned behaviors from one field (rural/traditional) impede adaptation to another field (urban/modern)" (Burawoy and Van Holdt 12).

15. Another important French ethnographer of Algeria of the same era, Germaine Tillion, also bases her analysis on a division between traditional Algerian culture and modern French society. Tillion published the influential study, *L'Algérie en 1957* (Algeria in 1957), in which she refused to attribute economic decline among Algerian Berbers to French colonialism (Goodman 17). This differs from Bourdieu, who *does* posit a correlation between economic decline and colonization. However, I have not found an explicit reference to either Bourdieu or Tillion in Fanon's writings.

16. Although the dates of the Algerian War are generally taken to be from 1954 to 1962, some historians date its beginning to the protests and subsequent massacres that occurred in May 1945, following the end of the World War II, referred to as the Sétif Massacres. Fanon's decision to place the beginning of the conflict on this date is no doubt a strategic one; he emphasizes that the war began with the French Army attacking innocent protesters.

17. Fanon often appeared to be far ahead of his time, whether discussing the nefarious role of the African bourgeoisie or anticipating the role of communications technologies in revolutions.

18. Freud developed the concept of object relations to describe how bodily drives satisfy their needs through a medium, an object, with a specific focus.

19. In his psychoanalysis of Algerian attitudes toward the radio in terms of object relations theory, Fanon appropriates some of the defense mechanisms for coping with phobias that Klein describes. Klein's analysis considers the notion of "self-projection," in which the ego "splits itself and the object into a good part and a bad part and projects all its badness into the outside world so that the hated breast becomes the hateful and hating breast" (20), a process that is applicable to the colonial situation for Fanon. In the case of the colonized, the identity of the self is split between the "good part"—that is, what is authentic to his/her own culture—and the "bad part," what has been taken from the French. Once the "badness" originating in the colonizer's culture is projected into the outside word, every object associated with this "badness"—for instance the radio—becomes "hateful" and "hating." Not only does the object remain separate from the colonized culture, but its very existence is denied.

20. In *A Thousand Plateaus: Capitalism and Schizophrenia* (1980) Deleuze and Guattari famously refer to machines as "assemblages" (*agencements*) that comprise both the material components of the object and organic elements

that make it function as a part of a system. For instance, a bicycle's material components consist of its pedals, handlebars, and wheels; while the rider's feet, legs and arms constitute the organic elements.

21. Bourdieu views the stable working class as modernist, and the peasantry as stuck in the eternal cycle of the present. Consequently, he considers the Algerian working class to be revolutionary but argues that the peasantry or urban subproletariat can do nothing more than break out into purposeless revolt.

22. In *Imagined Communities,* Anderson writes: "In an anthropological spirit, then, I propose the following definition of the nation: it is an imagined political community—and imagined as both inherently limited and sovereign. It is *imagined* because the members of even the smallest nation will never know most of their fellow-members, meet them, or even hear of them, yet in the minds of each lives the image of their communion" (5–6).

23. A major shortcoming of Fanon's analysis is his failure to consider the question of Arabization, which will become a central issue in Algeria following independence, enjoying considerable support from the FLN.

24. Fanon's troubles with Arabic are well documented; despite sincere attempts to learn the language, he was forced to work with an interpreter during his therapeutic sessions with patients and was never able to attain a conversational level.

25. See, in particular, "The Lived Experience of the Black Man" in *Black Skin, White Masks.*

26. In "In/Visibility and Super/Vision: Fanon on Race, Veils and Discourses of Resistance" (Gordon, Sharpley-Whiting, and White, eds., *Fanon: A Critical Reader*), David Theo Goldberg writes: "Radio and television are technologies that can promote invisibility and produce depersonalization" (190); and "Technology offers a medium for the dissemination of information but at once mediates the message" (191).

27. See chapter 2, in which I describe how Césaire uses theater to provoke a "coming to consciousness" leading to "self-confidence."

28. This is consistent with what the eminent historian on Algeria, Benjamin Stora, has written on underdevelopment in Algeria: "In 1962 Algeria was heir to an outward-oriented economy set up in relation to the metropolis, and existed as a function of the million of Europeans living there. In the first half of the twentieth century, the gradual integration into the French economy had brought about a rapid decline in local craft industries, which faced competition from French manufactured products. A dual and largely agricultural economy took shape. Side by side with a modern sector of large farm operations in the hands of the colons, a traditional section with low productivity attempted to provide for the local population's subsistence" (123). Thus, according to Stora, the "traditional" social formation was largely the result of colonial oppression.

29. See my section on Sartre in chapter 2.

30. Stora strongly agrees with Sartre and Fanon on this point (123).

31. Fanon did not consider himself a Marxist since he ascribed a large role to race in historical developments and felt that Marx did not take racism into consideration in his analysis. Nevertheless, Fanon's analysis is fundamentally Marxist in his frequent use of Marx's vocabulary and terminology (proletariat, bourgeoisie, etc.) and his focus on the struggle between classes as a definitive force in social upheavals.

32. Fanon states elsewhere that they lack a spirit of invention: "The dynamic and pioneering side, the inventive side and discoverer of worlds that one finds in all national bourgeoisie is unfortunately absent here" (149).

33. See, for instance, Amadou Hampâté Bâ, *The Fortunes of Wangrin* (1973); or Cheikh Hamidou Kane, *Ambiguous Adventure* (1961).

34. In chapter 3 of *Fanon: The Postcolonial Imagination,* Gibson examines Fanon's portrayal of Negritude throughout his career. He writes, "In *The Wretched*, negritude is much more historicized and directly criticized from the standpoint of the Algerian revolution, with criticisms lodged explicitly against negritude's leaders (like Senghor) who continued to support the idea of Algeria as French" (80); and "Fanon considers negritude important, but concedes that it is not a sufficient condition of liberation from the shackles of an imposed essence of Blackness" (81).

35. Sekyi-Otu performs a detailed analysis of this passage: "In the passage on the bridge—an allegorical inquiry concerning technology—Fanon adumbrates what may be called a postnationalist account of development and appropriation that mirrors Marx's etiology of estrangement" (209).

36. See the discussion of Headrick in the introduction.

37. Gibson likewise makes this connection between Fanon and the Arab Spring in the introduction to *Living Fanon: Global Perspectives* (New York: Palgrave Macmillan, 2011) and in an interview with Yasser Munif published online, "Frantz Fanon and the Arab Uprisings: An Interview with Nigel Gibson," *Jadaliyya*, August 17, 2012.

4. MACHINES AND MEDIA IN OUSMANE SEMBÈNE

1. In 1964, Sembène published a novel that recounts the story of this referendum: *L'Harmattan* (Paris: Présence africaine, 1964).

2. See, for instance, Victor O. Aire, "Didactic Realism in Ousmane Sembene's *Les bouts de bois de Dieu*," *Canadian Journal of African Studies* 11.2 (1977) 283–94; and Kenneth W. Harrow, "Art and Ideology in *Les bouts de bois de Dieu*: Realism's Artifices," *French Review* 62.3 (1989): 483–93.

3. See, for instance, Victor O. Aire, "Ousmane's Sembene's *Les bouts de bois de Dieu:* A Lesson in Consciousness," *Modern Language Studies* 8.2 (1978): 72–79.

4. See, for instance, Gibreel M. Kamara, "The Feminist Struggle in the Senegalese Novel: Mariama Bâ and Sembene Ousmane," *Journal of Black Stud-*

ies 32.2 (2001): 212–28; Renée Linkhorn, "L'Afrique de Demain: Femmes en marche dans l'œuvre de Sembène Ousmane," *Modern Language Studies* 16.3 (1986): 69–76; and Karen Sacks, "Women and Class Struggle in Sembene's *God's Bits of Wood*," *Signs* 4.2 (1978): 363–70.

5. This use of the term *la machine* to refer to both the railway line and the trains that run on it echoes Émile Zola's *The Human Best*, which recounts a story taking place along the railway line from Paris to Le Havre.

6. These perspectives are notably different from the portrayal of the railway in Camara Laye's *The Dark Child*. In this novel, the train functions as a metonym of modernity and the world outside the village of the protagonist/narrator. In the first few pages, he recounts how the shacks where the villagers lived would catch fire when the train passed, such that they had to put out the fire quickly before it spread. There are also the serpents on the train tracks, which his mother says possess the spirit of his father. When he grows older, as he waits for the train that will take him six hundred kilometers away to study in Conakry, he prays that it will be late so that he can be with his family a little longer. Murphy writes, "Beside this 'authentic' African village lies a railway track which Camara Laye seems to suggest is outside the influence of the West, luring his childhood self away from the 'purity' of the African village to the world of Western knowledge in the city" (*Imagining Alternatives* 32). Murphy considers the train to be the first wheel of the "*engrenage*" that culminates on the last page in Laye's arrival in France. While the train (which is mentioned only in passing in *The Dark Child*) represents modernity in both Laye's and Sembène's work, the characters of *God's Bits of Wood* are much more in tune to the workings of the railway and the life surrounding it; it does not possess the same sense of mystery and association with an outside world that it does for Laye.

7. This imagery recalls that of Émile Zola's *Germinal*, an obvious inspiration for Sembène's novel.

8. Although the precise origin of the term *toubabs* in West Africa to refer to white settlers is unknown, it may be derived from the word "Tougal," the Wolof word for Europe.

9. I will discuss this issue at further length in the next section.

10. Sembène's choice of a young woman as a mouthpiece is significant, since he has spoken out about the important role of women in African development in several interviews: "Africa can't develop without the participation of her women" (Busch and Annas 160); "in the society we are going to build, women will play an important role" (160).

11. For an interesting discussion of how the *moolaadé* resonates with the UN's Universal Human Rights Declaration's notion of the right to "asylum from persecution," see Borden, "At the Global Market."

12. Sembène's use of the term "Negro-African" here alludes to Senghor's use of the term.

5. DAMS AND MOTORBOATS IN OLYMPE BHÊLY-QUÉNUM AND AKÉ LOBA

1. See, for instance, Claude Ake, *Democracy and Development in Africa* (Washington DC: Brookings Institution, 1996); and Colin Legum, *Africa since Independence* (Bloomington: Indiana UP, 1999).

2. For an overview of this genre, see "The Francophone African Colonialist Novel," in *An Introduction to the African Prose Narrative,* ed. Lokangaka Losambe (Pretoria: Kagiso Tertiary, 1996).

3. For more biographical information about Bhêly-Quénum, see *Olympe Bhêly-Quénum par lui-même,* ed. Bernard Lecherbonnier (Paris: Nathan, 1979).

4. See, for instance, Amadou Hampaté Bâ, *The Fortunes of Wangrin;* and Cheikh Hamidou Kane, *Ambiguous Adventure.*

5. In the French colonial system, the colonies were divided up into *cercles* headed by a European official; these *cercles* were in turn divided into *cantons* consisting of a few villages. The French administrators appointed an African *chef du canton* to lead these units; this represented the highest position attainable by an African in the French government at the time.

6. GLOBALIZATION AND THE INTERNET IN ÉDOUARD GLISSANT

1. About this transition, Celia Britton has written: "*Le Discours antillais* was, as its title suggests, exclusively concerned with the French Antilles, and in fact mainly with Glissant's own home island, Martinique, and it gave an extremely pessimistic evaluation of Martinique as a 'morbid,' politically stagnant, alienated, and isolated society. The major texts of the 1990s, in striking contrast, expand their focus to encompass the whole world, and are dominated by a far more up-beat, exuberant celebration of hybridity and cross-cultural contact" ("Transnational Languages" 62).

2. See Hallward, "Édouard Glissant: From Nation to Relation."

3. As Britton explains, "The Relation to other people includes, most crucially, other people whose languages we do not know; *Poetics of Relation* insists that 'understanding,' at least in the conventional sense, is unnecessary and even harmful to the proper exercise of Relation, which is ethically bound to respect the other's opacity" ("Transnational Languages" 80).

4. The following builds on Helmtrud Rumpf, "Technology-Based Orality: A Force for Social Change in the Caribbean," who notes that for Glissant "it is no longer a matter of a hierarchical relationship in which one person informs another, but of reciprocal communication—an equal relationship (mise-en-relation)" (262).

5. Britton writes that, for Glissant, "contact between cultures has irreversibly put an end to the isolation that was such a dominant feature in the Martinique of his youth" (*Glissant and Postcolonial Theory* 179).

6. See also Britton, *Glissant and Postcolonial Theory* 179.

7. As Britton has noted, for Glissant, "'Writing in the presence of all the world's languages' means that my text is 'inflected' by other languages, not because it incorporates lexical borrowings, for instance, but in the more negative sense that it is haunted by the knowledge that other languages, offering a vision of reality that lies beyond the scope of my own, are endangered" ("Transnational Languages" 66).

8. See Aimé Césaire, "Poésie et connaissance," *Tropiques* 12 (1945): 157–70.

9. He alludes to this opposition in interviews from the 1990s onward and finally articulates it clearly in writing in *La Cohée du Lamentin* (2005). I will explore this distinction further in my discussion of *La Cohée du Lamentin* later in this chapter.

10. Derived from the French word for cement, *béton,* this refers to the massive construction of highways, shopping malls, and resorts in Martinique.

11. Glissant's analysis of how certain predominantly oral cultures might bypass the written form altogether to use new media to communicate greatly echoes Fanon's description of the Arabs of Algeria. According to Fanon, this people already possessed a highly developed means of communicating via oral culture, which allowed them to make an easy transition to appropriating the radio once the technology was stripped of its associations with the colonizer.

12. Rumpf: "Media-based orality, however, is not restricted to a national space, but connects its virtual members to the whole-world. The ongoing exchange opens new and unforeseeable horizons for the smallest and most isolated peoples" (267).

13. Much like what Mikhail Bhaktin once wrote about the novel with regard to genres.

14. For Glissant, the flash agents are that which transform "active relays" into "neutral relays" (*Poetics* 178).

15. See Marshall McLuhan, *Understanding Media: The Extensions of Man* (1964; Cambridge: MIT Press, 1994).

16. See chapter 1.

17. For more on Heidegger's analysis of the dangers of modern technologies, and its relationship to my readings of postcolonial literary texts, see the section of the introduction titled "What Is 'Technology'?" as well as the section "Senghor and Heidegger" in chapter 2.

18. See Seanna Sumalee Oakley, "Commonplaces: Rhetorical Figures of Difference in Heidegger and Glissant," *Philosophy and Rhetoric* 41.1 (2008): 1–21.

19. The Internet becomes one of the primary ways that Glissant tries to anchor his theories of the *tout-monde* in the real world, making them less abstract.

20. See "Manifeste pour une littérature-monde en français," *Le Monde* March 16, 2007.

21. In Headrick's terms (see the introduction to this volume), Glissant's no-

tion of globalization could be said to entail the geographic relocation of technologies by Western experts without any cultural diffusion to non-Western experts, a remnant of the colonial era with disastrous consequences.

22. Clark writes, "Such thinking, [Glissant] argues, is 'untenable in the Caribbean'—and undesirable, for such would-be sacred rootedness all too often means a territorial intolerance of others" (133).

23. This manifesto, published online by *Le Monde* on February 16, 2009, was coauthored by nine prominent Antillean intellectuals: Ernest Breleur, Chamoiseau, Serge Domi, Gérard Delver, Glissant, Guillaume Pigeard de Gurbert, Olivier Portecop, Olivier Pulvar, and Jean-Claude William.

24. Published online by the Institut du Tout-Monde on October 4, 2007.

7. URBAN SPACE AND CYBERSPACE IN PATRICK CHAMOISEAU

1. Watts describes the Old Warrior as a "composite figure whose utterances could seem, at times, to emanate from an Édouard Glissant, yet whose relationship to Glissant and with Chamoiseau, for that matter, are unclear" ("Wounds of Locality" 116).

2. As Watts points out, Glissant also makes this observation in *Caribbean Discourse* (119–24) ("Wounds of Locality" 115, 128).

3. In my analysis of Chamoiseau and Glissant, I consider their point of view on technology and globalization to be much more positive than does Katherine Gyssels in "The World Wide Web and Rhizomatic Identity: *Traité du tout-monde* by Édouard Glissant." According to Gyssels, Chamoiseau and other *créoliste* group members Raphaël Confiant and Jean Bernabé observe that "the Internet traps ex-colonized populations; it gives them a false impression of autonomy and better access to, and control of, the surrounding world." She also states that Glissant believes that "globalization and the Net may generate the complete reverse of what creolization was initially meant to be: recognition of and respect for diversity, the capacity to discover the Other and accept his/her difference, cultural heterogeneity, and the hybrid parts that make up societies." While this is certainly true for what Glissant calls globalization, Gyssels says nothing of globality, the positive mode of international community formation that Glissant views as the protector of local languages and culture.

4. Ultimately, the essence of Chamoiseau's critique of Glissant's theories of globalization is not that different—although very different in tone—from Hallward's (mentioned in the previous chapter). While Hallward emphasizes the extent to which Glissant's 1990s writings on globalization become largely apolitical as they lose their specificity, Chamoiseau signals the need to maintain a local component and fight like a warrior for what Glissant takes for granted (the *mise en relation* of peoples).

5. Chamoiseau states in his "Déclaration pour la méta-nation" (Declaration for the meta-nation), published on the website Mediapart on November 22,

2010, that he identifies as an "independentist" because it just makes things easier. In reality, he advocates true sovereignty (political and economical) for Martinique and other formerly colonized nations, which he believes is the only way to be free from colonial subjugation.

6. In "For What the Land Tells: An Ecocritical Approach to Patrick Chamoiseau's *Chronicle of the Seven Sorrows*," Renée K. Gosson focuses on the figure of the garden in Chamoiseau's novel, as the battleground between the competing environmental stances of the departmental administration (including Césaire) and Creole culture.

7. In "Flashbacks of an Orchid: Rhizomatic Narration in Patrick Chamoiseau's *Biblique des derniers gestes*," Heidi Bojsen shows how Chamoiseau "presents a narrative mode that challenges the Romantic legacy inherent in the terms 'territory,' 'landscape,' and 'independence'" (213).

8. In "'Toutes ces eaux!': Ecology and Empire in Patrick Chamoiseau's *Biblique des derniers gestes*," Watts makes the intriguing argument that the representation of water in the *Biblique* illustrates the complicated relationship between the local (where water exists in concrete from) and the global, where various competing forces work to control its distribution. He makes the fascinating observation that the exclamation "*Toutes ces eaux!*" (All these waters!) appears intermittently throughout the narration, as if submerging the warrior in water, and that the narrative itself becomes more fluid when describing water issues.

9. Watts, like Bojsen, explores the figure of the orchid, which he calls "an intermediate point between root and rhizome or between complete immobility and total dissemination" ("Toutes ces eaux!" 903).

EPILOGUE

1. Cazenave and Célérier write: "Together with *Africultures*, these Internet sites give the pulse of the moment and affect the shaping of the canon quite effectively" (173).

WORKS CITED

Adell, Sandra. *Double-Consciousness/Double Bind: Theoretical Issues in Twentieth-Century Black Literature.* Urbana: U of Illinois P, 1994.

Aguiar, Marian. "Smoke of the Savannah: Traveling Modernity in Sembène Ousmane's *Gods' Bits of Wood.*" *MFS Modern Fiction Studies* 49.2 (2003): 284–305.

Alessandri, Anthony, ed. *Frantz Fanon: Critical Perspectives.* London: Routledge, 1999.

Ananou, David. *Le fils du fétiche: Roman.* Paris: Nouvelles éditions latines, 1971.

Anderson, Benedict. *Imagined Communities: Reflections on the Origin and Spread of Nationalism.* London: Verso, 1991.

Arendt, Hannah. *On Violence.* San Diego: Harcourt, Brace, Jovanovich, 1970.

Arnold, James. "Césaire and Shakespeare: Two Tempests." *Comparative Literature* 30.3 (1978): 236–48.

———. *Modernism and Negritude: The Poetry and Poetics of Aimé Césaire.* Cambridge: Harvard UP, 1982.

Auclaire-Tamaroff, Elisabeth, and Barthélémy Auclaire-Tamaroff. *Jean-Marie Serreau: Découvreur de théâtres.* Paris: L'Arbre Verdoyant, 1986.

Bâ, Silvia Washington. *The Concept of Negritude in the Poetry of Léopold Sédar Senghor.* Princeton, NJ: Princeton UP, 1973.

Bairoch, Paul. *Révolution industrielle et sous-développement.* Paris: Mouton, 1974.

Benjamin, Walter. "The Author as Producer." Ed. Michael W. Jennings et al. *Selected Writings.* Vol. 2. Cambridge: Belknap P of Harvard UP, 2005.

———. "The Work of Art in the Age of Mechanical Reproduction." *Illumina-*

tions. Trans. Hannah Arendt and Harry Zohn. New York: Harcourt, Brace and World, 1968.

Bhabha, Homi K. *The Location of Culture.* London: Routledge, 1994.

Bhêly-Quénum, Olympe. *Le chant du lac.* Paris: Présence africaine, 1965.

Bimber, Bruce. "Marx and the Three Faces of Technological Determinism." *Social Studies of Science* 20 (1990): 333–51.

Boal, Augusto. *Theater of the Oppressed.* Trans. Charles A. and Maria-Odilia Leal McBride. New York: Urizen, 1979.

Bojsen, Heidi. "Flashbacks of an Orchid: Rhizomatic Narration in Patrick Chamoiseau's *Biblique des derniers gestes.*" *Caribbean Literature and the Environment: Between Nature and Culture.* Ed. Elizabeth DeLoughrey, Renée K. Gosson, and George B. Handley. Charlottesville: U of Virginia P, 2005. 213–24.

Bongie, Chris. "Spectres of Glissant: Dealing in Relation." *Friends and Enemies: The Scribal Politics of Post/Colonial Literature.* Liverpool: Liverpool UP, 2008. 322–70.

Borden, Amy. "At the Global Market: Ousmane Sembène's *Moolaadé* and the Economics of Women's Rights." *Jump Cut: A Review of Contemporary Media* 53 (2011).

Bourdieu, Pierre. *Sociologie de l'Algérie.* Paris: Presses Universitaires de France, 1958.

Bourdieu, Pierre, Alain Darbel, Jean-Pierre Rivet, and Claude Seibel. *Travail et travailleurs en Algérie.* Paris: Mouton, 1963.

Bourdieu, Pierre, and Abdelmalek Sayad. *Le déracinement: La crise de l'agriculture traditionnelle en Algérie.* Paris: Éditions de Minuit, 1964.

Bourdieu, Pierre, and Marie-Claire Bourdieu. "Le Paysan et la photographie." *Revue française de sociologie* 6.2 (1965): 164–74.

Bradby, David. *Modern French Drama, 1940–1990.* Cambridge: Cambridge UP, 1991.

Brecht, Bertolt. "The Modern Theatre Is the Epic Theatre: Notes to the Opera *Rise and Fall of the Town of Mahagonny (1930).*" *Modern Theories of Drama: A Selection of Writings on Drama and Theatre, 1850–1990.* Ed. George W. Brandt. Oxford: Clarendon; New York: Oxford UP, 1999. 224–31.

Breleur, Ernest, et al. "A Plea for 'Products' of High Necessity." Trans. Isabelle Métral. *L'humanité in English.* www.humaniteinenglish.com/spip.php?article1163.

Britton, Celia. *Édouard Glissant and Postcolonial Theory: Strategies of Language and Resistance.* Charlottesville: U of Virginia P, 1999.

———. *The Sense of Community in French Caribbean Fiction.* Liverpool: Liverpool UP, 2010.

———. "Transnational Languages in Glissant's 'Tout-monde.'" Ed. Mary Gallagher. *World Writing: Poetics, Ethics, Globalization.* Toronto: Toronto UP, 2008. 62–85.

Burawoy, Michael, and Karl Von Holdt. "Conversation 4: Colonialism and Revolution, Fanon meets Bourdieu." *Conversations with Bourdieu: The Johannesburg Moment.* Johannesburg: Wits UP, 2012. 75–90.

Burnett, Robert, and P. David Marshall. *Web Theory: An Introduction.* London: Routledge, 2003.

Busch, Annett, and Max Annas, eds. *Ousmane Sembène: Interviews.* Jackson: U of Mississippi, 2008.

Camara, Laye. *The Dark Child.* New York: Noonday, 1994.

Cazenave, Odile M., and Patricia Célérier. "The Fashioning of an Engaging Literature: The Publishing Industry, the Internet, and Criticism." *Contemporary Francophone African Writers and the Burden of Commitment.* Charlottesville: U of Virginia P, 2011. 139–76.

Césaire, Aimé. *Discourse on colonialism.* Trans. Joan Pinkham. New York: MR, 1972.

———. "L'homme de culture et ses responsabilités." *Présence Africaine* 24–25 (1959): 116–22.

———. *Notebook of a Return to My Native Land.* Trans. Mireille Rosello with Annie Pritchard. Newcastle upon Tyne, UK: Bloodaxe, 1995.

———. "Société et littérature dans les Antilles." *Études Littéraires* 6 (1973): 9–20.

———. *A Tempest.* Trans. Philip Crispin. London: Oberon, 2000.

———. *The Tragedy of King Christophe.* Trans. Ralph Manheim. New York: Grove, 1970.

Chamoiseau, Patrick. *Chronicle of the Seven Sorrows.* Trans. and with an afterword by Linda Coverdale; foreword by Édouard Glissant. Lincoln: U of Nebraska P, 1999.

———. "Déclaration pour la méta-nation." Mediapart website. Nov. 22, 2010.

———. *Écrire en pays dominé.* Paris: Gallimard, 1997.

———. *Les neuf consciences du Malfini: Roman.* Paris: Gallimard, 2009.

———. *Solibo Magnificent.* Trans. Rose-Myriam Réjouis and Val Vinokur. New York: Pantheon, 1997.

———. *Texaco.* Trans. Rose-Myriam Réjouis, and Val Vinokur. New York: Pantheon, 1997.

Ciaffa, Jay A. "Tradition and Modernity in Postcolonial African Philosophy." *Humanitas* 21.1/2 (2008): 121–45.

Clark, Timothy. "Questions of Scale: The Local, the National and the Global." *Cambridge Introduction to Literature and the Environment.* Cambridge: Cambridge UP, 2011. 130–42.

Conteh-Morgan, John. "A Note on the Image of the Builder in Aimé Césaire's *La tragédie du roi Christophe.*" *French Review* 57.2 (1983): 224–30.

Conteh-Morgan, John, and Dominic R. D. Thomas. *New Francophone African and Caribbean Theatres.* Bloomington: Indiana UP, 2010.

Corcoran, Patrick. *The Cambridge Introduction to Francophone Literature.* Cambridge: Cambridge UP, 2007.

Couffon, Claude. *Visite à Édouard Glissant: Entretiens réunis par Gérard Cléry.* Paris: Éditions Caractères, 2001.

Curtin, Philip. *The Image of Africa: British Ideas and Action, 1780–1850.* Madison: U of Wisconsin P, 1964.

Dash, Michael J. "*Villes, Poèmes:* The Postwar Routes of Caribbean Creolization." *Creolization as Cultural Creativity.* Ed. Robert Baron and Ana C. Cara. Jackson: UP of Mississippi, 2011. 228–42.

Deleuze, Gilles, and Félix Guattari. *A Thousand Plateaus: Capitalism and Schizophrenia.* Trans. Brian Massumi. Minneapolis: U of Minnesota P, 1987.

Diese, Barbara. "Césaire's Concept of Négritude in *Cahier d'un retour au pays natal.*" *Journal of Caribbean Studies* 13.2 (1993): 40–57.

Dunn, David L., and Aimé Césaire. "Interview with Aimé Césaire on a New Approach to *La tragédie du Roi Christophe* and *Une saison au Congo.*" *Cahiers Césairiens* 4 (1980): 1–10.

Ellul, Jacques. *The Technological Society: A Penetrating Analysis of Our Technical Civilization and of the Effect of an Increasingly Standardized Culture on the Future of Man.* Trans. John Wilkinson. New York: Vintage, 2003.

Epskamp, Kees P. *Theatre in Search of Social Change: The Relative Significance of Different Theatrical Approaches.* The Hague: Center for the Study of Education in Developing Countries, 1989.

Ezra, Elizabeth. *The Colonial Unconscious: Race and Culture in Interwar France.* Ithaca: Cornell UP, 2000.

Fanon, Frantz. *Black Skin, White Masks.* Trans. Charles Lam Markmann. New York: Grove Weidenfeld, 1982.

———. *A Dying Colonialism.* Trans. Haakon Chevalier and G. M. Carstairs. Harmondsworth: Penguin, 1970.

———. *Toward the African Revolution: Political Essays.* Trans. Haakon Chevalier. New York: Monthly Review, 1967.

———. *The Wretched of the Earth.* New York: Grove Weidenfel, 1991.

Farías, Victor. *Heidegger and Nazism.* Philadelphia: Temple UP, 1989.

Fitzpatrick, Kathleen. "The Humanities, Done Digitally." Ed. Matthew Gold. *Debates in the Digital Humanities.* Minneapolis and London: U of Minnesota P, 2012.

Fox-Genovese, Elizabeth. *Feminism without Illusions: A Critique of Individualism.* Chapel Hill: U of North Carolina P, 1991.

Freire, Paulo. *Pedagogy of the Oppressed.* New York: Continuum, 1970.

Fumagalli, Maria Christina. *Caribbean Perspectives on Modernity: Returning Medusa's Gaze.* Charlottesville: U of Virginia P, 2009.

Fuss, Diana. "Interior Colonies: Frantz Fanon and the Politics of Identification." *Diacritics* 24.2 (1994): 19–42.

Fuyet, Hervé, Nicole Fuyet, Guy Levilain, and Mary Levilain. "Décolonisation et classes sociales dans *La tragédie du Roi Christophe* d'Aimé Césaire." *French Review* 46.6 (1973): 1101–16.

Gadjigo, Samba, and Fatoumata Coulibaly. *The Making of Moolaade.* New York: New Yorker Films, 2004. Film.

Gérard, Albert S. *European-Language Writing in Sub-Saharan Africa.* Budapest: Akadémiaki Kiadó, 1986.

Gibson, Nigel C. *Fanon: The Postcolonial Imagination.* Oxford: Polity and Blackwell, 2003.

Gikandi, Simon. "African Literature and Modernity." *Texts, Tasks, and Theories: Versions and Subversions in African Literatures.* Ed. Tobias Robert Klein and Viola Pruschenk. Amsterdam and New York: Rodopi, 2008. 3–19.

Glissant, Édouard. *La Cohée du Lamentin: Poétique V.* Paris: Gallimard, 2005.

———. *Caribbean Discourse: Selected Essays.* Trans. J. M. Dash. Charlottesville: U of Virginia P, 1999.

———. *L'imaginaire des langues: Entretiens avec Lise Gauvin (1991–2009).* Paris: Gallimard, 2010.

———. *Introduction à une poétique du divers.* Paris: Gallimard, 1996.

———. *Nouvelle région du monde: Esthétique I.* Paris: Gallimard, 2005.

———. *Poetics of Relation.* Ann Arbor: U of Michigan P, 1997.

———. *Traité du tout-monde: Poétique IV.* Paris: Gallimard, 1997.

Glissant, Édouard, et al. "Manifeste pour une littérature-monde." *Le Monde* March 15, 2007.

Glissant, Édouard, and Patrick Chamoiseau. *Quand les murs tombent. L'identité nationale hors-la-loi?* Paris: Galaade, 2007.

Glissant, Édouard, and Alexandre Lepin. *Les entretiens de Baton Rouge.* Paris: Gallimard, 2008.

Goodman, Jane E. *Bourdieu in Algeria: Colonial Politics, Ethnographic Practices, Theoretical Developments.* Lincoln: U of Nebraska P, 2009.

Goody, Alex. *Technology, Literature and Culture.* Cambridge, UK: Polity, 2011.

Gordon, Lewis R., T. Denean Sharpley-Whiting, and Renée T. White, eds. *Fanon: A Critical Reader.* Oxford: Blackwell, 1996.

Gosson, Renée K. "For What the Land Tells: An Ecocritical Approach to Patrick Chamoiseau's *Chronicle of the Seven Sorrows.*" *Callaloo* 26.1 (2003): 219–34.

Guattari, Félix. "On Machines." *Journal of Philosophy and the Visual Arts* 6 (1990): 8–17.

Gyekye, Kwame. *Tradition and Modernity: Philosophical Reflections on the African Experience.* New York: Oxford UP, 1997.

Gyssels, Kathleen. "The World Wide Web and Rhizomatic Identity: *Traité du tout-monde* by Édouard Glissant." *Mots Pluriels* 18 (2001).

Hallward, Peter. "Édouard Glissant: From Nation to Relation." *Absolutely Postcolonial: Writing between the Singular and the Specific.* Manchester: Manchester UP, 2001. 66–132.

Harding, Sandra. *Sciences from Below: Feminisms, Postcolonialities, and Modernities.* Durham: Duke UP, 2008.

Hardt, Michael, and Antonio Negri. *Empire.* Cambridge: Harvard UP, 2007.

Harvey, David. "The Fetish of Technology: Causes and Consequences." *Macalester International* 13.7 (2003).

Headrick, Daniel. *The Tentacles of Progress: Technology Transfer in the Age of Imperialism, 1850–1940.* Oxford: Oxford UP, 1999.

Hegel, Georg Wilhelm Friedrich. *Philosophy of Right.* Trans. T. M. Knox. Oxford: Clarendon, 1967.

Heidegger, Martin. "*Der Spiegel* Interview with Martin Heidegger." *The Heidegger Reader.* Ed. Günter Figal. Bloomington: Indiana University Press. 313–33.

———. "Interview." *Der Spiegel.* May 31, 1976: 204.

———. *Introduction to Metaphysics.* Trans. Richard Polt and Gregory Fried. New Haven: Yale UP, 2000.

———. "Letter on Humanism." *Basic Writings.* Trans. David Farrell Krell. New York: Harper Collins, 1977. 195–205.

———. "The Origin of the Work of Art." *Off the Beaten Track.* Ed. and trans. Julian Young and Kenneth Haynes. Cambridge: Cambridge UP, 2002.

———. *Poetry, Language, Thought.* Trans. and introd. Albert Hofstadter. New York: Harper Colophon, 1971.

———. "The Question Concerning Technology." *The Question Concerning Technology and Other Essays.* Trans. and ed. William Lovitt. New York: Garland, 1977. 115–54.

———. "The Self-Assertion of the German University: Address, Delivered on the Solemn Assumption of the Rectorate of the University Freiburg the Rectorate 1933/34: Facts and Thoughts." Trans. Karsten Harries and Hermann Heidegger. *Review of Metaphysics* 38.3 (1985): 467–502.

Hiepko, Andrea Schwieger. "Europe and the Antilles: An Interview with Édouard Glissant." Trans. Julin Everett. *The Creolization of Theory.* Ed. Françoise Lionnet and Shu-mei Shih. Durham: Duke University Press, 2011. 255–61.

Hountondji, Victor. *African Philosophy: Myth and Reality.* 2nd ed. Bloomington: Indiana UP, 1996.

Hymans, Jacques Louis. *Léopold Sédar Senghor: An Intellectual Biography.* Edinburgh: Edinburgh UP, 1971.

Irele, Abiola. "What is *Negritude?*" *The African Experience in Literature and Ideology.* Bloomington: Indiana UP, 1990.

Jones, Donna V. *The Racial Discourses of Life Philosophy: Négritude, Vitalism, and Modernity.* New York: Columbia UP, 2010.

Kesteloot, Lilyan. *Comprendre le "Cahier d'un retour au pays natal" d'Aimé Césaire.* Issy les Moulineaux: Classiques Africains, 1982.

Klein, Melanie. *Selected Melanie Klein.* Ed. Juliet Mitchell. New York: Free Press, 1986.

Knepper, Wendy. *Patrick Chamoiseau: A Critical Introduction.* Jackson: UP of Mississippi, 2012.
Kourouma, Ahmadou. *The Suns of Independence.* Trans. Adrian Adams. New York: Africana, 1981.
Laroche, Maximilien. "*La tragedie du roi Christophe* du point de vue de l'histoire de Haiti." *Études littéraires* 6.1 (1973): 35–47.
Laville, Pierre. "Aimé Césaire et Jean-Marie Serreau, un acte politique et poétique." *Les voies de la création théâtrale II.* Paris: Éditions du Centre National de la Recherche Scientifique, 1970.
Lazarus, Neil. *The Postcolonial Unconscious.* Cambridge: Cambridge UP, 2011.
Livingston, Robert Eric. "Decolonizing the Theatre: Césaire, Serreau and the Drama of Negritude." *Imperialism and Theatre: Essays on World Theatre, Drama, and Performance.* Ed. J. Ellen Gainor. London: Routledge, 1995. 182–98.
Loba, Aké. *Les fils de Kouretcha.* Paris: J.-B. Baillère et Fils, 1970.
Markovitz, Irving. *Léopold Sédar Senghor and the Politics of Negritude.* New York: Atheneum, 1969.
Marx, Karl. *Capital: A Critique of Political Economy.* New York: Penguin, 1993.
———. "The Future Results of British Rule in India." *New York Daily Tribune* Aug. 8, 1953.
Masson, Joel. "Les aventures et inventions de Jean-Marie Serreau." *Loisir* (Caen) 24: 12–13.
Mbembe, Achille. "Nicolas Sarkozy's Africa." Trans. Melissa Thackway. *Africultures.* www.africultures.com/php/?nav=article&no=6816.
McCulloch, Jock. *Black Soul and White Artifact: Fanon's Clinical Psychology and Social Theory.* Cambridge: Cambridge UP, 1983.
McCusker, Maeve. *Patrick Chamoiseau, Recovering Memory.* Liverpool: Liverpool UP, 2007.
Miller, Christopher L. *Theories of Africans: Francophone Literature and Anthropology in Africa.* Chicago: U of Chicago P, 1990.
Moore, Gérald. *African Literature and the Universities.* Ibadan, Nigeria: Ibadan UP, 1965.
Mortimer, Mildred. *Journeys through the French African Novel.* Portsmouth, NH: Heinemann; London: J. Currey, 1990.
Moura, Jean-Marc. *Littératures francophones et théorie postcoloniale.* Paris: Presses Universitaires de France, 2007.
Moutoussamy, Ernest. *Aimé Césaire: Député à l'Assemblée Nationale (1945–1993).* Paris: L'Harmattan, 2000.
Mowitt, John. *Radio: Essays in Bad Reception.* Berkeley: U of California P, 2011.
Mulvey, Laura. *Fetishism and Curiosity.* Bloomington: Indiana UP, 1996.
Murphie, Andrew, and John Potts. *Culture and Technology.* New York: Palgrave Macmillan, 2003.

Murphy, David. "Filming the Past, Present and Future of an African Village: Ousmane Sembène's *Moolaadé*." Ed. Amresh Sinha and Terence McSweeney. *Millennial Cinema: Memory in Global Film*. London: Wallflower, 2011.

———. *Sembene: Imagining Alternatives in Film and Fiction*. Oxford: J. Curry; Trenton, NJ: Africa World Press, 2001.

Nguyen Nghe. "Frantz Fanon et les problèmes de l'indépendance." *La Pensée* 107 (1963): 23–30.

Oakley, Seanna Sumalee. "Commonplaces: Rhetorical Figures of Difference in Heidegger and Glissant." *Philosophy and Rhetoric* 41.1 (2008): 1–21.

Owusu-Sarpong, Albert. *Le temps historique dans l'œuvre théâtrale d'Aimé Césaire*. Paris: L'Harmattan, 2002.

Pfaff, Françoise. *The Cinema of Ousmane Sembene, a Pioneer of African Film*. Westport, CT: Greenwood, 1984.

———. "Three Faces of Africa: Women in *Xala*." *Jump Cut: A Review of Contemporary Media* 27 (1982): 27–31.

———. "The Uniqueness of Ousmane Sembène's Cinema." *Ousmane Sembène: Dialogues with Critics and Writers*. Ed. Samba Gadjigo. Amherst: U of Massachusetts P, 1993.

Porton, Richard, and Jared Rapfogel. "The Power of Female Solidarity: An Interview with Ousmane Sembene." *Cineaste* 30.1 (2004): 20–27.

Pratt, Mary Louise. *Imperial Eyes: Travel Writing and Transculturation*. London: Routledge, 1992.

Prieto, Eric. "Édouard Glissant, Littérature-monde and Tout-monde." *Small Axe* 14.3 (2010): 111–20.

Renders, Marleen. "An Ambiguous Adventure: Muslim Organisations and the Discourse of 'Development' in Senegal." *Journal of Religion in Africa* 32.1 (2002): 61–82.

Riesz, János. "Senghor and the Germans." *Research in African Literatures* 33.4 (2002): 25–37.

Robinson, James E. "Caribbean Caliban: Shifting the 'I' of the Storm." *Comparative Drama* 33.4 (1999–2000): 431–53.

Rumpf, Helmtrud. "Technology-Based Orality: A Force for Social Change in the Caribbean." *A Pepper-Pot of Cultures: Aspects of Creolization in the Caribbean*. Ed. Gordon Collier and Ulrich Fleischmann. Amsterdam: Rodopi, 2003. 261–76.

Sarkozy, Nicolas. "The Unofficial English Translation of Sarkozy's Speech." Address by Mr. Nicolas Sarkozy, President of the French Republic, at the University of Cheikh Anta Diop, Senegal, on July 26, 2007. www.africaresource.com/essays-a-reviews/essays-a-discussions/437-the-unofficial-english-translation-of-sarkozys-speech?showall=&limitstart=.

Sartre, Jean-Paul, and John MacCombie. "Black Orpheus." *Massachusetts Review* 6.1 (1964–65): 13–52.

Schwieger Hiepko, Andrea. "Europe and the Antilles: An Interview with

Édouard Glissant." Trans. Julin Everett. Ed. Françoise Lionnet and Shumei Shi. *The Creolization of Theory.* Durham, NC: Duke UP, 2011.

Sekyi-Otu, Ato. *Fanon's Dialectic of Experience.* Cambridge: Harvard UP, 1996.

Sembène, Ousmane. "Entretiens avec Ousmane Sembène." *Jeune Afrique* (1979): 72–76.

———. *God's Bits of Wood.* Trans. Francis Price. London: Heinemann, 1995.

———. Interview by Bonnie Greer. June 5, 2005. *Guardian.* www.theguardian .com/film/2005/jun/05/features.

———. Interview by Daniel Graham. 2002. *Making of Moolaadé.* Trans. Samba Gadjigo. New Yorker Films, 2005. DVD.

———. "Interview with the Director by Samba Gadjigo 11 April 2004." *Artificial Eye,* n.d.

———. "Interview with Ousmane Sembène—Father of African Film." *Socialist Worker* 1955 (2005).

———. "Man Is Culture." *Man Is Culture.* Bloomington: African Studies Program, Indiana U, 1979.

———. *Moolaadé.* Dir. Ousmane Sembène. Perf. Fatoumata Coulibaly, Hélène Diarra, Aminata Dao, and Salimata Traoré. London: Artificial Eye, 2004. DVD.

———. *Ô pays, mon beau peuple!* Ed. Patrick Corcoran. London: Methuen Educational, 1986.

———. *Xala.* Dir. Ousmane Sembène and Paulin S. Vieyra. New York: New Yorker Films, 2005. DVD.

Senghor, Léopold Sédar. *Liberté 1: Négritude et humanisme.* Paris: Éditions du Seuil, 1964.

———. *Liberté 3: Négritude et Civilisation de l'Universel.* Paris: Éditions du Seuil, 1977.

———. *Liberté 5: Le Dialogue des cultures.* Paris: Éditions du Seuil, 1993.

———. "Marxisme et humanisme." *La Revue Socialiste* 19 (1948): 201–16.

———. *Œuvre poétique.* Paris: Éditions de Seuil, 1990.

———. *La poésie de l'action: Conversations avec Mohamed Aziza.* Paris: Stock, 1980.

———. *Pour une relecture africaine de Marx et d'Engels.* Dakar-Abidjan: Les Nouvelles Éditions Africaines, 1976.

———. *Selected Poems.* Trans. John Reed and Clive Wake. London: Oxford University Press, 1964.

Spengler, Oswald. *Man and Technics: A Contribution to a Philosophy of Life.* Trans. Charles Francis Atkinson. New York: Knopf, 1932.

Spivak, Gayatri. "Can the Subaltern Speak?" *Marxism and the Interpretation of Culture.* Ed. Cary Nelson and Lawrence Grossberg. Urbana: U of Illinois P, 1998.

Stora, Benjamin. *Algeria 1830–2000: A Short History.* Trans. Marie Todd. Ithaca: Cornell UP, 2004.

Syrotinski, Michael. *Singular Performances: Reinscribing the Subject in Francophone African Writing.* Charlottesville: U of Virginia P, 2002.

Taylor, Lucien. "Créolité Bites: A Conversation with Patrick Chamoiseau, Raphaël Confiant, and Jean Bernabé." *Transition* 74 (1997): 124–61.

Thiam, Cheikh. *Return to the Kingdom of Childhood: Re-Envisioning the Legacy and Philosophical Relevance of Negritude.* Columbus: Ohio State UP, 2014.

Thomas, Dominic R. D. *Africa and France: Postcolonial Cultures, Migration, and Racism.* Bloomington: Indiana UP, 2013.

———. *Nation-Building, Propaganda, and Literature in Francophone Africa.* Bloomington: Indiana UP, 2002.

———. "New Technologies and the Popular: Alain Mabanckou's Blog." *Research in African Literatures* 39.4 (2008): 58–71.

Tsunekawa, Kunio. "La 'Négritude' à deux vitesses: Aimé Césaire et Léopold Sédar Senghor." *Aimé Césaire: Une pensée pour le XXIe siècle: Actes du colloque en célébration du 90e anniversaire d'Aimé Césaire, Fort-de-France, du 24 au 26 juin 2003.* Ed. Christian Lapoussinière. Paris: Présence Africaine, 2004. 344–70.

Watts, Julia H. "An Interview with Raphaël Confiant." *Plantation Society in the Americas* 5 (1998): 41–59.

Watts, Richard. "Poisoned Animal, Polluted Form: Chamoiseau's Birds at the Limits of Allegory." *Pacific Coast Philology* (2012): 177–93.

———. "'Toutes ces Eaux!': Ecology and Empire in Patrick Chamoiseau's *Biblique des derniers gestes.*" *MLN* 118.4 (2003): 895–910.

———. "The 'Wounds of Locality': Living and Writing the Local in Patrick Chamoiseau's *Écrire en pays dominé.*" *French Forum* 28.1 (2003): 111–29.

Wilder, Gary. *Freedom Time: Negritude, Decolonization and the Future of the World.* Durham: Duke University Press, 2015.

Woodis, Jack. *New Theories of Revolution.* New York: International, 1972.

Wolitz, Seth. "The Hero of Negritude in the Theater of Aimé Césaire." *Kentucky Romance Quarterly* 16.3 (1969): 195–208.

Ziarek, Ewa Plonowska, ed. *Fanon and the Impasses of Modernity.* Special issue of *Parallax* 8.2 (2002).

INDEX